Mentoring Strategic Change in Health Care

Also available from ASQC Quality Press

Quality Improvement Handbook for Health Care Professionals
James P. Mozena and Debby L. Anderson

Show Me: The Complete Guide to Storyboarding and Problem Solving
Harry I. Forsha

Show Me: Storyboard Workbook and Template
Harry I. Forsha

The Change Agents' Handbook
David W. Hutton

Team Fitness: A How-To Manual for Building a Winning Work Team
Meg Hartzler and Jane E. Henry

Managing the Four Stages of TQM: How to Achieve World-Class Performance
Charles N. Weaver

The ASQC Total Quality Management Series

> *TQM: Leadership for the Quality Transformation*
> Richard S. Johnson
>
> *TQM: Management Processes for Quality Operations*
> Richard S. Johnson
>
> *TQM: The Mechanics of Quality Processes*
> Richard S. Johnson and Lawrence E. Kazense
>
> *TQM: Quality Training Practices*
> Richard S. Johnson

To request a complimentary catalog of publications, call 800-248-1946.

Mentoring Strategic Change in Health Care

An Action Guide

Chip Caldwell

ASQC Quality Press
Milwaukee, Wisconsin

Mentoring Strategic Change in Health Care: An Action Guide
Chip Caldwell

Library of Congress Cataloging-in-Publication Data

Caldwell, Chip.
    Mentoring strategic change in health care: an action guide / Chip
Caldwell.
      p. cm.
    Includes bibliographical references and index.
    ISBN 0-87389-224-0
    1. Health facilities—Administration.   2. Total quality management.
3. Organizational change.   4. Health services administration.
I. Title.
RA971.C28   1995
362.1'068—dc20   95-8969
                                                                    CIP

10 9 8 7 6 5 4 3 2

ISBN 0-87389-224-0

Acquisitions Editor: Susan Westergard
Project Editor: Kelley Cardinal

ASQC Mission: To facilitate continuous improvement and increase customer satisfaction by identifying, communicating, and promoting the use of quality principles, concepts, and technologies; and thereby be recognized throughout the world as the leading authority on, and champion for, quality.

Attention: Schools and Corporations
ASQC Quality Press books, audiotapes, videotapes, and software are available at quantity discounts with bulk purchases for business, educational, or instructional use. For information, please contact ASQC Quality Press at 800-248-1946, or write to ASQC Quality Press, P.O. Box 3005, Milwaukee, WI 53201-3005.

For a free copy of the ASQC Quality Press Publications Catalog, including ASQC membership information, call 800-248-1946.

Printed in the United States of America

 Printed on acid-free paper

 ASQC
Quality Press
611 East Wisconsin Avenue
Milwaukee, Wisconsin 53202

To Paul Batalden, M.D., a very good mentor

Contents

Figures and Tables

Chapter 5

Foreword

I have sympathy for leaders—especially those who intended to lead improvement. Advisors in quality management continually warn that the drive for quality is nondelegable, that old habits of control and exhortation must end, that long-term executive vision must replace a focus on quarterly reports, that teams take time to mature and therefore take great patience, and that purpose must be constant, especially when times are rough. All are burdens on leaders. Senior Executive Leadership is Category I in the criteria for the Malcolm Bladrige National Quality Award, and the placement is no accident. "Without leadership from the top," goes the refrain, "fundamental improvement is impossible."

All of this is almost certainly true (although we will always welcome the informative counterexample), but it leads to a very difficult problem. To wit: Improvement appears to require *exceptional* leaders, sure to be in relatively short supply. The issue is basic. In managing the improvements of processes and products, one assumption *not* permitted in the work plan is that "all workers will be well above average" (in skills, motivation, honesty, and self-sacrifice). No quality improvement plan is real that includes the step, "Find heroes."

And yet, when we look at the specifications for *leadership* of improvement, the job seems heroic in its proportions. Of 100 health care executives, or 100 chiefs of medicine, how many do we really believe can master the core issues of *customer-mindedness, process-mindedness,* and *statistical-mindedness,* that Chip Caldwell describes in this book? How many can formulate and manage the transformations and paradigm shifts, link vision to strategies, induce and sustain ongoing measurement of progress, assess readiness, and diagnose and treat inhibitors of progress? How many Caldwells have we got?

Not many. If the quality movement in health care succeeds, by helping health care reach needed new pinnacles of performance, its historians will write that there was an early breed of pioneering executives who broke away from the pack. Those executives, history will say, showed courage, curiosity, open-mindedness, and patience. They went out on limbs and left the company of their peers to try forms of leadership and organization that looked not just new, but crazy to many. Some paid a heavy price because courage is sometimes distinguished from foolhardiness only in retrospect.

Chip Caldwell will be named in that history. And he will be in surprisingly small company. As total quality management (TQM) swept into health care in the early 1990s, in a charge led by many who did not understand even the basics of what they espoused, a form of shallowness came to dominate the improvement scene, and the inevitable failures disillusioned many. Hundreds—perhaps thousands—of health care leaders learned the rhetoric, but only a few mastered the underlying theory, and only a few of *them* put the theory into action. Chip Caldwell carried through the whole way.

In this book, he tells his story, and the contents will surprise some readers. Opening a book on TQM one may expect tutorials on tools (flowcharts, Pareto diagrams, and histograms) or an elaboration on a quality improvement process (like FOCUS-PDCA or someone's seven-step process). One would expect lists of principles for top leaders, or rollout steps for organization-wide transformation. Little of that is here.

Instead, we see an original picture of leadership tasks as a great leader defined and experienced them. Caldwell, like all early architects of change, had to take a multiplicity of ideas and mold them together into a framework of action that made sense to him. No one has ever written the quality story the same way before, and no effective leader will write it again in just this way. Caldwell thought too hard to copy anything absolutely, and therefore his approach is original in the deepest way.

We cannot expect this of all health care leaders—not even of most. Whatever equipped Chip Caldwell to march out ahead of his peers makes his own, personal method inaccessible to others. If he were usual enough for us to copy, he would not have been unusual enough to cut his own path. It is a sort of tragedy: We want most to emulate that which is most inherently original.

So, the burden falls back on Caldwell. He must teach the ordinary leader about the lessons of extraordinary leadership. This book contains echoes of Plato's story of the cave, in which the only man with sight tries to describe shadows to the sightless others. Chip Caldwell would resist the drama in that analogy, but his problem is not so different. How to describe to others the results of a journey of discovery, when the journey itself is part of the discovery?

The task is impossible, but it is also necessary. The difficulty, and the possibilities, are most evident in the later chapters in this book—"Evidences of Readiness" and "Accelerators and Inhibitors." These are frustrating to read because they are aimed at the core concepts that leaders will have to build in their own way. What does "grow a shared vision" or "create constant discomfort with the present state" mean in operational, daily terms? An effective answer differs from leader to leader. Chip Caldwell knows that the best he can do, as was done for him by his own mentors, is to ask good-enough questions—good enough to stimulate the curiosity of people who want to become better leaders of improvement.

This—the raising of questions—he has done very well. The questions are a gift from one of the best of our contemporary American health care executives. For each reader who hopes to help others, this fragile gift now must be transformed into a new personal shape—informed by the early reports from a pioneer, but molded by each leader into his or her own image.

Which leads again to the basic issue: Can ordinary leaders—the vast, competent majority of us who lack Caldwell's frontiersmanship—lead extraordinary change?

My own opinion is yes, and Caldwell, since he takes the time here to tell his story, must share my optimism. Our confidence comes from a basic belief that the core process in improvement, when all is said and done, is *learning*. Chip Caldwell and I know that the most important precondition to the leadership of improvement is the authentic curiosity of the leader. And that is good news, because at least once, as children, we all were curious. With this book in hand, the average among us can open important doors of opportunity, finding improvement paths as the author did, in our own and special ways.

Donald M. Berwick, M.D.

In the 1900s as, in Joseph M. Juran's words, quality moves to center stage, more and more books appear on quality management. Many of these books address special topics, new or reexpressed ideas that deal with one part of the quality management puzzle. Many still address the question of why TQM or continuous quality improvement is a better way to achieve higher operating performance. A few even carefully explain what must be done.

But precious few confront the critical issue of *how* to do it. Caldwell, using his many years of experience as a chief executive officer (CEO), focuses directly on this issue throughout this remarkable text. This is a guide written not by the theorist or the philosopher on what should be done and why; instead, this is a practical guide written by one who has traveled the path and carefully documented the many twists and turns, forks, and dead ends.

For many senior executives, and especially for CEOs and presidents, this is going to be the guide for which they have been searching. In clear language, Caldwell covers the basic understanding needed by senior executives to create the customer focus, process thinking, and factual management so necessary for business success. Amply illustrated by many relevant examples, this book provides the means for the CEO and the executive quality council to develop a strategic deployment of the key goals to achieve meaningful results that are truly tied to organizational success.

An example of the clear, practical approach outlined in this book occurs early. Caldwell provides a list of discussion questions for a one-hour quality council meeting with suggestions for work to be done prior to the meeting. He then follows this with a discussion exercise for a one-hour department manager/team leader meeting. These specific suggestions, scattered liberally throughout the book, provide concrete, realistic action items that many health care leaders (and many leaders in other industries) have been searching for, often by time-consuming trial and error.

If this book was simply the documentation of one CEO's own journey toward quality management and the lessons learned, it would be well worth reading. But it is far more. Chip Caldwell has added to his considerable experience as a senior executive a new set of experiences, those of a consultant explaining to others how his experiences can be applied in their environments. This ability to teach, to explain, and to tailor his experience to different environments comes through clearly on every page.

In chapter 4 Caldwell takes much of the unnecessary mystery out of developing an organization's vision and strategic deployment system. In straightforward, bottom-line business language he discusses the links between market needs, customer outcomes, mission of the organization, guiding principles, the vision, and how to deploy the vision to achieve real results. Here again he focuses on concrete suggestions, even going so far as to suggest the five key strategic endeavors that should form the basis of any organization's strategic plan. I have personally worked with many organizations that could have saved weeks or even months of valuable time by starting with this list.

Again and again in this text Caldwell does not quibble. He gives specific advice on how to deploy goals to achieve results, who should do the work, how they should go about their task, and how much time it will take. This level of specificity is sorely missing in most books. Some readers of a more philosophical bent may argue with the details, but those readers with a need for practical advice will quickly recognize these suggestions as much needed realistic guidelines that can be used as the foundation for workable action plans.

In workshop after workshop the number one question raised is about measurement. Measurement appears to be one of the most difficult issues for most organizations. Caldwell makes a major contribution in his specific chapter on strategic measures deployment. He gives clear guidelines on how to merge the financial measures and the quality measures and provides a useful tool, the too-little-understood spider diagram, for displaying results at all levels in the organization. He illustrates this chapter on strategic measures deployment in great detail using 16 measures he developed as a chief executive.

For the leader truly interested in improving the performance of his or her organization rather than just studying the concepts of quality management, this is an invaluable book. It is a book to be read and used. Many organizations could benefit by having each member of the quality council read a chapter a week, discussing the chapter, and using the discussion questions at the end of each chapter as the agenda for their weekly quality council meetings. The progress they would make would be a welcome surprise.

A. Blanton Godfrey
Chairman and CEO
Juran Institute, Inc.

Preface

This book on TQM transformation has three purposes. First, I hope that the transformation model creates a mental model for health care and other strategists to capture the creative energies of the entire workforce to mobilize and achieve organizational visions. Second, I attempted to interpret vital concepts from Juran, Deming, Noriaki Kano, Kanatsu, Batalden, Berwick, and others and mold them into a cohesive web of utility. Finally, the book includes multiple examples of how many organizations have attempted to frame concepts contained in the transformation model to their respective organizations. I hope that these examples accelerate creativity in the reader's organization.

Toward the first purpose, CEOs and strategists often complain that TQM takes too long or that the results do not attend to the real issues of importance to customers. Many of your fellow CEOs and strategists faced the same dilemma. I know we did. I hope that the concepts and applications presented in this book in some small way help CEOs and strategists create new and exciting methods to engage everyone in the organization to recognize and improve customer needs, at whatever level they serve. It is a rewarding experience for a CEO to watch a team from dietary, maintenance, or nursing present a measurable improvement in a key process, knowing that they know they have made a fundamental difference and that they are mastering the tools to improve another process. Their growing confidence and self-esteem driven from analyzing and exceeding customer needs, for me, was an overwhelming experience. The problem still remains with CEOs and other senior leaders of how to convert the logic to effective improvement work.

Something snapped in me in 1987 when Batalden explained the cycle of continuous improvement. By mid-1988 something had snapped among the vice presidents as we searched for answers. By mid-1990, something had snapped in the minds of at least 25 percent of the department managers, physicians, and employees. Meeting customer needs became bigger than each of us. Clearly our own egos and self-interests blocked our path on more than one occasion, but I sensed all of us felt oddly uncomfortable when this was occurring. As we struggled to interpret the market need for our organization in the community, to convert our understanding of this customer need into a vision and strategic measures, and to widely deploy teams to meet these needs, we developed a passion to drive results. In other words, as we attempted to deploy the transformation model, we developed a common vision. While it was often not very pretty, it was effective.

It is also important to point out that not all the conventions contained in this book may work in your organization. The concepts presented in this book come from a small sample of only 20 or 30 health care organizations. Rather, I hope that the success factors and failure factors driving these conventions will serve as a baseline for readers to experiment within their own organizations. Real learning, at least from the experiences cataloged in this book, comes from the internalization of the logic of conventions, not merely the replication of a collection of them.

Acknowledgments

It is a very humbling endeavor to write a book. Obviously the author wants the effort to be appreciated and elevated to the best-seller list. I suspect most first-time authors, like me, however, are more worried about embarrassing themselves than they are about how to handle such profound notoriety that you can't even go to McDonald's without being rushed for autographs.

First and foremost, credit, must be directed to Paul Batalden, M.D., my mentor. I first met Paul in the fall of 1987 at a dinner meeting in Nashville with about four other CEOs. He had just been hired by Tommy Frist, M.D., president of the Hospital Corporation of America (HCA), and Paul was telling us what TQM was all about and made a few references to a guy named W. Edwards Deming. This Deming guy didn't think much of budgets, purchasing on the basis of price, or inspection. Frankly, I think the wine got to me before Paul did, but he seemed like a nice fellow. The next time I saw Paul was at the HCA Eastern Group meeting in Nashville. Paul made a three-hour presentation on Deming's 14 principles. I was awestruck; Deming had created the purest integration between marketing and operations I had ever seen in the form of the cycle of continuous improvement. After the meeting, I sought out Paul and asked him to help us at West Paces Medical Center to apply these principles. He was eager to assist. It would be another book entirely to relate the stories that followed. Paul is the preeminent mentor and far too humble. The learning that occurred at his hands has literally changed the lives of thousands of people.

Sometime during 1988, Paul hosted another meeting of CEOs and quality managers who were attempting to deploy TQM in their hospitals. I was fortunate to sit beside. Don Berwick, M.D., then of the Harvard Community Health Plan. He was totally immersed in what we were doing at West Paces Medical Center. I was slightly embarrassed because we had just begun and none of us felt very comfortable with strategic linkages or the way in which deployment would drive results. Don has remained a dedicated mentor over the years. Many of the concepts represented in this book sprung from Don's observations about the way health care organizations and physicians interact.

An acknowledgments section without listing Jack Bovender would be inappropriate. Jack served as the president of the HCA Eastern Group and later as HCA chief operating officer. His supportive style enabled the managers and employees of West Paces Medical Center to test new ground, make mistakes, and recover. He was always willing to play whatever part we felt was appropriate. Once he even agreed to fly to Atlanta to review department storyboards; he probably felt like this was a small contribution, but managers acknowledged his attentions for months. His efforts were rewarded. From the time we implemented our TQM initiative in 1987 until fiscal year 1993, West Paces' earnings before depreciation, interest, and taxes grew from $9 million to over $20 million.

Paul Makens of the HCA Quality Resource Group deserves acknowledgment for introducing me to Takashi Kanatsu's book, which contains the first spider diagram I ever saw. From this beginning point, Paul and Gene Nelson, now at Dartmouth Hitchcock Medical Center, helped us understand how to construct a strategic measures deployment scheme.

Vicki Davis, perhaps the first TQM coach in a U.S. hospital, invested in a new career. Formerly the material manager, she met Paul's description of the "cream rising to the top." In some ways, many of us should be angry with her. The use of TQM tools came naturally to her. She didn't have to struggle with any of it. She became the facilitators' facilitator.

The members of the West Paces Medical Center Quality Council over the years deserve special recognition for bringing results to the TQM theory. They were always willing warriors in a quest to conquer unseen lands. Peggy Hindsman, Mitch Mitchell, Jim Browne, Joe Calcutt, Edward McEachern, John Anderson, Lorraine Schiff, Andy Johnston, Rodney Ray, Pam Kerns, Carol Allen, and countless others, each contributed immeasurably, not only to the results achieved at West Paces, but to my growing knowledge and understanding of accelerators and inhibitors. The department managers, physicians, and employees invested heavily in themselves to learn how to use new and foreign tools and became willing instructors to the hundreds of visitors who sought them out.

Acknowledgment should also be given to those who willingly shared materials and concepts for this book. Employees at Wesley Medical Center, Juran Institute, SunHealth, StorageTek, Ft. Sanders Health System, Suburban Medical Center, Mike Midas, TEC 152, and many other people were eager to accelerate others' learning by sharing their work.

The person perhaps most responsible for getting this book to this point is my wife, Donna. Always encouraging, always supportive, blowing her cool at appropriate times—everyone who knows Donna, from her children to her casual acquaintances, knows that she can be counted on to be supportive of them. Donna has stood beside me for more than 20 years. In fact, she probably knows more about TQM than most people I know. I know for a fact that she could run a hospital as well as many CEOs. To Donna goes a lot of acknowledgment.

Chapter 1

Need for Change

This book is certainly not the first about invoking the power of total quality management (TQM) to transform an organization's effective deployment of strategy, and I doubt it will be the last. It does, however, embroil us in perhaps the most important aspects of any effective strategic deployment—how to drive the organization's strategic imperatives through a transformation of management behaviors at the very highest levels of the organization to each and every member. This view of management may best be thought of as *mentoring*. Effective mentoring requires a radical departure from the thought processes inbred in most of us. Perhaps an effective metaphor would be that true mentors envision their behaviors as "seed and water, seed and water." That is, our roles with members of the organization have evolved from "Follow me" to "How can I help you better interpret and exceed customer needs?" This link between customer-driven strategic imperatives and people working efficiently and effectively together to achieve the strategy is the heart of TQM's power.

The successful implementation of TQM in any organization requires the successful introduction and management of two critical components: (1) The effective use of a specific TQM model (for example, Joseph M. Juran's quality trilogy or Florida Power & Light's measures/countermeasures) and (2) evolution to a mature TQM organizational environment. Significant research has been completed in the first area, TQM models, and, therefore, while the creators of the various models might object, it makes very little difference which one is selected as long as the model requires disciplined conformance to three features.

1. Customer-mindedness: Recognition of customers, both internal and external, and the identification of their needs and expectations

2. Process-mindedness: Inclusion of steps and methods that ensure that profound knowledge of the processes under study is achieved

3. Statistical-mindedness: Insistence on the use of basic statistics to uncover root causes of variation and failure to meet customer expectations in the performance of these processes, combined with techniques to reduce variation

As long as the TQM model achieves these three requirements, it will meet the intended use.

Equally important is the establishment of a TQM organizational environment capable of sustaining a culture of continuous improvement. Paul Makens, formerly of Hospital Corporation of America (HCA) Quality Resource Group, states that TQM effectiveness is a formula of [use of tools] × [the environment].[1] An organization that maintains effective use of tools 100 percent of the time by 10 percent of the workforce will lag behind an organization that maintains effective use of tools 75 percent of the time by 75 percent of the workforce. Therefore, management must not only concern itself with selection of tools to employ, but also the environment in which the tools are deployed. Maintenance and enhancement of the environment requires significantly more management attention because, unlike a TQM model, no single prescription for the evolution of an organization can be researched and installed. Techniques and conventions that are successfully applied in one organization may create havoc in another organization due to the unique nature of organizational cultures. Perhaps this complexity is at the heart of the disillusionment of many senior leaders. Many have complained that TQM is not effective in driving their organizations' vision, market share, cost of poor quality, or shareholder value. In fact, some leaders function under the disillusionment that TQM is dead and reengineering is in. These managers, faced with the pressing need to drive innovation throughout the workplace, have been led to believe that all their organizations need is a new program or set of steps to follow and their strategies will fall into place. Yet the old adage, "if it appears too good to be true" certainly deserves a place in TQM application. The requirement to transform the workplace before TQM tools and techniques can be maximized demands senior management's time and creativity. The transformation is hard work, as most leaders who have attempted to implement a TQM program will attest; in fact, many have given up, claiming that TQM does not work. But, TQM is more than tools; it requires great attention to detail.

Understanding the personality characteristics and the likely response to organizational change is the sole domain of management and depends largely upon the unique personality of the organization. The attention to personality characteristics, both organizational and for each and every individual, is the art and science of mentoring. Effective mentoring requires that senior leaders bring together the organization's strategic imperatives and the organization's collective personality and vision. Our understanding of the need for the existence of our organization in the marketplace, based on a sound knowledge of customer needs, converted into the social needs of the workforce in an understandable way to each and every member of the company can be thought of as the division between the successful enterprise of the future and the organization that may cease to exist in the years ahead. At the heart of this success will be our effective learning of mentoring behaviors.

For those leaders who invest the time to transform the organization, the payoff has, in some cases, proven astounding. Xerox doubled its market share between 1979 and 1986. Westinghouse Commercial Nuclear Fuel Division captured 40 percent of the U.S. market and 20 percent of the world market, driving a tenfold improvement in the reliability of its products.[2] Similarly, a study conducted between June 1990 and February 1991 of leading U.S. companies, including Corning, Xerox, IBM, Westinghouse, Kodak, General Motors, Ford, Milliken, and DEC concluded that companies hosting mature TQM environments enjoyed an average annual increase in market share of 13.7 percent, an 11.6 percent decrease in customer complaints, a 12 percent reduction in order processing cycle time, and a 10.3 percent drop in product defects.[3]

Ample evidence exists that TQM, upon management of both dimensions of tools and environment, can drive strategic results, but too many leaders allow themselves to be lulled into interpreting unpreventible events as a failing of TQM as a strategic deployment methodology. For example, IBM, the biggest chip of the blue chips, tumbled long and far as its market faced unprecedented changes. Its failing, in fact, can clearly be attributed to the failure to surpass its competitors in two of TQM's predominant offerings—increasing the rate of innovation and listening to the voice of the customer. Big Blue failed to innovate as fast as its competitors for two reasons. First, it committed itself to a mainframe market strategy based on unpredictably faulty market assumptions and, second, once leaders recognized a need to alter strategic direction, the organizational infrastructure prevented them from innovating fast enough to respond before chaos struck. Federal Express, a Malcolm Baldrige National Quality Award recipient, also suffered at the hands of unpredictable environmental forces. Florida Power & Light, the first non-Japanese company to ever win the coveted Deming Prize, similarly found itself immersed in a strategy that did not accurately translate the voice of the customer into its internal operating language. Each of these examples of organizational trauma do not highlight the weaknesses of TQM, but rather firmly illustrate how vital the very centerpoints of TQM constructs are. Expertise in translating the voice of the customer and aligning organizational structures to drive the rate of innovation ahead of competitors are vital.

In spite of the path laid out for us through the lessons of successful applications, as well as the lessons from market traumas, little work continues to surface in the literature in this vital area of transforming the organizational environment. Yet, molding an effective TQM environment commands greater planning and attention than applying the TQM model, but our understanding of the transformation can best be initiated by the recognition that deployment of TQM is, in fact, a transformation. That is, to capture the use of TQM tools and techniques, leaders, employees, suppliers, and other organizational affiliates must recognize that they are charged to complete an organizational transformation and that each has a precise role and responsibility in the transformation.

In order to understand the task at hand, it is important to relate the transition of the many paradigm shifts that occur in an organization as it moves through a TQM transformation. As first pointed out to me by my mentor, Paul Batalden, M.D., formerly HCA vice president (VP) of quality care and now with Dartmouth Medical School, introduction of TQM does not create conversion of Organization A to Organization $A_{plus\ TQM}$, but rather it is a cultural transformation in which Organization A becomes a different organization, Organization B (see Figure 1.1).[4] In other words, because TQM produces use of

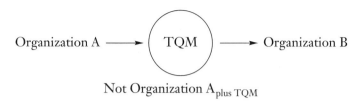

Figure 1.1. TQM: The transformation.

tools deployed widely within the organization and dependent upon internalization of TQM concepts by the entire workforce, the result is not a new program but a new organization culture. Japanese companies have clearly recognized the vital formula of tools times environment and this recognition was best articulated by the Japanese leader, Konosuke Matsushita, in 1982.

> We are going to win and the industrial West is going to lose out; there's not much you can do about it because the reasons for your failure are within yourselves. Your firms are built upon the Taylor model. Even worse, so are your heads. With your bosses doing the thinking while the workers wield the screwdrivers, you're convinced deep down this is the right way to run a business. For you the essence of management is getting the ideas out of the heads of the bosses and into the hands of the labor.
>
> We are beyond your mind-set. Business, we know, is now so complex and difficult, the survival of firms so hazardous in an environment increasingly unpredictable, competitive and fraught with danger, that their continued existence depends upon the day to day mobilization of every ounce of intelligence.[5]

Introduction of TQM in an organization requires systematic conversion from its current culture to a TQM environment in which widespread innovation is fostered. This involves internalization of many new paradigms at every level of the organization: chief executive officer (CEO), senior management, middle management, employees, volunteers, and physicians. Some of the important paradigm shifts are

1. Internalization of the Shewhart cycle of continuous improvement[6]
2. Understanding and reducing variation

3. Understanding and mastering error-free design, and reducing cost-inefficient inspection

4. A commitment to understanding the importance of Noriaki Kano's levels of customer knowledge—Expected, Requested, and Delighted[7]

5. Establishment and maintenance of an employee empowered organization

Once an organization has selected an available TQM model or developed one of its own and established an education program to advance understanding of the model and its use, the organization must set the stage for the transformation. This involves the careful study of those factors that accelerate the transformation and those factors that inhibit the organization from achievement of widespread use of TQM methods.

This book concentrates on the accelerators and inhibitors in evolution of a TQM environment featuring employee empowerment. It is about how to grow from a leadership management model to a mentor model. Students of the concepts discussed in this text will learn to learn from themselves, to teach others to learn from themselves, and to observe subtle differences in organizational performance and behavior that drive achievement of the organization's strategy. Mentor behaviors as discussed herein require serious practice to break old paradigms, values, and concepts. As Peter M. Senge observes, good managers possess both advocacy skills and inquiry skills.[8] While leaders of organizations employing the more familiar and traditional management by objectives strategic deployment model, by nature must be strong in advocacy skills; a successful TQM deployment requires a different set of skills, just as moving to a leadership style from a control style required the acquisition of new skills. Mentoring, the management style of TQM deployment, requires movement to a more central inquiry skill set. This skill requires much more patience and certainly greater discernment skill. That is, mentoring through inquiry possesses as its desired result organizational learning—employees and teams learn to learn from their own actions. Discerning through observation not only takes patience but also recognition of subtle signs that individuals are, in fact, applying TQM methods to their work. These observable signs may not be evident for several weeks or even months, as illustrated in Figure 1.2, but once the organization begins to learn from itself, the rate of innovation becomes logarithmic.

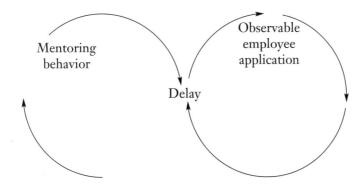

Figure 1.2. The mentoring behavior chain.

This book is about strategic deployment, the achievement of the results needed by the organization to drive its strategic vision. The greatest gap in most TQM deployments is the failure to link the organization's strategic needs to the deployment of teams, use of tools and techniques, and so on. In other words, many organizations create a TQM initiative outside the CEO's suite, seemingly as a program to be carried out in a vacuum. Several of these organizations have invested millions of dollars in training every employee in the workplace, but have failed to provide a means for those trained to apply their knowledge to improving those processes most important to the organization's vision of meeting customer needs. Many have achieved profound improvements, but often upon processes that are not vital to its strategy. Therefore, one of the purposes of this book is to place the quality agenda firmly on the CEO's desk. By recognizing the power that exists in an extensively trained workforce, CEOs and senior leaders in mature TQM organizations have shown that market share goes up, customer satisfaction goes up, costs go down, and employee satisfaction swells. These results can be achieved only when the quality council and the executive council are one and the same, and the leaders of the organization set the quality agenda.

Discussion Exercise for a One-Hour Quality Council Meeting

Assign an operations person or team of people on the quality council to report on the following quality audit prior to the meeting. If possible, the quality improvement team case study should be made available to each council member one week in advance of the discussion. The assigned council member or team leads a discussion at the council meeting on the following points.

1. Review your quality improvement model's steps with the council.

2. By reviewing the completed work of a recent quality improvement team, is there evidence that disciplined completion of each step in each improvement cycle concludes with

a. Customer-mindedness

— Is there evidence that each improvement team and team leader has followed tools that first identify the customer or customers of the process under improvement?

— Is there evidence that the team began its quest with the stated needs of the customer or customers in the customer's words?

— Did the team then translate these stated customer needs into the team's operational language?

b. Process-mindedness

— What evidence exists that the team understood the process producing satisfaction of the customer's needs?

— Did the team's charter or mission statement give adequate guidance about the boundaries of the process to be improved so that the team clearly understood its input point and its output point?

— Did the team include persons representing each major step in the process?

— Did the team's flowchart adequately detail the points of inspection, rework, duplication, waiting loops, and disposition of rejected inputs?

c. Statistical-mindedness

— Did the team use a structured approach to uncover root causes of variation or poor quality, which gives the quality council satisfaction that unbiased alternatives were identified? Did the team follow Kaoru Ishikawa's concept of asking why five times before concluding its investigation of symptoms?

— Did the team use data to test these theories? How comfortable, on a scale of 1 to 5, does the quality council feel that this team was unbiased in its testing?

— Upon determining a root cause, is there evidence that the team used a structured process (for example, an alternatives form) to generate multiple alternatives to remedy the root cause? Does the form include several evaluative factors upon which to select a remedy (for example, ease of introduction, cost and conformance to existing organization policy)?

— Did the team determine process output characteristics to measure in the form of run charts or control charts? Are these charts inclusive of data points before and after the piloted remedy? Did the chart show an improvement after the remedy? If not, did the team return to the improvement model for a refined diagnosis?

3. As a result of the weaknesses, if any, of the quality audit, brainstorm and nominally group three to four improvements that can be made to strengthen your existing model. Assign a quality council member to sponsor or champion each improvement and report back to the quality council in a finite period of time. Identify and assign, if necessary, a technical person to assist the council member.

Discussion Exercise for a One-Hour Department Manager/Team Leader Meeting

For this exercise, it is best if the meeting is led by the quality council member or team of council members who facilitated the previous exercise. This method gives department managers and team leaders the opportunity to see various council members in leadership roles, highlighting the notion that the TQM initiative is vested in all senior leaders. As facilitator or facilitators for this meeting, it is important to note that the intent of this exercise is to drive notions of customer-mindedness, process-mindedness, and statistical-mindedness to the department manager and team leader audience. It is not to be critical of the current model or its application. Therefore, it is vital to avoid any critical comments of their ideas. You are simply planting seeds so that, as these leaders serve on future teams, they might begin to learn from themselves by asking these questions of each other.

1. Review your organization's quality improvement model.
2. Brainstorm the ways in which your organization's model identifies customer needs and interprets those needs from the words of your customers to the words of the organization.
3. Brainstorm ways in which your organization's model fully explores the process under improvement and includes team members who are most knowledgeable of the process.
4. Brainstorm how the use of statistical methods prevents teams from preselecting biased remedies to process problems.

Discussion Exercise for a Governing Board Meeting

Assign the chairperson of the quality improvement committee, or an interested governing body member, to lead the discussion, with the quality director as facilitator at the flip chart.

1. Review your quality improvement model steps with the governing body and illustrate them through one or two very brief case examples. If the governing body meeting is an extended meeting, consider two presentations by a physician-led clinical team and a support department team.
2. Brainstorm and clarify what methods and processes the governing body engages in to assess the degree to which
   a. The organization understands and interprets customer needs.
   b. These needs are met, compared to customer expectations and competitor performance, in quantified form.
   c. All stakeholders—community, governing body, senior leaders, employees, medical staff, suppliers—understand their roles in meeting customer needs.

3. Based on this informal analysis, complete the following exercise.

   a. Brainstorm where gaps exist in the organization's methods and processes to achieve the items on the previous list.

   b. Clarify gaps so that each governing body member fully understands all entries.

   c. Nominally group the most important gaps by asking each member to vote on his or her top three gaps. Record responses on the flip chart to rank the top five to six gaps.

Notes

1. Paul Makens, site visit interview with author, Atlanta, Ga., March 1990.

2. Donald M. Berwick, A. Blanton Godfrey, and Jane Roessner, *Curing Health Care* (San Francisco: Jossey-Bass, 1990), 29–30.

3. B. Usilaner and M. Dulworth, "What's the Bottom Line Payback for TQM?" *Journal for Quality and Participation* 15 (March 1992): 82–90.

4. Paul B. Batalden, "Hospital-Wide Quality Improvement" (Paper presented at HCA Eastern Group CEOs, Nashville, Tenn., October 29, 1990).

5. Ibid.

6. Mary Walton, *The Deming Management Method* (New York: Dodd, Mead & Company, 1986), 86–88.

7. Berwick, Godfrey, and Roessner, *Curing Health Care*, 55.

8. Peter M. Senge, *The Fifth Discipline: The Art and Practice of the Learning Organization* (New York: Doubleday, 1990), 198.

Chapter 2

The Transformation Model

In order to incorporate the accelerator and inhibitor conventions presented in this text and to grow this body of knowledge in the literature, it is important to frame these conventions along organizational transformation concepts. As suggested by Kurt Lewin, organizational change requires not only creation of accelerating forces, but also management of inhibiting forces.[1] Attempts by many organizations to generate change simply by adding accelerators without consideration of the necessity of removing inhibitors has presented formidable complications. As illustrated in Figure 2.1, effective organizational change requires the acknowledgment of the current state, followed by an unfreezing of predominate attitudes before the organizational transformation can begin.[2] Upon successful evolution through the transformation stage, a process of refreezing of organizational values and attitudes occurs before the future state is achieved.

During the transformation stage at West Paces Medical Center, after many false starts, we found management must focus on the conventions that accelerate this change and understand the attitudes that inhibit transition. We, like most organizations, began our TQM initiative by introducing a vast number of accelerators—quality council, storyboards, road maps, storyboard review, quality management director, and an introduction of an endless number of new TQM tools and techniques at all levels. After two years of frustration at the seeming slowness of team cycles, we began to recognize the vital nature of Lewin's concepts. Uncovering and removing inhibitors is as important, if not more important, than merely introducing new concepts and conventions to accelerate the change. The nature of this unfreez-

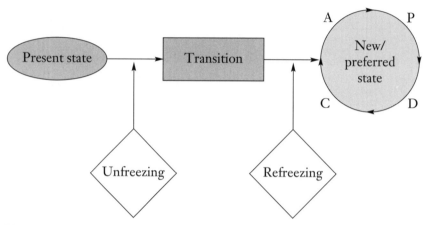

Figure 2.1. Lewin's change model.

ing-refreezing work is further complicated by the fact that old paradigms number in the hundreds and must be prioritized before modification (see Figure 2.2). This complexity alone can be enough to frustrate the most sturdy manager.

Paradigm Management

Since full maturity in TQM requires a successful shift in paradigm thinking, organizations evolving through TQM are moving through the unfreezing and refreezing phases along each of these different paradigms with transitions occurring at different points in time and at different rates of speed. In other words, management is constantly faced

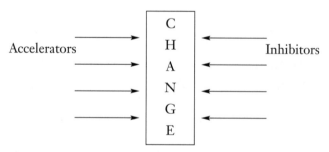

Figure 2.2. Accelerators and inhibitors.

with old paradigm issues within one paradigm while at the same time managing refreezing issues in another paradigm. For example, integrating quality assurance into quality improvement requires the management of one entire set of paradigm thinking issues. These issues are being dealt with at the same time the organization is attempting to instill the discipline to understand and reduce variation, which is occurring at the same time the organization is attempting to understand vendor certification issues, which is occurring at the same time the organization is struggling with human resource compensation concepts. As Figure 2.3 shows, the cumulative complexity of managing these inhibitors along multiple paradigm shifts at the same time can become overwhelming.

As the organization's leaders critically examine readiness for each new phase of TQM transformation, many leaders have analyzed and interpreted the organization's status in light of the location of the workforce along this continuum and in relation to its status in other phases. In our case the accelerator of most help was the TQM strategic road map, a Gantt chart of sorts that listed major deployment tasks and steps projected over the upcoming 24 months. Using the road map to identify paradigm issues and the actions intended to address them allows senior leaders to visualize the organization's efforts without becoming overwhelmed by the magnitude of the task. That is, our quality council was well aware that our performance appraisal and compensation was not aligned with our strategic vision, but during the early phases of TQM deployment, we simply could not undertake the

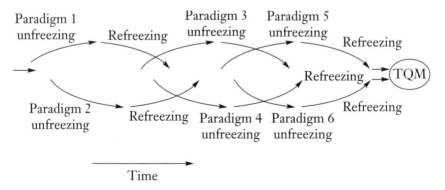

Figure 2.3. Paradigm transformation.

massive task of human resource function restructuring. Members of the council felt at ease, however, knowing that we had included this task on our road map, with work to begin in 18 months.

The Transformation Model

The first place to begin is to conceptualize a transformation model necessary to move the organization from its current state to the desired state. This mental model not only serves as the framework of this book, it is intended to serve as a framework for CEOs, strategists, quality management professionals, and quality councils as strategic deployment initiatives are generated. The elements are not wholly original, of course, as it will become apparent that the model weaves together the outputs of your current elements—strategic planning, market assessment, operations planning, budgeting and financial management, human resource management, and supplier manage-ment—all woven together in a TQM blanket intended to describe, align, and manage the customer's needs throughout each organiza-tional element. It is also necessary to point out that whether or not a CEO, organizational strategist, quality management professional, or quality council records a mental model as expressed here, some model is used by each individual charged with managing the organization. The model might not be recorded, it might have never been expressed, but it exists nonetheless. Each manager follows a predeter-mined set of principles in constructing any change model, action plan, road map, or strategic plan. The failure to record and reach organiza-tional agreement on the model being used is, in fact, a great inhibitor in itself. Ask any group of senior leaders to brainstorm their frustra-tions regarding how organizational plans are conceived, planned, deployed, carried out, and measured, and it becomes apparent that great variation exists regarding the model in use. Ask any group of department managers to brainstorm their frustrations regarding how organizational plans are conceived, planned, deployed, carried out, and measured, and it becomes apparent that great variation in under-standing is present at this level as well. This, of course, is not to sug-gest that models in use, whether recorded or not, are ill-conceived, but rather that, by recording and communicating the organization's model, a significant inhibitor to generating organization-wide under-standing is removed.

Although each element of Figure 2.4 will be discussed in great detail throughout the remainder of this book, a brief glossary is in order at this point to explain the meaning of each element. Even before generating a discussion glossary, it is perhaps important to confess that I, and most others on the quality council, experienced great frustration before an understanding of the model became apparent. Vicki Davis, the quality director, invested hours and hours to explain the various elements of the transformation model and the need for each of the elements. She had been tutored extensively by Batalden before she could lead discussions with the quality council. For some, the transformation model may be intuitive, but for others, it may make little sense and you may not see the logic of struggling with its precepts. If you invest the time, I believe the benefits will far outweigh the costs in the long run. This document became such an important communication tool for me when I was CEO of West Paces Medical Center that the flip chart paper upon which it was drawn hung in a

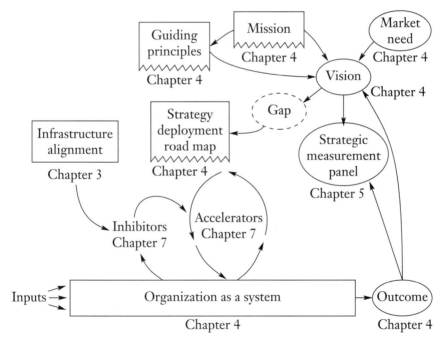

Figure 2.4. The transformation model.

Source: Adapted from HCA documents. Reprinted with permission.[3]

room adjacent to my office for four years. This document, over the years, helped senior leaders transform the strategic thrust of the organization as we began to recognize the weaknesses in our outcomes and the direction of the health care market toward physician-hospital integration and the need to innovate cost reductions while maintaining quality.

Perhaps the best point at which to begin a discussion of the transformation model is a focus on market need since TQM conventions intended to advance our understanding of customer needs is at the heart of our efforts. Recording the ultimate need for the organization, in the words of the market, is a vital first step and should include a set of statements from market research about the status of the market—its current and anticipated needs, and the identification of market, technology, competitor, and environmental issues necessary to express the needs—in the customer's words. Needs should, at this point, be expressed in customers' language since there is the opportunity to translate the customer's language to the organization's language in the outcomes element. No rocket science here, simply basic strategic planning methodology.

Mission to most organizations is self-evident, so I will not explain.

Outcome is the measurable result of the transformation of the various inputs into the organization's product or service.

The organization as a system is a phrase coined to describe the seamless interweaving of the multiplicity of department processes and subprocesses that come together to produce a given outcome.

Inputs represent, of course, the raw materials and human power that are transformed by the organization to produce outcomes, as well as the introduction point of the customer into the organization as a system.

Guiding principles represent the document that some organizations create to express their culture and attitudes toward their customers, human resources, suppliers, or other ideological expressions. In its purest form, an organization with a maximum degree of shared guiding principles by its workforce and suppliers would have no need for a policy and procedure manual.

Vision is a long-term (generally five or more years) statement of the organization's strategic intent. For example, Florida Power & Light's vision was something like "to be the best-value public utility and to be recognized as such." Often, vision statements are placed on the back of business cards, on plaques in the lobby, and customer communications documents or advertisements. Organizations tend to look to become best in class or world-class when conceptualizing their visions.

The strategic measurement panel is perhaps the most subtle element of the model and will be discussed in great detail later in the text. To be most effective, many organizations have found it helpful to identify a set of 10 to 15 quantitative measures to capture the degree of conformance to the stated vision, which becomes the vehicle against which senior leaders drive strategic plans.

The gap represents the difference, best measured quantitatively, between the organization's vision and current outcomes. This difference, or gap, is one of the methods quality councils use to determine which key business processes should be a high priority of reengineering teams, or in which areas development capital is most needed.

The strategy deployment road map is the action plan that ties each element together. This plan, generally projecting activities 12 to 24 months out, is the result of the organization's best thinkers about how to close the gap between current outcomes and the vision within the time frame mandated by the vision. This plan is very detailed in scope and accountability and is considered to be a dynamic instrument versus a static tool so that as conditions change it changes with them.

Infrastructure alignment refers to the elements of the organization that must be aligned to achieve the vision. Generally, organizations determine that their organizational structures, legal structures, performance appraisal concepts, compensation philosophies, capital allocation policies, and so on are not only *not* aligned to achieve the organization's vision, but, in fact, are an impediment to success.

Accelerators and inhibitors are those conditions and factors that together drive or repel the strategic deployment road map's intent. Closely following and managing accelerators and inhibitors as suggested in Lewin's model may perhaps be the most important ingredient in an organization's efforts. These notions, of course, are one of the features of this book.

Not only does this mental model serve as a strategic deployment metric, it serves several other useful purposes, as well. The model helps clarify the relationships between the various elements that come together to generate outcomes. It infuses a discipline of systems' thinking upon all managers who are engaged to bring the vision to reality. It ensures a consistent language or glossary among all organizational stakeholders, senior leaders, trustees and directors, employees, and suppliers. Finally, the entire metric, or excerpts from it, can be used effectively to communicate to stakeholders and external publics. In all, the transformation model is well worth its weight in flip chart paper.

Notes

1. D. Cartwright and A. Zander, *Group Dynamics: Research and Theory* (New York: Harper & Row, 1968), 149.

2 Paul B. Batalden, "Hospital-Wide Quality Improvement" (paper presented at HCA Eastern Group CEOs, Nashville, Tenn., October 29, 1990).

3. Paul B. Batalden, *Organizing Hospital Care as a System: An Annotated Guide* (Nashville, Tenn.: HCA Quality Resource Group, 1992), 3, 22.

Chapter 3

Paradigm Shift Management

The importance of becoming educated about paradigms, paradigm shifts, and paradigm shift management has been well documented in literature by almost every contemporary management writer. It has become a focus of strategic planning meetings attended by most CEOs and senior leaders since almost every industry is faced with unprecedented market evolution and consumer sophistication. Gaining an understanding of these paradigms and the implications they have on failure to achieve an organization's strategic vision is perhaps one of the most difficult challenges facing senior leaders. Yet, as discussed in the next chapter on strategy and visioning, transforming an organization with these in mind will probably ensure an organization's survival. While volumes of text could be written on this topic, there are eight concepts that serve our purposes in this text.

1. Importance of velocity of innovation
2. Reduction of cost of poor quality
3. Elements of customer judgment
4. Progressive systems integration
5. Alignment of support infrastructure
6. Understanding the cycle of continuous improvement

7. Reduction of variation

8. Employee empowerment

Paradigm 1: Importance of Velocity of Innovation

One of the enlightenment books of the 1980s was the landmark study by Tom Peters and Robert Waterman *In Search of Excellence.*[1] Every manager with any degree of integrity scrutinized this comparative work of America's most successful companies and lusted after replication. Peters and Waterman found that there were indeed some common factors to be found among America's top 43 companies. Upon discovering this revelation, we drooled, stayed up late at night, begged our subordinates, masterminded strategies, bored our boards, and otherwise made absolute fools of ourselves in the quest to become one of the vital few. We managed by walking around ourselves to death to the delight of shoe manufacturers the world over.

But what has become of the 43 companies scrutinized by Peters and Waterman 10 years hence? In a study conducted by Richard Pascale, another startling revelation becomes known to us. Of the original 43, only 14 are still recognized as leaders within their own industries, let alone considered world-class.[2] What became of the unlucky 29? Did they fall asleep at the switch? Did they cease to follow the valued truths? Not in any meaningful way. What is more likely is that they failed to recognize perhaps the most important paradigm of our time—the importance of the *velocity of innovation.* As discussed in chapter 1, IBM succumbed to it, mostly due to its massive infrastructure. Eastern Airlines was trampled by it. Others, in turn, failed, not at failing to recognize customer needs, but in not recognizing and acting upon them as fast as their competitors. The familiar kaizen diagram so popular in Juran's talks and writings, shown in Figure 3.1, illustrates that, while Company A produces a reasonable rate of innovation, its rate is dwarfed by Company B.[3]

As you can see from Figure 3.1, Company A does not cease to innovate, it merely innovates slower than its competitors; hence, Company A, without changing its business line, finding a new market, or otherwise manipulating its given circumstances, will succumb to Company B's overt competitiveness. A definition of innovation may be

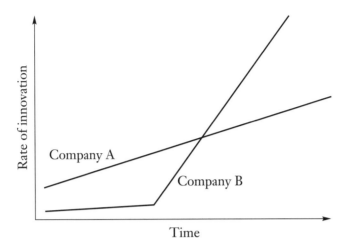

Figure 3.1. Company A versus Company B.

helpful at this juncture. Some may think of innovation as break-throughs of astounding proportions; reengineering afficionados often claim that the only road to innovation is radical departure from the current state. Some may think the term applies to technology intro-duction or capital building programs or creating more services. Others may simply believe the term means the cumulative work of endless quality improvement teams and hundreds of individuals applying TQM tools on a small scale in their daily work. In fact, innovation means all of this combined. In a rapidly changing competitive envi-ronment, the methods and intensity of innovation at Company A must surpass or equal that of Company B, or Company A will simply perish.

For those who grow exceedingly nervous around this discussion, it may be some comfort to acknowledge that your competitors face the same threats from you. It is only the competitive arena that defines the rate of innovation. An instructional metaphor often repeated by scuba instructors illustrates the point. On a scuba expedition, one diver asked her dive buddy, "What will you do if you see a shark?" The dive buddy remarks, "I will swim away as fast as I can." The first diver laughed. "You can't outswim a shark!" she said. "I don't have to outswim the shark, pal, I only have to outswim you," concluded the dive buddy. Keeping a close eye on market research trends of your customer's satisfaction with your products and services compared to your competitors remains, as always, a fundamental strategic task.

Another complexity surrounding the intensity of innovation in competitive markets today is well illustrated by a conversation reported to me by Batalden with a London physicist he met who postulated that the acquisition of knowledge, or learning, by individuals, organizations, and societies, is not keeping pace with the rate of information generation. As illustrated in Figure 3.2, if one assumes that the rate of information generation from the 1930s through the 1970s follows the lower slope and the rate of learning accelerates at the same rate, then we can conclude that these slopes are relatively equal. However, microprocessor technology, cellular technology, and the mass application of information technology has produced a logarithmic explosion of information availability. The availability of information continues to dramatically accelerate. The shaded ellipse at the far right of the figure demonstrates the zone of comparison of your organization's rate of innovation compared to your competitors. If your training methods for employees do not keep pace with the availability of information, how can you expect your knowledge transfer rate to change? Or, perhaps a more important question: Can you

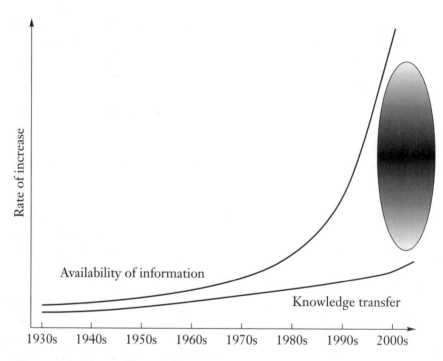

Figure 3.2. Slope of knowledge transfer.

afford to train your employees and deploy your strategy in the same old ways while your competitors embark on creative training methods and deploy TQM methods to capitalize on the creative energies of their entire workforces?

Almost anyone with a modem and a PC can instantaneously obtain access to incredibly sophisticated research and download the information. Services such as CompuServe, Prodigy, America On-Line, and others link millions of people to the Internet, the world's richest database. These services not only provide access to a library of libraries, but also to numerous user groups on every known subject and perhaps even some virtual subjects. In short order, computer-literate individuals can access a set of research materials, obtain the most recent demographic information at city block detail, formulate theories, and obtain feedback via online user groups regarding their theories, all within a matter of a few hours.

Recently I observed a student at Georgia Tech registering for classes for the upcoming semester. Among the materials handed her was an orientation document that contained a chapter on how to access the university's InterNet system. Instructions included how to navigate not only the state of Georgia University Library archives, but also an outline of services available through the Library of Congress, various science and technology databases, periodicals, government documents, census and demographic profiling, and corporate information databases, all via a local telephone connection.

Just 24 hours later, I was drafting a TQM proposal tailored to the specific needs of a demanding client. After a one-hour telephone conference with the organization's quality director, I signed on to the Juran Institute mainframe to search the subdirectory housing draft proposals and the subdirectory of course descriptions. Within 30 minutes I was able to locate and download five files, import them into WordPerfect 6.0, suture the documents together using bridging language, and, within another hour, uploaded the completed contract for execution by Juran's officers. The client received a precise agreement conforming to his stated needs within 24 hours of the original conference call.

We have come to expect this level of service from those with whom we choose to partner. No longer is this degree of service considered heroic, it has become an expectation, and yet only two to three years ago this level of service was not even possible. Innovation has become perhaps the most important management indicator, rivaling cash flow generation, net revenue growth, and return on investment. Failure to recognize the importance of the velocity of innovation, in fact, has predictable results. Examine almost any industry. Can you recall when the process to cash a check required a trip to the bank during its operating hours, standing in a long line, and enduring several frustrating steps of identification verification? Now one can acquire cash at automated teller machines (ATMs) located in airports, foreign countries, and grocery stores. At some large grocery chains, you can even pay via a small self-operated ATM device at the checkout counter. No longer will we be satisfied with cumbersome service. This has become my new paradigm.

These new levels of service are not restricted, however, to industry-specific customer expectations. Customers generalize across industry groups, demanding transference of technological innovation from industry to industry. Health care consumers cannot understand why a simple registration process can take 30 minutes, particularly since the data collected were retrieved by the physician only 10 minutes ago. Airline travelers expect a seamless flow of information from registration through baggage claim and, in fact, continue to question why a boarding pass is required since the travel office receives seat assignments via computer. Ritz Carlton boasts of its customer-specific database that registers incredible detail about its frequent guests. Upon check-in, the registration desk is informed whether the guest prefers smoking or nonsmoking, ground floor, near the elevator, and even whether the customer prefers black or blue ink in room pens![4]

The importance of these advanced learning methods is not only the mystique of the new order, but, more importantly, from an organizational perspective, the ability for those enlightened organizations to accelerate the velocity of their organizational learning. This premise lies at the heart of Senge's concepts of the learning organization. Those organizations that recognize and invest capital, energy, and training to evolve their organizational learning processes to take advantage of the information explosion will undoubtedly dominate their markets in the future.[5]

Likewise, those organizations that rely on the same old methods of learning and training will be unable to capitalize on these new technologies, and the gap between them and their competitors will continue to expand. Unfortunately for these lagging organizations, by the time they recognize that they are losing the battle, the war will be lost. Think about it. How long does it take from the time a new program is introduced in an organization until it acquires the necessary critical mass of utilization to become effective? Nine months? Two years? Ten years, as Deming asserted? How long after the U.S. auto manufacturers recognized that their Japanese competitors were making radical innovations through the use of TQM methods, quality circles, and employee empowerment methods was it before they were able to replicate these learning processes? Years!

Without new methods of learning introduced by schools and universities, organizations, and individuals, the gap grows. . . and grows. . . and grows. Therefore, if the accelerated achievement of strategy is not the compelling reason to alter your methods of training and learning, then is it compelling enough to understand that if your organization does not, your competitor may? In other words, can we learn anything from a follow-up study of the original *In Search of Excellence* heroes?[6]

Paradigm 2: Reduction of Cost of Poor Quality

A second paradigm that management must master is the notion of cost of poor quality (COPQ). At the very heart of many of W. Edwards Deming's 14 principles is an understanding of cost of poor quality.[7] Principle 3, "Cease dependence on inspection alone" and Principle 4, "End the practice of awarding business on the basis of price alone," attempt to drive management's thinking to the recognition that we often invent subprocesses and subroutines to remedy errors inherent in upstream processes. An equivalent investment in removing the variation and errors of upstream processes by chief financial officers (CFOs), instead of laying on more bureaucracy, more inspection, and additional steps, will produce a far greater return on investment.

For purposes of our discussion, we will rely on the definition of cost of poor quality as those costs, manifest by unnecessary steps, needless inspection, rework, waste, and duplication, that do not contribute to the value of the good or service being produced. If removed, this cost of poor quality would reduce cycle time, reduce cost, reduce customer dissatisfaction, and improve throughput.

And, as Juran points out, cost of poor quality, or defects, are not only a recordable cost from a financial point of view, but in lost customer loyalty as well.[8] Removal of cost of poor quality, or defects, is a management activity that not only addresses cost, but, in turn, reduces customer dissatisfaction.

Traditional notions of accounting do not uncover these costs. Budgeting and profit-and-loss statements provide exceptional detail about the efficiency of the processes we perform, but tell us nothing about their efficacy, that is, whether these processes should have been performed in the first place. Traditional accounting methods advise managers at all levels about process efficiency, like personnel cost as a percent of revenue, or staff hours per line item sold, supply costs per X-ray film used, and so on. As illustrated in Figures 3.3 and 3.4, cost of poor quality attempts to show us how needless process steps creep into our organizations without detection. Many will recognize the concept as one our generation of managers have been taught as "managing the white spaces," but the implications of cost of poor quality go far beyond organizational communications complexity. Studies from the Juran Institute on customer loyalty and cost of poor quality demonstrate very effectively that cost of poor quality consistently approaches more than 30 percent of operating costs! That is, in very well-managed companies, known industrywide for efficiency, anywhere from 20 to 40 percent of costs are absorbed in processes that should never have been performed or in capital assets that should never have been acquired, regardless of the efficiency achieved.[9]

In Figure 3.3 we see that traditional oversight and financial accountability constructs are created vertically. Consequently, organizations tend to compartmentalize. Department budgets report such efficiency indicators as cost per unit sold, and managers attempt to generate improvement in these budgetary features through comparison to historical costs and/or through comparative analysis of depart-

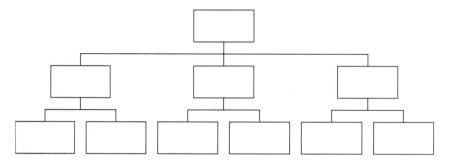

Figure 3.3. Traditional organization chart.

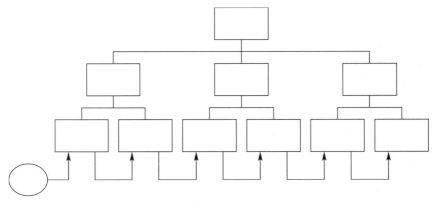

Operating room patient flow

Figure 3.4. A cross-functional view of a hospital operating room.

ments in the same company or industry. In contrast, Figure 3.4 high-lights the view of the organization through the eyes of the customer. The customer enters the organization through some scheduling or order-taking function, is passed on to a registration function, and is further passed down the line through production, assembly, distribution, and cash collection. Since many of the departments operate in compartmentalized divisions, the customer experiences wait loops, repetitive data collection and verification processes, and additional inspection. These cost of poor quality events have the effect of producing customer dissatisfaction, and anything the organization can do to eliminate these events have the effect of decreasing customer dissatisfaction.

Batalden told a story once of a large soft goods manufacturer who learned the hard way about the impact of customer dissatisfaction caused by the cumulative impact of organizational compartmentalization. This manufacturer's most important customer was one of the largest retail chains in the United States. This manufacturer, as a result of many years of application of TQM tools at the department level, prided itself on a high degree of department performance to meet customer needs. Each department had identified several key processes under its jurisdiction and constructed statistical process control (SPC) charts of the performance of each of these processes. Not one of these departments failed to produce a 95 percent or greater performance. The manufacturer was horrified when it almost lost the business of its most important customer as a result of poor order-to-delivery cycle time; the manufacturer assembled its SPC performance measures and verified that each department had indeed met the company's 95 percent goal. Senior management was in a quandary to define the problem until a manager with some analytical insight expressed the company's cumulative performance in the form of an equation. The number of processes to deliver an order to the customer, from the time the order was placed until the product appeared on the customer's shelf, totaled seven. The equation produced the cumulative company performance as a result of each of these departments performing at the 95 percent level.

$$\text{Customer view of performance} = [95\%] \times [95\%] \times [95\%] \times [95\%] \\ \times [95\%] \times [95\%] \times [95\%]$$

The result demonstrated that, in the eyes of the customer, the company produced a 70 percent level of quality and, as a result, almost lost its most important account. Therefore, the effect of organizational compartmentalization, as produced through the organizational structure of Figure 3.3, is customer dissatisfaction. The cumulative effect of ongoing and persistent cost of poor quality is known as customer disloyalty, the point at which customers are repelled. This hidden cost of poor quality element, resulting in lost revenue, is not measured in most traditional cost of poor quality studies.

Viewing the organization in this manner offers another bonus. Each of these cost of poor quality events adds cost to the production of services and products, but do nothing to add value to the outcome; they are simply costs incurred to correct other failed processes in existence in the organization, hence, the term *cost of poor quality*. Therefore, not only do these events generate customer dissatisfaction, they generate needless cost, which if removed would make the organization more competitive. These costs are not accounted for in the traditional budgeting system as it exists in Figure 3.3.

If we examine, for example, the cross-functional operating room (OR) process illustrated in Figure 3.4, the monthly budget report received by the OR supervisor indicated the unit cost per OR case. The degree of satisfaction with the performance of the OR was derived from historical comparison of the OR cost per case and a comparative report of OR costs from our parent company, HCA. However, the budget report told us nothing of cost of poor quality. It gave us no clue as to which steps in the OR process were being performed that would not have been required if an upstream process had not failed. As it existed at West Paces Medical Center in Atlanta in 1988, the average number of minutes each surgery patient waited in the OR holding area was 23 minutes. A significant portion of this time was devoted to inspecting the medical chart to verify the presence of preoperative laboratory, X-ray, electrocardiogram (EKG), and other diagnostic reports. These reports provide vital documentation for surgeons and anesthesiologists that the patient is fit for surgery. A cost-of-poor-quality researcher would inquire, "Why is this inspection necessary in the first place?" In other words, what resources would have been saved had these upstream departments managed error-free processes that ensured the presence of the diagnostic data, thereby eliminating the need for any inspection in the OR holding area? In the case under discussion, a quality improvement team reduced the average OR holding area time from 23 minutes to 16 minutes for each and every case, producing not only a labor savings, but a perception of increased quality on the part of the patient.

These cost of poor quality events occur every minute in organizations. I recall my first exposure to cost of poor quality, although at the time I did not have a label for it. While touring the hospital, I watched a nursing unit secretary input a dietary order into the hospital's computer system, which sent the order directly to the dietary department for processing. Upon completion of the computer input, she picked up the phone and called dietary to inform them that a diet change order had just been sent through the hospital computer system. I asked her why she called dietary to verify the order. She replied that on a few occasions her diet change orders had not been executed so she called dietary on each case to ensure they knew an order change had been sent. She was, of course, only being conscientious about caring for her patients and could not be faulted that processes established by management did not perform to the level of customer needs.

In the health care industry the cost of poor quality quotient is staggering. As reported by Don Berwick, M.D., president of the Institute for Healthcare Improvement, a collection of independent studies demonstrated that there existed no scientific justification in the medical literature for 17 percent of the coronary angiograms performed within the study group, 17 percent of upper gastrointestinal endoscopies, 32 percent of carotid endarterectomies, and 50 percent of blood transfusions.[10] The opportunities to be exploited by thoughtful systems thinkers in the reduction of cost of poor quality permit the industry to start almost anywhere within the system to drive out waste.

In addition to cost-of-poor-quality studies, the organization must give consideration to how the organization is managed. That is, we understand cost-of-poor-quality issues and have even completed an extensive study highlighting our greatest opportunities for improvement. Now what? This is one of the fundamental arguments for business process quality management teams, as the Juran Institute refers to key business processes. The introduction of the process of reengineering is the remedy endorsed by many leaders in the field of cost of poor quality and TQM for the effective management of cost of poor quality and customer loyalty issues.

Of course, simply acknowledging the existence of cross-functional cost of poor quality is only the diagnostic component. Every organization possesses its own unique set of organizational personality issues, often referred to as *turf issues*. There will always be competition between departments and individual managers for capital, recognition, and autonomy. The behaviors stemming from these issues are the fabric of human nature and will not simply disappear because the organization has engaged in cross-functional process analysis. A critical step in any effective quality improvement model and a vital awareness for senior leaders is the recognition and downplaying of these issues and behaviors as they are recognized.

Several accelerators exist to tame the effect of cost of poor quality, and they will be discussed in chapter 7 on accelerators and inhibitors. A training program of which I am particularly fond drives the recognition by middle managers that their processes collectively form a department system, and they, in turn, are a component of a larger system. Figure 3.5 is a section of the training tool developed by our mentors to accomplish this recognition. Apparent from close scrutiny of the system map is that many processes, both upstream and downstream, come together. This tool is helpful to enable managers to visualize processes they perform, which, in the absence of a failed upstream process like X-ray results charting, would not be required and is, thus, cost of poor quality. Likewise, managers are challenged to identify their own processes that are failure prone, in an effort to drive cost of poor quality reduction action planning. This systems management logic is called *business process quality management* (BPQM) and generally requires the assignment of an accountable manager to oversee system integration as articulated previously.

One of the most important paradigms managers must recognize, measure, reduce, and manage is cost of poor quality, and the most

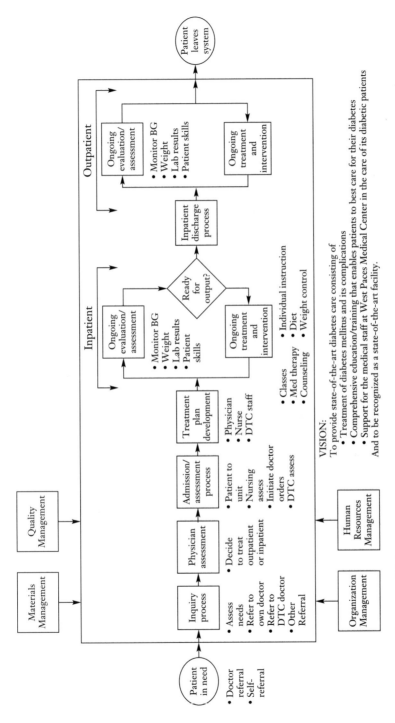

Figure 3.5. System of diabetes treatment center.

successful companies will be those that demand their upstream and downstream partners do the same, devoting teaching resources to help them do it.

Paradigm 3: Elements of Customer Judgment

Most companies when they hit hard times abandon all logic and "slash and burn," without considering the delayed negative impact of key decisions on customer loyalty. Action plans almost always involve an across-the-board reduction in employees and other costs by department. For example, each department reduces 5 percent of its workforce and 5 percent of its supply usage. Rarely, if ever, is the impact on customer satisfaction measured. Surely, key customers are contacted and persuaded that major cost reductions are necessary, but their service levels will remain constant. However, service levels are not measured, and, therefore, the impact on lost sales in the future is unknown. These programs are often given classy names, like *reengineering* or *right sizing;* some companies even veil these actions under the umbrella of *outsourcing,* even when it is known that outsourcing will result in increased unit costs, but at a decreased total cost because the outsource vendor will drop employees, thereby saving the parent company the difficult task of eliminating jobs.

Of course, responding to environmental changes is the essence of good management practice and must be faced rapidly if an organization is to weather the inevitable storms on the corporate battlefield. No one can be criticized for taking decisive action in the midst of changing conditions. The enlightened manager, however, will save the company millions over the years by constructing scenarios that consider all variables, including future customer loyalty, before deciding on the proper course.

The necessity to generate rapid change will become more and more pronounced in the future as technology and entrepreneurs become more closely wed in the race to innovate. These rapid innovations of existing products and the introduction of new products will render others obsolete, so the astute manager will embrace a new paradigm of customer judgments.

It is most instructive to begin any dissertation on customer judgments by examining Juran's definition of quality, what he calls the

Big Q.[11] Quality must be viewed as the customer views us, and, as most of us recognize, this view is not shared by our organizational structure—the customer is almost hidden from us by the very nature of the way we perform our work. Departments hand the customer to each other in an endless stream of often disconnected processes, and the only way we can discern the customer's satisfaction is to invest large sums of money for customer surveys, focus groups, and the like. Unfortunately, even when we are able to uncover a rough spot, department managers look desperately for the faulty department, responding, "it was not our department's fault."

I recall an incident while I was the CEO of West Paces Medical Center that caused my blood to boil. A patient had written a complaint letter to me about being "lost" between the radiology department and labor and delivery. She had been retrieved from radiology by a hospital volunteer after a routine ultrasound and transported back to labor and delivery, where she sat undiscovered for several hours. I am sure the number of hours was an exaggeration. The more probable fact, in this case, was probably fifteen minutes; nevertheless, her complaint was certainly valid enough. Upon requesting an investigation, I received a typed letter from the head of radiology indicating that "it was not my fault. . . ." This inherent compartmentalization continued to frustrate many of us on the quality council, as well as our customers. This event, too, can be expressed in terms of the previous paradigm on cost of poor quality.

In order to construct a framework for managing customer judgments, we found it helpful to utilize Kano's levels of customer judgment as the theoretical construct worthy of comprehension and mastery.[12, 13] In an effort to help us understand levels of customer needs and expectations, Kano defined customer judgments along three levels.

Level I   Expected—must have

Level II   Requested—nice to have

Level III   Delighted—customers brag about

He defined Level I as qualities that a customer expects. Asked another way, "What features of our processes must be present in order that our customers will not be repelled by our services?" Understanding this level of customer need leads us to understand what features of our products or services must be in place or our customers will reject us. The way one measures achievement of Level I satisfiers is through an effective complaint management system.

Level II customer needs are those features of our products or services that might be requested by our customers. The absence of these features would not repel our customers nor would they achieve a higher level, but they meet intermediate needs. An organization measures its Level II customer judgments by asking in customer surveys, "Were you satisfied?"

Level III customer needs are those needs that, if present, would cause our customers to express delight about our products or services to everyone they meet. The question becomes, "What features of our products, if offered, would cause our customers to brag about our services?" Kano suggests that process owners be driven to develop a complete understanding of Level III customer needs. HCA's Gene Nelson taught us to uncover Level III needs by analyzing underlying answers to the question, "Was the care so good at West Paces Medical Center that you would brag about it to your family and friends?" He also has taught us to affinitize into logical process groupings responses to the questions, "What good surprises occurred during your stay? What bad surprises occurred during your stay?" The affinitization process enabled us to realize that, among our four customer groups, there were 23 hospitalwide measures of quality. These 23 hospitalwide measures were continuously plotted, studied, and posted for all managers, employees, physicians, and customers to see.

Paradigm 4: Progressive Systems Integration

The rush is certainly on in the health care industry to consolidate and form legal structures to embrace the physician components and the hospital components. Much of this consolidation is occurring because competitors are generating the need for a "me-too" initiative. But, for many, the alignment of organizational elements, and the creation of new ones, is seen as a logical and progressive evolution of organizational theory within the industry to bring about long-needed efficiencies. For the enlightened ones, the payoff will be massive, beyond their wildest expectations. For others, who may not have grasped the theoretical underpinnings of systems thinking, the result may not be so sweet. Systems logic, of course, has been espoused for decades in other industries by Juran, Deming, Senge, and others. The question remains, at least in this industry, what will we do after the attorneys have completed the legal structures for holding companies, physician-hospital organizations (PHOs) to receive and hold managed care contracts, medical service organizations (MSOs) to run back-office operations for claims administration, physician and payor contracting, and utilization management? The competitive edge will fall to those who master the paradigm shifts suggested in this chapter and, in particular, this paradigm on progressive systems integration.

Most of the effort thus far in the health care industry has centered around vertical integration, that is, the acquisition and merger of community hospitals within a defined market. The underlying assumption for this strategy is, of course, that the economies of scale gained through supplier contracting and consolidation of administrative functions like purchasing, human resources, and billing and collections will drive the new entity to community-best value in terms of cost competitiveness and joint payor contracting. The logic of this strategy is sound enough; however, the economies are somewhat minute compared to the benefits of horizontal integration. Vertical process savings might fall into the range of 10 percent of revenues. As clearly demonstrated in the section on cost of poor quality, the really big hits occur upon restructuring to align the system horizontally.

As demonstrated in Figure 3.6, the history of quality management in other industries provides the insight that cost of poor quality occurs at handoff points, rework loops, inspection, and waste inputs. The cumulative effects of these events, as discussed in the cost-of-poor-quality paradigm, may exceed 30 percent of an organization's operating budget.

Process productivity

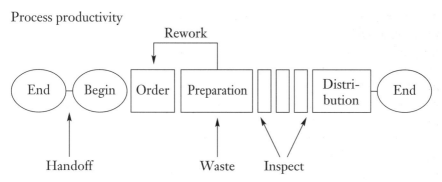

Figure 3.6. The systems thinking model.

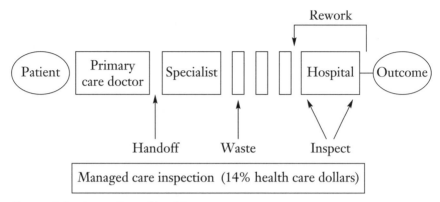

Figure 3.7. An unaligned health care system.

Figure 3.7 illustrates the unaligned health system as it currently exists in most communities. Primary care physicians, or family practitioners, generally serve as the introduction point for most customers (patients) at a point when a physical symptom is present. Approximately one third of all encounters result in a referral to a specialist, with some proportion admitted to a hospital for treatment. Each of these entities operate independently of one another, with a significant degree of autonomy. Health maintenance organizations (HMOs) attempt to tie the system together by inserting a management and utilization layer above the entire system through a series of contracts, discounts, and inspection. This attempt at systems integration has proven somewhat effective, reducing specialist and hospital referrals by as much 30 percent, however, the cost of this layer of inspection approaches 14 percent for most managed care entities, again generating an unnecessary element of cost of poor quality.

As suggested in Figure 3.8, as the health care system matures and enlightened managers apply systems thinking to the production of health care processes, these independent entities become dependent upon each other for contractual relationships between patients and payers. A properly aligned health system contains legal structures, compensation philosophies, and entrepreneurial rewards for the elimination of cost of poor quality, improvement of patient outcomes, and continuous innovation. These entities will be able to eliminate much of the costly HMO inspection layer of 14 percent through reengineering along business process quality management lines.

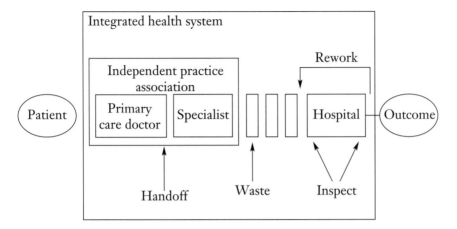

Figure 3.8. An aligned health care system.

Paradigm 5: Alignment of Support Infrastructure

Another paradigm issue to be taken under consideration is the organizational infrastructure. Infrastructure includes the organizational design itself as illustrated in Figures 3.3 and 3.4, performance appraisal and compensation philosophies, capital allocation principles, supplier relationships, recruitment and interviewing processes, customer judgments measurement systems, and so on. It is the alignment of the infrastructure to support rather than inhibit the achievement of the organization's vision and strategic deployment road map. The quality council must invest time to ask the critical questions related to infrastructure. Does our current organization design support our vision and strategic deployment road map? Do our budgeting and financial reporting systems highlight cost of poor quality across department lines? Do our policies for performance appraisal, compensation, recognition, and promotion support our vision, or do they encourage compartmentalization? Upon examination of our current capital budget, does it support optimization of the organization as a system, or do we allocate capital simply on the basis of unit return on assets? Does our legal structure, including all subsidiaries, support our vision? These, and other infrastructure issues, combine to either accelerate or inhibit the achievement of our vision and are worthy of CEO and quality council attention.

Most organizations are clearly not aligned along the path of the organization as viewed by the customer. As discussed, this fallacy produces customer disloyalty and cost of poor quality. One remedy is to create additional organizational structures to manage across cost-of-poor-quality lines, for example, the creation of a quality council, business process quality management reengineering teams, cross-functional teams, department teams, and individual quality in daily work structures to produce a view of the organization consistent with customer needs.

Another dilemma for organizations is the issue of performance appraisal and compensation philosophies. Should we reward teams? Should we eliminate individual merit pay? Should we compensate individuals on the basis of the team or department performance as a whole? A recent formal survey of several Baldrige Award winners and other recognized organizations by the Juran Institute revealed great variation among our nation's leaders about just how to manage this issue. Several indicated that the human resource department had not yet been engaged in the TQM process![14] Ken Blanchard, author of *The One Minute Manager*, remarked recently, "When I ask people how they like the way their performance is evaluated, everyone laughs; no one seems to have anything good to say about appraisal systems."[15]

These questions plagued us most at West Paces Medical Center and still disturb most organizations. Several recent studies are surfacing, however, that provide some theoretical framework upon which to base our deliberations. One by Peter R. Scholtes challenges several assumptions we make about performance in general.[16] First, he questions whether performance appraisals are consistently applied across the entire organization or by even the same manager over time. Second, he questions the variation from rater to rater in appraisals resultant from rater bias, due to the rater's self-image, the rater's own past performance appraisal, the rater's ability or willingness to be direct rather than shy about performance issues, and the rater's effectiveness in applying quantitative data versus subjective means to derive ratee scores. Third, and perhaps most importantly, he questions the very assumptions upon which a performance appraisal system is built. He analyzed, in cause-and-effect diagram fashion, the degree of control an employee has over his or her own performance and concluded, as did Deming, that process errors are mostly beyond the control of the employee. Process failures result from the inadequacy of processes designed by management, the effectiveness of the company education department, and the capabilities of the machines, tools, and materials given to the employee. This paradigm, among them all, may be the most difficult to manage. Several have tried team compensation, self-directed work team construction, gain sharing, and other innovations, but much remains to be tested before a solid conclusion can be drawn. Some argue that this is one of the most vital undertakings an organization can sponsor.

Paradigm 6: Understanding the Cycle of Continuous Improvement

When Batalden first introduced Shewhart's cycle of continuous improvement to me in 1987, as shown in Figure 3.9, my first reaction was that it was the purest integration between marketing and operations I had ever seen.[17] The health industry is plagued with wasted resources in the area of promotion and advertising. As the health industry has become more competitive, hospitals have rushed to promote their services but often without first understanding the patient's needs or expectations of the service. Adhering to the discipline required by the cycle of continuous improvement is one central paradigm shift that should be recognized at all levels of the organization before effective TQM transformation can occur.

The cycle begins with first defining the boundaries of the process that is to be designed or redesigned. What is the first step in the process? Who supplies the action to initiate the process? What is the last step of the process? The answers to these questions define the

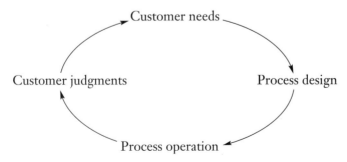

Figure 3.9. Shewhart's cycle of continuous improvement.

boundaries of the process improvement effort. Once known, the process owner can more effectively address the question of the needs and expectations of the customers of the process.

Once customer needs have been understood, the process design phase can began. Incorporation of features into the process design that meet the needs and expectations of customers is the second step of the process.

The cycle is completed upon obtaining customer judgments about performance of the process in meeting the identified needs and expectations of customers that will allow the improvement cycle to be reinitiated.

It is this redesign paradigm, based on customer judgments and customer needs, that so differs with the way American managers have been trained. Unfortunately we have never developed the patience to invest the time necessary to fully understand needs and expectations of customers before designing the process, so we design processes without adequate knowledge. Once the process has been designed, we place it into service and wait until we receive a complaint. A complaint is a form of customer judgment, as we see from Kano's model, albeit the lowest form of customer judgment (see Figure 3.10). Once a complaint is received, we are quick to add steps to the process that ensure that this complaint will never recur. Then we wait for another complaint and redesign the process once more to ensure that the second complaint never recurs, and this process of adding steps endlessly to

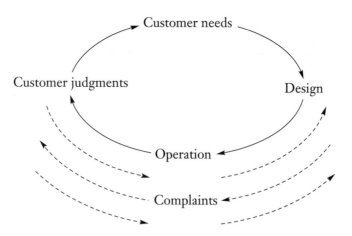

Figure 3.10. Cost-of-poor-quality generation from a complaint cycle.

resolve complaints is the prominent way of the problem-solving American. The result of this way of thinking is waste, rework, and needless complexity almost everywhere we look. Shewhart would have us, using TQM methods, uncover root causes of the original failure and remedy them rather than add another layer of inspection and cost to the process.

An example of this way of thinking can be illustrated through an analysis of the nutrition process at West Paces Medical Center in 1988. Depending upon who the patient asked—a nurse, a food service worker, a volunteer, a telephone operator—there were 22 different subprocesses to gain access to a soda. Another example was the surgery process. From the time the patient entered the admitting department until a surgical operation began, health care professionals inspected the medical record eight separate times for the presence of lab, X-ray, and EKG results: These eight inspections were performed by three different persons, and the other two individuals inspecting the medical record were unaware that the third individual was inspecting the process until it was uncovered through the flowchart constructed by the quality improvement team.

Paradigm 7: Reduction of Variation

Another important paradigm to internalize is the importance of process variation. While it is not uncommon for manufacturing companies to have adequate data on variation from engineering specifications, variation in sales processes, customer service processes, administrative processes, and health care processes is almost nonexistent. Most organizations are not even aware of the mean or median length of time it takes to perform a given process, let alone the variation from trial-to-trial or day-to-day. For example, most hospitals could not point to the mean length of time for the delivery of a medication ordered from a physician. But, more importantly, even if the process average is known, knowledge of variation from this average is a foreign request.

What is startling about this discovery about service and health care processes is that most of us define quality on the basis of variation. When I conducted the employee orientation session for new employees, I asked them to list the brand names of companies that they believed provide high quality products. I received answers like Toyota,

IBM, HCA, Westinghouse, Xerox, and Kodak. To the right of these responses, which were recorded on a flip chart, I recorded characteristics of the products or services delivered by these companies that would lead anyone to think they produced high quality. The list usually included such entries as dependability, consistency, knowledge of what quality means to me, responsiveness to service requests, and warranties. With a red marker, I circled the words *dependability* and *consistency* and asked, "Why is it that in service processes and health care processes we haven't the faintest idea whether our processes are consistent or dependable? Why is it that we never measure how the performance of our processes varies over time?"

As demonstrated in Figure 3.11, the customers of the cleaning process in labor and delivery experienced a variation cycle time from 25 minutes to just over 35 minutes. The medication delivery process for new IVs produced a variation from 20 minutes to more than 8 hours! The average of both of these processes told them nothing of the variation in the processes. Yet the customers of these processes defined quality as consistency.

The recognition of the importance of understanding and reducing variation is a central thesis of Deming's work.

Paradigm 8: Employee Empowerment

We have touched upon Makens' formula of [tools] × [environment] in a previous chapter. The part of the formula that an organization would input into the equation under environment would be the percent of the workforce effectively using tools. Now that we know and understand the use of quality improvement tools, how many people and teams within the organization are effectively using them? This is what the Baldrige Award criteria refer to as *deployment*. Only with widespread use of tools can an organization achieve TQM maturity.

A story was told by Batalden during one of his courses about an award granted in Japan to the company with the highest number of employee suggestions. Matsushita came in first with 5 million suggestions. Toyota came in second with only 1.5 million; however, they implemented 95 percent of them. I often told employees in orientation that, if I were to receive 1.5 million employee suggestions in our suggestion boxes, everyone in senior management would resign. The difference at Toyota and in TQM-rich environments is that employees

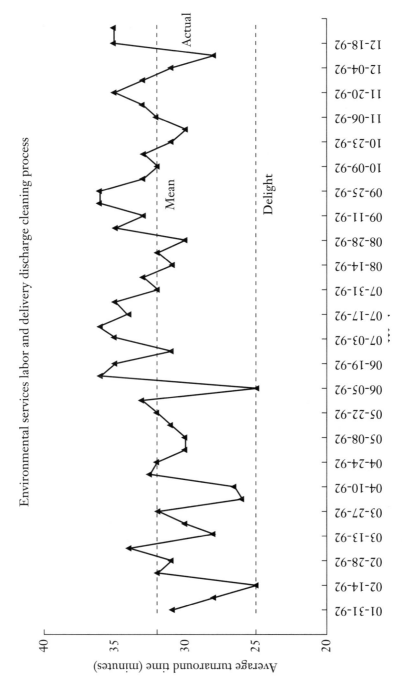

Figure 3.11. Process variation.

are not only empowered to make suggestions, they also have been trained to innovate within their own processes and to carry their innovations and suggestions to other process owners for implementation. In Juran's address, "The Upcoming Century of Quality" at the 1994 ASQC Annual Quality Conference, he identified eight factors necessary to drive the quality agenda in the United States in the next century. Two of those can be related to the paradigm of empowerment: the workforce must be educated in TQM techniques and empowered to use them, and the reward system must be revised to reflect the growing need for innovation at the worksite.[18]

The notion of employee empowerment strikes hard at the orthodox American management model. All of us have been raised on the Taylor model, and we are unaccustomed to relinquishing control; however, creating an effective TQM organization mandates personal reflection in this area.

Up until the 1970s, management work was characterized as control-oriented; managers were trained that the primary focus of their work, once the planning, organization, and coordination steps were concluded, was to control the process of work (see Figure 3.12). Managers were trained with methods to control the activities of the workforce. Success under this management style was embodied as someone who established elaborate control feedback processes and achieved results through fear. This style of management was directorial in nature.

Control-oriented management thought was replaced in the 1980s with the leadership model: Emerging managers of the '80s were told that effective management was a combination of technical skills, management skills, and leadership skills. We were taught that effective managers were able to lead their workforce to higher planes of achievement and performance. To become more effective, enlightened managers studied interpersonal skills development, communication skills, and negotiating. Successful managers under the leadership

Management models

1970s	1980s	1990s
Control	*Leadership*	*Mentoring*
"I must control your activities."	"Let me show you how."	"How can I help you improve?"

Figure 3.12. Management models.

model were those who were able to achieve results by persuading others, building trust and confidence, and serving as the problem solver. The mentoring model is characterized by many, most notably by Senge, as the advocacy model of management.[19]

Effective management in a TQM environment will lead managers to focus on a new set of skills. These skills can be classified under the mentoring model of management. Mentoring skills will lead organizations to realize the full potential of their creativity. Successful managers under the mentoring model are able to build learning organizations. They teach individuals at all levels of the organization how to innovate. More importantly, improved productivity is achieved through motivation by building a common shared vision. Everyone understands the vision of the organization and his or her role in achieving the vision. Furthermore, everyone's personal values are tied to the organization's values. Successful managers do not just lead, they mentor by asking employees, "What do you make? Why are your processes important to the customer, and how do they tie to the end result? What would it take to perform this process in half the time? With zero errors?" Mentoring questions like these drive knowledge of process, variation, and supplier-customer interlinkage into the organization. More importantly, by mentoring rather than leading, everyone in the organization learns to ask and answer his or her own questions. The management style of mentoring can also be thought of as *management by inquiry*.

There are other logical reasons to invest in the creation and generation of a mentoring model of management. Several studies demonstrate the improvement in employee innovativeness and performance when engaged to participate and govern their processes. The most known of these is the popular monolith by Frederick Herzberg, "One More Time: How Do You Motivate Employees?" In this landmark study, as shown in Figure 3.13, Herzberg successfully argues that *Achievement, Recognition, Work itself,* and *Responsibility* are the top employee satisfiers, while *Company policy, Supervision,* and *Relationship with supervisor* head the dissatisfier list.[20] Juran recorded research indicating that, of four work groups studied, the one permitting participation produced increased efficiency, while the other three groups showed decreased efficiency, increased hostility, increased turnover, and greater grievances.[21]

Not only is it important for senior management to understand these paradigms, it is equally important that department managers, quality improvement team leaders, and employees rethink their notions along these paradigms because they see them from the oppo-

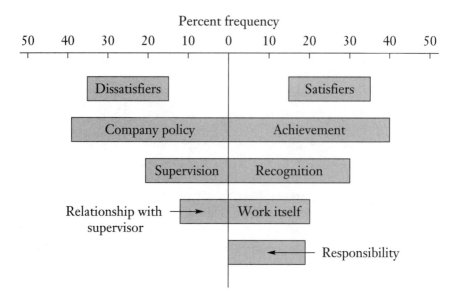

Figure 3.13. Employee satisfiers and dissatisfiers.

site point of view. As Batalden points out, "Fear is a major quality thief."[22] We have trained individuals at every level in the organization to be fearful of making suggestions or making waves. They too live in the world of the Taylor model, but at the opposite end.[23] One of our greatest challenges is to walk side by side with our workforce in reaching a new plane of improvement activity.

Discussion Exercise for a One-Hour Quality Council Meeting About Paradigm Mastery Analysis

1. Divide the paradigms among the participants at this council meeting. Each group or individual presents the discussion paradigm and reveals one observation from your own organization. Consider both positive and negative observations. Take only three minutes per paradigm.

2. Brainstorm and record on a flip chart as many observations from your organization the council members can list for evidences of

    a. Innovation

   b. Cost of poor quality

3. Assign someone on the council to save the flip charts from item two. Bring them back to the council for a second look in nine months.

Discussion Exercise for a One-Hour Quality Council Meeting About Infrastructure Assessment

It is the alignment of the infrastructure to support rather than inhibit the achievement of the organization's vision and strategic deployment road map that drives the speed of results. These, and other infrastructure issues, combine to either accelerate or inhibit the achievement of our vision and are worthy of CEO and quality council attention. The quality council must invest time to ask the critical questions related to infrastructure. In a one-hour session, discuss the following issues.

1. Does our current organization design support our vision and strategic deployment road map?
2. Do our budgeting and financial reporting systems highlight cost of poor quality across department lines?
3. Do our policies for performance appraisal, compensation, recognition, and promotion support our vision or do they encourage compartmentalization?
4. Upon examination of our current capital budget, does it support optimization of the organization as a system or do we allocate capital simply on the basis of unit return on assets?
5. Does our legal structure, including all subsidiaries, support our vision?

Discussion Exercise for a One-Hour Department Manager/Team Leader Meeting

Someone from the quality council, preferably an operations manager, is assigned to facilitate this exercise. Other council members rotate among the tables to help facilitate each group's discussions. As in the exercise in chapter 1, it is unimportant whether participants get right or wrong answers. This is a mentoring activity, that is, "seed and water, seed and water." Simply asking managers to wrestle with these issues will go a long way toward creating discomfort with the current state. The desired outcome is for these managers to reflect on these paradigms as they lead teams in the future.

1. The council facilitator briefly presents in 10 minutes or less the concepts of cost of poor quality and customer dissatisfaction using the process productivity and systems mapping figure in this chapter.

2. Divide the department managers/team leaders into groups of 8 to 10 people. Individuals are instructed, using a copy of the system map included in this chapter, to draw the processes performed in their departments.

3. Within their groups, managers are to identify and discuss among themselves probable points of cost of poor quality and customer dissatisfaction that occur in their departments as a result of an upstream process failure from another department.

4. Within their groups, managers are to identify and discuss among themselves probable points of cost of poor quality and customer dissatisfaction that occur in a downstream department as a result of a process failure in their own departments.

5. Each table elects one member to present their ideas to the larger group as a whole.

6. Time permitting, the council member facilitating this session records responses on a flip chart from the whole group to the question: "What conclusions can we draw from the discussion today?"

Discussion Exercise for a Governing Board Meeting

Assign the chairperson of the quality improvement committee or equivalent, or an interested governing body member to lead the discussion, with the quality director as facilitator at the flip chart.

1. Brainstorm.

   a. What are the evidences of an increasing rate of innovation or improvement throughout the organization?

   b. What statistical evidence do we periodically review to ensure ourselves that these improvements are important to customers?

   c. What analysis do we possess about cost of poor quality or nonvalue-added cost in our organization?

2. Examine briefly the following paradigm topic areas.

   a. Importance of velocity of innovation

   b. Reduction of cost of poor quality

   c. Elements of customer judgment

   d. Progressive systems integration

   e. Alignment of support infrastructure

   f. Understanding the cycle of continuous improvement

   g. Reduction of variation

   h. Employee empowerment

3. In order to advance the knowledge of the governing board as a whole, brainstorm on, "What continuing education and discussion exercises might be provided during the next several meeting to advance our knowledge?"

Notes

1. Thomas J. Peters and Robert H. Waterman, *In Search of Excellence* (New York: Harper & Row, 1982).

2. Richard Pascale, *Managing on the Edge* (New York: Simon & Schuster, 1990).

3. Joseph M. Juran, *Juran on Quality by Design* (New York: The Free Press, 1992), 19.

4. Howland Blackiston, *Puttin on the Ritz*, segment 2 of *Quality Minutes*, Wilton, CT: Juran Institute, Vol 1:7 1994, videocassette.

5. Peter M. Senge, *The Fifth Discipline: The Art and Practice of the Learning Organization* (New York: Doubleday, 1990), 198.

6. Peters and Waterman, *In Search of Excellence*.

7. W. Edwards Deming, *Out of the Crisis* (Cambridge, Mass.: MIT Center for Advanced Engineering Study, 1982), 28–49.

8. Juran, *Quality by Design*, 72–121.

9. Maureen Bisognano, "Accellerating Improvement" (paper presented at the National Forum for Healthcare Improvement, San Diego, December 6, 1994), 2.

10. Donald M. Berwick, "Improving the Appropiateness of Care," *Quality Connection* 3:1 (winter 1994): 2–3.

11. Juran, *Quality by Design*, 11–12.

12. Paul B. Batalden, "Hospital-Wide Quality Improvement" (paper presented at HCA Eastern Group CEOs, Nashville, Tenn., October 29, 1990).

13. Donald M. Berwick, A. Blanton Godfrey, and Jane Roessner, *Curing Health Care* (San Francisco: Jossey-Bass, 1990), 55.

14. Juran Institute, *The Road to Total Quality: A Self-Assessment Guide* (Wilton, Conn.: Juran Institute, 1993).

15. Ken Blanchard, "Performance Appraisals Are No Laughing Matter," *Quality Digest* 14 (May 1994): 17.

16. Peter R. Scholtes, *A New View of Performance Evaluation* (Madison, Wisc.: Joiner Associates, 1987), 1–33.

17. Deming, *Out of the Crisis*, 88.

18. J. M. Juran, "The Upcoming Century of Quality" (address at 1994 ASQC Annual Congress, May 24, 1994), 14.

19. Senge, *The Fifth Discipline*, 198–202.

20. Frederick Herzberg, "One More Time: How Do You Motivate Employees?" *Harvard Business Review* 65 (Sept-Oct 1987): 109–120.

21. J. M. Juran, *Managerial Breakthrough* (New York: McGraw-Hill, 1964), 153.

22. Batalden, "Hospital-Wide Quality Improvement."

23. Senge, *The Fifth Discipline*, 350.

Chapter 4

Strategy and Visioning

One of the greatest challenges organizations currently face in their TQM deployment initiatives is generating the link between their strategic plans and their quality plans. So often companies that I mentor treat the quality plan, if indeed one exists at all, as a document and process entirely separate from their strategic plan and financial plan.

As Juran has pointed out for years, organizations are very effective in the deployment of financial plans and many are very good at deploying strategic plans. Few, however, have mastered the integration of all three into a cohesive approach based upon the quantified needs of customers. Juran encourages upper managers to think of the construction of the quality plan as a parallel process to the construction of the financial plan.[1] The process to create an integrated quality plan follows the same steps as generating the budget. A greater degree of coordination is required in that, first, customer needs are quantified, quality goals and objectives are articulated, and these requirements become the framework to compile financial requirements.

Every activity in which an organization embarks should be centered around the achievement of the vision and strategic deployment road map. One of the results of this separation may be the loss of interest by the CEO and other senior leaders in the TQM initiative. It becomes quite apparent to everyone in the organization that the CEO is not attending quality council meetings or leading other TQM communications activities. This observation might have the effect of sending a sign that the organization's TQM priorities and the organization's strategic priorities have taken different roads. Rather than

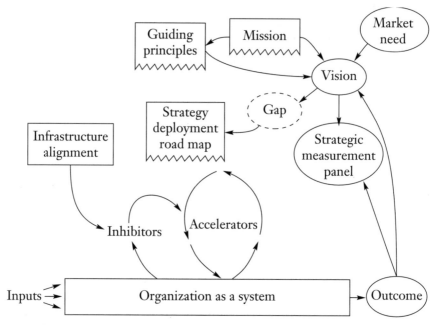

Figure 4.1. The transformation model.

proceed down different paths at ever greater rates of speed, the best advice an organization can follow is to reassess the strategic agenda and the quality agenda and synchronize the two. If the CEO does not see the TQM agenda as the best vehicle to drive strategic results, if the CFO does not claim that the TQM program's reduction of cost of poor quality is the highest rate of return of any of his or her investments this budget year, if the operations VPs do not recite daily how TQM teams and other visible evidences of use of TQM tools and techniques are accelerating their divisions' efforts, then basic examination of the focus of the quality council's recent agendas, minutes, and future plans might help assess the degree to which strategic issues are being addressed.

For purposes of review, see Figure 4.1 to continue to build the mental model of strategic deployment.

Chapter 2 on the transformation model revealed Figure 4.1 as a mental model for tying all of these issues together. In this chapter on strategy and visioning, we will make some observations about the link between

1. Market need
2. Current outcomes
3. Mission
4. Guiding principles
5. Organization's vision
6. Organization as a system
7. Strategy deployment road map

This discussion will be followed in the next chapter on the creation of a strategic measurement panel to be deployed from the CEO level to the operating department level in an effort to manage the achievement of results to drive the organization vision.

Focus on Results

Often organizations that do not possess an integrated strategic deployment road map consisting of quality, financial, and strategic imperatives seem to not have a proper alignment of key priorities or their priorities appear to focus on strategies unrelated to customers. History provides adequate examples for us to examine, but our own experiences may provide an ever richer pool. Consider the organizations that, due to the CEO's own lack of vision or the organization's failure to embrace it, obviously strayed from a customer-focused mind-set, embracing perhaps financial targets or internal political achievements above the deeper sense of customer commitment. These organizations seem to possess no thirst to exceed customer expectations, and employees do not appear to share a common mind-set that the key customers' needs stand above all else. Rather, employees privately remark that senior leaders care only about the bottom line or that customer complaints are not taken seriously. The organizations that come to mind for me have either ceased to do business or have radically revised their cultures.

Consider, on the other extreme, those organizations in which customer needs have become the focal point of all activity and planning. Those organizations have an unexplainable vibrancy that permeates the workforce. Employees appear confident in their own jobs and express delight about working in the organization.

This latter organization is representative of the model for emulation, one that has articulated customer needs into the very fabric of all organizational activity—from the strategic plan, the budget, capital allocation, employee rewards and recognition to the anecdotes that are heard in the cafeteria and at new employee orientation. This organization has introduced processes that uniquely match its own culture, but focus on results as interpreted from customer needs assessments.

How might we begin to quantifiably assess the degree to which customer needs are being met? One method is to use current and future cash flow as a proxy for the degree to which customer needs are being met. Cash flow is a measurement with a common denominator for both current and future examination. For the most part, a discussion of desired strategic results can be centered around the question, What might we manage today that will ensure positive cash flow today, tomorrow, and in the future? In 1988 at West Paces Medical Center we initiated our understanding at the time of the transformation model. The board of trustees, particularly the chairman, Bill Reid, M.D., became enamored with a story that highlighted a Japanese company with a 500-year strategic plan. We discussed how this might be possible for the next several months at formal and informal gatherings. Upon creating the strategic measurement panel, to be discussed in the next chapter, we focused our attention on the notion that measurements of continued cash flow generation over a 10-year horizon would serve our purposes. Therefore, we conceptualized the development model illustrated in Figure 4.2.

As suggested in the figure, we were interested in uncovering measures of optimal cash flow in 1994, 1997, and 2000. Our conclusions

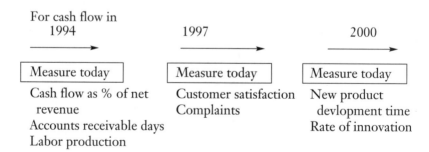

Figure 4.2. Strategic measures deployment.

reasoned that, to stay in business in 1994, we needed to focus our measurement set on current efficiency and selected, among other measures, cash flow as a percent of net revenue, accounts receivable days, and labor productivity for the 1994 set. We next asked ourselves, if we wish to ensure cash flow in 1997, at what must we excel in 1994? We recognized that, due to word of mouth and the strength of market reputation, we must manage and improve the perception of 1994 customers in order to ensure a steady stream of customers in 1997. That is, if we excel today at customer service, customers will express delight about us publicly and will, therefore, accelerate market share growth. Thus, our 1997 measurement set included, among other measures, customer satisfaction scores and customer complaints. Finally we asked ourselves, at what must we excel in 1994 in order to ensure cash flow in the year 2000? We concluded that we must drive up the rate of innovation and drive down new product introduction cycle time if we are to surpass our competitors' strategic efforts. Therefore, we constructed measurements for the number of new products and the number of months to develop them, as well as the volume of quality improvement team improvements and the number of days per team cycle.

Many organizations upon constructing a strategic plan, after considering market needs, skip over measurement, and go directly to "What are we going to do?" Are we going to introduce new product X in 24 months? Construct an outpatient surgery center? Form a PHO? Each element would fall under the category of tactical plans. These organizations, in an effort to be proactive, fail to ask, "Based on what we believe the market is doing, how might we best measure the impact of our strategic tactical plans?" In reality, the second stop after speaking to customers is to construct the strategic measurement template to assess the degree of effectiveness of the tactical actions.

Our efforts over the years and the observations from organizations I now mentor have led to the acknowledgment that five key strategic endeavors, which, if followed with absolute aggressiveness required of all serious strategic thrusts, should form the basis of any organization's 500-year plan. They are the following:

1. Increase the rate of innovation 20 percent per year.

2. Reduce cost of poor quality 20 percent per year.

3. Increase customer satisfaction 20 percent per year.

4. Progressively integrate the organization as a system.

5. Exceed stakeholder cash flow expectations 20 percent per year.

Increase the Rate of Innovation 20 Percent per Year

The sustainable growth targets of most businesses require a fundamental understanding of the ideation and introduction of new products and services into the marketplace. I am referring here to not only product breakthroughs, but the entire scope of innovations that can and should be managed in an organization—new products, new markets, employee suggestions, quality improvement team improvement cycle time—and the dimension of innovation deserving the focus of our efforts is not only the value of an individual innovation, but, more importantly, its cycle time compared to our previous innovation work. What is the average number of days for a quality improvement team to complete a cycle? How many days did this team trim off the cycle compared to its last cycle? What is the rate of increase in the number of customer-driven employee suggestions? How many months does it take us to introduce a new or modified product or service compared to this time last year?

Reflecting on the paradigm discussed in the last chapter, if we can learn anything from historical evidence, increasing the rate of innovation should become the cornerstone of every organization's strategy, as again suggested in the Figure 4.3.

In the movie *City Slickers*, one scene in particular highlights the critical nature of this strategy. At dusk, after a tough cattle drive throughout the day, the three city men sat around the campfire with their trusty, but frighteningly rugged and asocial guide, sharing stories of awe at their discovery of the peaceful, but austere, existence enjoyed by the cowboy on an open range surrounded by hundreds of aimless cattle. They had come to respect the cowboy life as one, not only filled with adventure, danger, and unpredictability, but of great responsibility. They realized that the survival of hundreds of animals depended on the cowboy's skill, judgment, and tirelessness over unforgiving natural elements. They came to learn that, without these attributes, everyone and everything on the cattle drive would quickly perish. At the conclusion of the scene, Billy Crystal, a city slicker, turned to the old, wrinkled cowhand played by Jack Palance and inquired, "Your life seems so peaceful and full of contentment: How

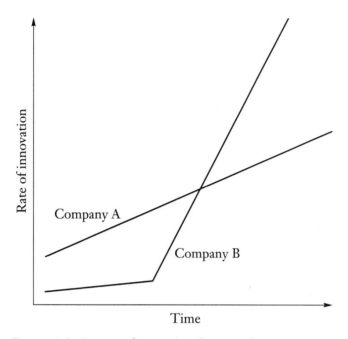

Figure 4.3. Impact of increasing the rate of innovation.

can I achieve the peace of life you have captured?" The old cowhand appeared to reflect for a moment, then answered simply, "It's just one thing." Crystal inquired further, "What one thing? What do you mean, 'It's just one thing?' What's the one thing?" to which the cowhand quietly advised, "That's up to you. But to be truly happy, a person must pursue just one thing."

Likewise, if a CEO or senior strategist were to ask me, "To be truly, I mean truly, successful, what must we do?" I would respond, "It's just one thing. Increase your rate of innovation faster than your competitors."

Reduce Cost of Poor Quality 20 Percent per Year

Continuing the discussion from the previous chapter on the cost of poor quality paradigm, as a measurement of customer dissatisfaction and needless cost, most organizations would be best served by radically decreasing their dependence on traditional vertical budget reporting systems and focus on the more customer-oriented and wasteful horizontal view enabled through cost of poor quality analysis.

As we will discuss in the next chapter on measurement, a definitive cost of poor quality figure should be visibly placed at the highest level of the financial measures hierarchy. To be maximally effective, the fewer strategic measures at the top level, the more scrutiny and activity will be directed toward improving cost of poor quality and, therefore, I recommend that CEOs and CFOs subordinate many measures currently located at the highest level to be reviewed only upon deviation from targeted performance thresholds.

Most financial accounting systems possess inadequate structures to capture cost of poor quality accurately. Activity-based costing (ABC) systems were created for this purpose, but most organizations, even large ones like Coca-Cola, might be best served by manually calculating cost of poor quality once per year for each major division or engaging an outside firm to produce an annual breakdown, as opposed to investing millions of dollars of scarce capital for an ABC system.

Whichever route the organization takes, however, is not as important as recognition itself that cost of poor quality management is a strategic must.

Increase Customer Satisfaction 20 percent per Year

If an organization wishes to continually focus on one factor that will drive cash flow three years hence, it is customer satisfaction and market recognition of the value of the organization's goods and services. A lot is written and recorded about the need to meet customer satisfaction, but most organizations have not gone far enough, as observed by Deming, Juran, and others. They have not engaged an insightful, profound knowledge of the customer's need or desire for the product or service.

This translation skill set is becoming more complex as customers become more sophisticated and production methods permit increased product segmentation. Customer needs are also consistently generalized across industries. Customers are experiencing tremendous improvements in convenience and the reduction of waiting times. Supermarkets and airports offer ATMs, gasoline stations provide at-the-pump cash payment methods, and almost every industry highlights time-saving innovations. Customers have come to expect that reductions in waiting time and greater product options in one industry should be generalized to other industries. Companies have responded to these needs in great order. Market segmentation has become so widespread that we need a new term to accurately label it. Consider, for example, Coca-Cola. In the early 1980s, you bought Coke. By the mid-1980s, you could buy Diet Coke or Sprite or Minute Maid Orange. Next, of course, came New Coke (although I still refuse to believe that this admitted error was not a secret market genius). Then you could buy Diet Sprite and Diet Minute Maid Orange. Then, you could buy caffeine-free Coke and caffeine-free New Coke. Next, you could buy Diet Caffeine-free Coke and Diet Caffeine-free New Coke. Finally, although I am sure this is not the final segmentation of the soft drink market, consumers were offered the "cherry" option. At the present moment, there are 22 varieties! Consumers have come to expect that their needs will be met and the market responds with market segmentation.

Companies often make the leap from a basic understanding of customer needs to their own interpretation of customer needs. This translation, as Juran refers to it, deserves an entire science devoted to ascertaining the customer's need for the product or service.[2] Berwick and A. Blanton Godfrey go to considerable lengths to explore the nature of defined versus perceived customer needs and how best to utilize this customer knowledge as one basis for the chartering and formation of quality improvement teams.[3]

As we attempted to gain a firmer understanding of how to measure and improve customer satisfaction at West Paces Medical Center, Nelson guided us toward the use of Kano's levels of customer judgment discussed in the last chapter as a viable framework.[4] Two of the 300 questions posed in the patient satisfaction instrument he helped engineer for HCA inquired, "What good surprises did you experience during your stay?" and "What bad surprises did you experience during your stay?" The cumulative responses to these questions were affinitized by Carol Allen, our customer service recovery expert, and placed on a storyboard to serve as a portable communication tool throughout the organization. In addition, these responses served as one source of ideas for the formation of team activities.

No customer research, regardless of how small, is unworthy of communication and scrutiny at each level of the organization in a continuous quest to drive customer satisfaction to higher performance.

Progressively Integrate the Organization As a System

Building on the discussion of the paradigm of systems thinking from the previous chapter, each organization must continually improve its position within the marketplace. Automobile manufacturers are a wonderful example of this phenomenon. One of the largest markets in the United States is the automobile aftermarket, that is, the installation of accessories into cars after delivery by the car dealer (see Figure 4.4). A major growth strategy for the automobile industry is to track the aftermarket and pick and choose which features carry enough margin and volume to meet their investment objectives. Once the aftermarket has matured to a high degree of market acceptance and demand, the automakers move in and offer the aftermarket product as a deluxe option.

For example, in the late 1970s and early 1980s, one of the fastest growing automobile aftermarkets was the installation of tape decks: As the market matured, auto manufacturers began offering tape decks during the production phase. Of course, the audiotape market fully recognized the trend and began marketing compact disk (CD) players, which, of course, is now a standard auto dealer accessory. Also, in the automobile industry, the growing prevalence of cellular telephones has led manufacturers to offer preinstalled cellular phones, usually hidden in a compartment and equipped with a hidden, hands-free microphone and speaker.

The growth of the superstore model and the tactics of WalMart are further examples of systems integration, but in the opposite direction. Superstores, most common in the PC market, sprang up a few years ago to capitalize on a market whose penetration grew to the point that customer-accessible warehousing became possible (see Figures 4.5 and 4.6); availability or options went up, while unit costs went down. The consumer wins on both counts. CompUSA and Home Depot are examples of this direction of system integration.

The health care industry has gone berserk with both horizontal integration, like these mentioned, and vertical integration. PHOs, MSOs, independent practice associations (IPAs), and integrated health systems (IHSs) are all examples of horizontal integration.

As discussed in chapter 3, the most effective use of systems integration is horizontal integration because the greatest cost of poor quality and customer dissatisfiers occur as the customer moves longi-

Figure 4.4. Automobile audio aftermarket.

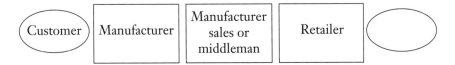

Figure 4.5. Pre-superstore.

tudinally through the system. The examples listed can best be conceptualized through mastery of a mental model like the one in Figure 4.6.

The health care industry, due to the nature of its evolution as a cottage industry of fiercely independent entities, presents many interesting and challenging dilemmas. Should a hospital form a PHO? Can the same objectives be achieved without the expensive legal arrangements necessary for the establishment of a PHO? Should specialists be permitted an equal vote in the governance to primary care physicians? Should primary care physicians be organized separately from specialists? Should the organization establish an MSO to manage capitation contracting? If so, should it organize its own or bring in an outside firm? What are the advantages and disadvantages of both options? Will the marketing function of the integrated health system market to both employers and external HMOs/personal provider options (PPOs)? Should we establish our own HMO? What are the risks and rewards of competing directly against while trying to contract with HMOs?

Exceed Stakeholder Cash Flow Expectations 20 Percent per Year

Perhaps the need for cash flow as a key strategic imperative is obvious, but what may not be as obvious is the importance of regenerating the organization's view of cash flow as a key indicator from a financial mind-set to a quality mind-set. Most organizations cannot continue to exist without strong fiscal conservatism. Historically financial needs, strategic needs, and quality needs are rarely, if ever, expressed in recognition of each other and, yet, a customer-driven mind-set would seem to suggest the importance of integrating all needs. Some organizations

Figure 4.6. Superstore market integration.

boldly communicate quality goals to employees, but stop short of educating employees of the organization's cash flow needs. Presumably, the financial plan analyzes expected cash flow, which is determined from anticipated changes in the balance sheet, and expects that some part of the cash flow budget fuels programs and process changes intended to meet anticipated customer needs and meets debt service requirements and fund growth needs for nonprofit organizations or investor return for investor-owned organizations. An educated workforce, brought to understand the need for cash just as it understands the need to improve customer satisfaction, should also be able to contribute more fully and grow in its contributions to achieving the organization's vision.

Now that we have concluded the discussion on strategic results, it is a good point at which to address one component of infrastructure, the organization chart, and roles and responsibilities of various entities created to support the TQM deployment. These entities are the quality council, BPQM teams (if your organization has embarked upon reengineering), cross-functional quality improvement team leaders and members, department quality improvement team leaders and members, and individuals engaged in quality in daily work (QDW) improvement activities. As Table 4.1 suggests, and as a main tenet of the discussion on the importance of focusing on at least five strategic thrusts, the quality council owns the degree of achievement of results and should invest most of its meeting time to discussing the results of teams and other strategic activities. Many quality councils get trapped into analyzing the type of tools by teams, the type and construction of TQM education activities, and so on. This is not to suggest that these latter activities are irrelevant, but rather that they are the domain of the quality management department, facilitators, and team leaders. Similarly, the quality council must invest a significant proportion of its time analyzing and effecting change to the infrastructure necessary to accelerate the achievement of the organization's vision. This task cannot be delegated to subordinate levels of the organization.

Some observers might question the allocations as less than desirable for their particular organization and the suggestions are certainly not intended to be rigid expectations, but rather a means by which an organization can conceptualize the various roles and responsibilities in carrying out the strategic deployment road map. Others may argue that teams could not possibly contribute to vision achievement by investing only 20 percent of their available time to results, and these guidelines, too, are always open to debate. In keeping with the lessons

Table 4.1. Time allocation chart.

Time allocation	Results	Methods	Infrastructure
I. Quality council	50%	10%	40%
II. Quality management director	10%	70%	20%
III. Facilitators	10%	90%	0%
IV. BPQM teams	20%	70%	10%
V. Cost-of-poor-quality teams	20%	70%	10%
VI. Cross-functional teams	20%	70%	10%
VII. Department teams	20%	70%	10%

Results include: 1. Rate of innovation   2. Cost of poor quality
3. Customer satisfaction   4. Systems integration   5. Cash flow
Methods include: 1. QI teams   2. Quality planning teams   3. BPQM
teams   4. Cost-of-poor-quality teams   5. Benchmarking
6. Networking   7. Education
Infrastructure includes: 1. Organizational design   2. Compensation
3. Performance appraisal   4. Capital allocation   5. Legal structure
6. Supplier relations   7. Facilities

so profound in Deming's teachings, focus on the process. Teams should be driven to address process changes through the use of TQM tools in order to achieve results.

Market Needs

Referring again to the transformation model in Figure 4.1, the logical place to start any dialogue about strategic visioning is the ultimate desired results from our efforts—continually meeting market needs. Knowledge of customers is the cornerstone of every effective strategy. An in-depth discussion of market assessment is far beyond our purposes here, except to ensure that the reader and quality councils engaging this text clearly recognize that the strategic plan and quality plan should be one and the same, and, further, that every effort undertaken by the organization, including TQM, should be measured by its contribution to the achievement of the organization's vision. As company planners uncover strengths, weaknesses, opportunities, and threats for the segments of environment, competition, information systems, and key products, they should be mindful of the prominent role of the paradigms discussed in the previous chapter relative to organization positioning in the market.

Many mature TQM strategists, particularly the Japanese, would have us believe that non-TQM strategists are beneath their mind-sets. That is, evidence suggests that traditional strategic processes do not go far enough to help translate the needs of customers into the company's operational language. Harvard Business School's Ben Shapiro observes that truly exceptional companies hold a management philosophy that encourages strategists, managers, and employees to look intensely at their organization as a system through the eyes of the customer. He notes that great performing companies are those that understand what it is like to be a customer from order to postsales service.[5] Many Japanese companies go to great lengths to observe even the smallest customer interfaces. A TQM convention called *kokai watch* is utilized by Bridgestone Tire Company.[6] It involves the structured observation by several persons not normally involved in the production of a particular process, that is, the observers are outsiders. The process is generally very minute and finite, requiring from a few minutes to a couple of hours to complete one cycle. The watchers, with pad and pen, watch intensely as the process is performed and attempt to identify even the smallest and most insignificant improvement suggestions. As related to me by Mary Walton, the reporter of the watch on the process to die rubber for Bridgestone tires is concerned with any component that requires two or more minutes. Over the years, Bridgestone has reduced the process from several hours to two hours. Its Japanese counterpart has driven the process down to 18 minutes and becomes concerned with components that take more than six seconds! As customer expectations increase, so, too, must our procedures for anticipating customer needs.

To close this discussion on market needs, I came as close to understanding the meaning of market need when asked by Batalden, "What would happen if West Paces were to close today? Would anyone notice?" This sobering question is worth repetition. What would happen if your organization closed today? Who would notice?

Current Outcomes

As demonstrated in the transformation model in Figure 4.1, the end result of the collective performance of the organization as a system can and should be expressed in measurable terms, that is, from their language to our operations language. This is akin to translating Spanish to French. These measurements are reflected in the strategic measurement panel and form the basis for quality council action. The issue of what to measure is perhaps more elusive than we might imagine, particularly as our organization engages more responsive measures of the degree to which we meet Kano's Level I and Level III needs. Juran places the task of translating customer needs among the most underestimated.[7] Howland Blackiston, president of Juran Institute, tells the horror story of SAS Scandinavian Airlines' strategic measure for the cargo division.[8] It seems that to track the effectiveness of the package delivery process the cargo group measured its success on the basis of degree of cargo capacity filled on each plane. The greater the percentage full, the better the workers felt about themselves. Unfortunately, the business was not growing as fast as SAS had hoped, so a quality improvement team was formed to improve the process. SAS' promise to customers was that packages would be received the next day, but after several complaints, the team decided to test the process. To its surprise, packages took four days! Why? The package handlers had been instructed to hold packages until there were enough to fill its cargo planes, which was precisely how their performance was measured—by full planes. SAS was guilty of understanding customer needs, but measuring its success on its own needs. How often do other organizations fail to measure more than one dimension of quality? Do your financial systems measure labor productivity, like the number of staffhours per patient day, full-time equivalents (FTEs) per occupied bed, or returned goods costs as a percent of net sales? What do these measures tell your organization about how well the customer's needs were met? The point here is not CFO-bashing, they get bashed enough from the CEO and the board. The discussion question is, "How do you know?"

Mission Statement

The issue about the mission statement is not so much of what it says, but rather, does it play a role in shaping the company's strategy? Does each and every stakeholder know the mission of the organization? Your vision? Your commitment to understanding and meeting customers' needs? How do you know they know? As shown in Figure 4.7, the mission statement at West Paces Medical Center enjoyed a promi-

Strategic Plan Abstract

Mission	To provide excellence in health care.
	To improve the standards of health care in the Atlanta community.
	To provide superior service to enable physicians to best serve the needs of their patients.
	To encourage continuing education and training to staff members and to maintain quality assurance.
	To generate measurable benefits for the medical staff, the employees, and, most importantly, the patients.
Vision	To be the best-value Atlanta health system by 1996 and be recognized as such.
Quality Definition	At West Paces Medical Center, achieving quality means adding value to all that we do through a commitment to the continuous improvement of services that meet the needs and expectations of our patients, physicians, payers, employees, and the community we serve.
Approach	1. Through quality function deployment, identify and measure all needs of patients, physicians, purchasers, employees, regulators, and stockholders.
	2. Improve every quality indicator.
	3. Decrease cycle time and variation in every process.
	4. Concentrate on error-free process design.
	5. Attain 100 percent effective participation and teamwork.

Figure 4.7. Sample mission statement.

nent place in the strategic plan, appearing above the vision, quality definition, and strategic approach.

Guiding Principles

As illustrated in the transformation model in Figure 4.1, guiding principles form the bridge between the mission statement and vision. In their purest form, guiding principles can replace the need for extensive policy and procedures manuals because each and every individual in the organization is charged and empowered to perform his or her respective processes with the guiding principles in mind.

We did not institute guiding principles at West Paces Medical Center until much later in our TQM deployment than is customary.

We simply did not see the need for such a "soft" convention, and the quality council did not push the issue. My more astute colleagues, Jim Biltz, then CEO of Wesley Medical Center in Wichita, Kansas, and John Kausch, CEO of West Florida Medical Center in Pensacola, Florida, invested time and energy to create widespread buy-in of their organizational guiding principles. These efforts seemed to generate a strong rate of return. Shown in Figure 4.8, Wesley's guiding principles suggest a heightened appreciation for Deming's 14 principles. Figures 4.9 and 4.10 reveal different approaches to the application of the concept of guiding principles from StorageTek and Corning, while Figure 4.11 shows an example of guiding principles from an integrated health system, the HCA MedFirst Health System. An interesting integrated health system employee involvement policy from Fort Sanders Health System can be reviewed in Appendix C.

Organization's Vision

The creation of the organization's vision requires the adoption of processes intended to generate widespread buy-in throughout the organization. As Senge observes, a vision is more than just the CEO's idea of where the organization is headed, it only becomes a powerful tool upon articulating the combined values of the members of the organization.[9] The vision is based on the market need for your organization's goods and services in its words, translated into your operating language in the form of outcomes and the mission statement.

At West Paces Medical Center, our vision was "to be the best-value Atlanta health system by 1996 and to be recognized as such." It was crafted from key words generated by the 54 department managers and senior leaders at our TQM retreat on May 5, 1988.

The vision should be expressed in quantifiable terms in the strategic measurement panel, which is the focus of the next chapter. The measurement panel provides a graphic picture of each of the strategic thrusts discussed earlier. These measures are expressed in terms of Kano's Level I needs and Level III needs, that is, each measure is given a lower level, below which customers are being repelled or the strategy is in grave danger. At the upper extreme, Level III measures the target that suggests that customers are being delighted or the organization has reached world-class performance for that particular indicator. As we shall see, West Paces Medical Center monitored 16 CEO-level measures to track vision accomplishment.

To help achieve continuous improvement and innovation in all that we do, we have developed guiding principles. These principles and our quality improvement process are based on the ideas of W. Edwards Deming. Dr. Deming is the American statistician who helped Japanese industries develop systems to build quality into the products that now dominate world markets. He developed a theory of management designed to transform an organization. Our principles reflect his beliefs:

The HCA Wesley Guiding Principles

1 Place quality first

We make the quality of our products and services our number one priority. We will strive to eliminate barriers, rework and complexity in the belief that benefits to our patients, market share and profitability will follow.

2 Focus on the customer

We recognize that there are many internal and external customers of the medical center and we will strive to meet their needs. We will identify opportunities for improvement by listening to the voice of the customer.

3 Recognize our people as our most valuable asset

We respect the talents people bring to their jobs and believe that people want to do their best. We will focus on systems improvements.

4 Acknowledge physicians as partners as well as customers

We recognize the essential relationship between the medical center and the medical staff. We will involve physicians in the constant improvement of systems.

5 Become partners with suppliers committed to continuous improvement

We believe the value of a product or service is measured by more than price alone. We will build mutually beneficial relationships with suppliers committed to quality improvement.

6 Manage through leadership

We show the way by example. We will share our vision, enable others to act, and promote teamwork.

7 Encourage pride of workmanship

We believe in creating an environment that allows people to take pride in their work. We will empower people to identify and remove barriers to quality.

8 Treat one another with trust and respect

We respect the worth of every individual. We will continuously improve our working relationships based on this principle.

9 Value honesty, trustworthiness and integrity

We are dedicated to doing the best for all concerned. We will treat patients, other customers, and one another as we would wish to be treated, recognizing that how we act is the Wesley product.

10 Seek continuous improvement in all we do

We understand that quality is ever evolving. We will strive for excellence.

11 Utilize statistical processes to monitor systems and identify opportunities for improvement

We seek continuous improvement of the process through reduction of variation. We will use data to understand the process.

12 Cease reliance on inspection to achieve quality

We recognize that we cannot effectively achieve quality through inspection alone. We will use inspection as one means for listening to the voice of the system.

13 Understand that defects come from processes, not people

We believe that waste, rework and inefficiencies originate in defective systems. We will encourage people to improve the process.

14 Support education and training

We value the growth and development of people. We will invest in job training and encourage self-improvement.

15 Promote innovation

We support creative thinking in the improvement of systems and development of services. We will pay particular attention to the ideas of those closest to the work.

16 Celebrate achievements

We believe in the value of recognizing improvements. We will take time to celebrate successes.

These guiding principles will trigger Dr. Deming's chain reaction. They will help lead us through our transformation. Such a transformation, however, will not happen overnight; it is a journey that will take many years. This movement from old to new ways is rooted in our understanding of and commitment to these guiding principles and to our continual application of them.

Figure 4.8. Wesley Medical Center guiding principles.

Source: HCA Wesley Medical Center, Wichita, Kans. Reprinted with permission.

Operating Principles

StorageTek is dedicated to serving its *Customers* worldwide by continuing to be the preferred provider of high-performance information storage subsystems, printers, and supporting services and by adhering to the following principles:

Quality: Our standards of quality will ensure our competitiveness. We will sacrifice short-term gain for reliability and excellence in serving our *Customers'* needs.

People: People are the key to StorageTek's success. Individual recognition and advancement will be based upon performance that supports *StorageTek's* commitments to our *Customers* and investors.

Accountability: Our business will be managed to achieve planned growth and long-term profitability. We will grow by building upon demonstrated strengths and meeting *Customers'* needs.

Action: Each of us will participate in and contribute to the cost-effective, timely resolution of challenges and opportunities which continuously improve our *Customer* commitment.

Practices: We will act with integrity to ensure credibility in our relationships with our *Customers*, investors, fellow employees, suppliers and those communities in which we operate worldwide.

Figure 4.9. StorageTek's guiding principles.

Source: StorageTek, Boulder, Colo. Reprinted with permission.

Organization As a System

In drawing a system map of the organization, or a high-level flow-chart, as it is sometimes called, the organization becomes very close to the customer and begins to experience what it is like to be a recipient of the organization's processes.

The first step identifies the input, best thought of as the ignition switch that causes the organization to go into action. This input is generally the business the organization is in. For a hospital, for example, it would be "patients with health care need," for an HMO, "populations at health risk;" for a computer retail firm, "customers with automation need;" for a restaurant, "hungry customers." As discussed

Corning "Making Quality Happen" Goals

1. By 1991, increase employee training for meeting job requirements to an average of 5 percent of time worked.
2. By 1991, achieve a 90 percent reduction in the most critical errors preventing the attainment of total quality in products, processes, and services.
3. By 1991, the first-day quality of new goods and services will meet customer requirements, and will be equal to or better than the quality of competitive products or the quality of the products being replaced.

Corning "Making Quality Happen" Principles

1. Provide visible, unquestioned leadership.
2. Focus on customer results.
3. Train all employees.
4. Achieve and recognize employee participation.
5. Communicate about quality internally and externally.
6. Provide a quality process and quality tools.

Figure 4.10. Corning's goals and principles.

Source: David Luther, "Making Quality a Competitive Strategy" (address of the Congressional Subcommittee on Science, Research, and Technology, Washington, D.C., April 18, 1989), 7–15.

in the paradigm on systems thinking, learning to manage upstream will be a key strategic activity, but for the purposes of the current system, it is important to stay focused on the business you are actually in, not the business you would like to be in. For example, a hospital might say it is in the business of maintaining community health, and, thus, would list as an input, "population at health risk," but, unfortunately, this is not the what the customer is paying for. Customers and their proxies, the employers, are paying for hospitals to manage "patients with health care needs." Many hospitals provide wonderful community services in the area of preventive care, community education, and the like, but this is no different than IBM funding the arts in its communities or Delta Airlines providing a grant to a local community college. These are higher order obligations hopefully felt by every organization, but it is not yet your business.

Upon completion of the identification of the input, construct a high-level flowchart, as illustrated in Figure 4.12, of how the customer moves through your organization, from "customer awareness" of the services you offer, "needs identification," "product creation," "product

HCA MedFirst Health System Quality Improvement Plan

I. *Vision:* To be the best value Atlanta health system by 1996 and recognized as such.

II. *Guiding Principles:*

    a. TQM-based, in the pursuit of error-free design and reduction of variation in clinical and support processes.

    b. Physician and specialist selection will follow an inclusive methodology rather than an exclusive one.

    c. Tailor made integrated health systems are our primary product and we will strive to include all desired providers if they make quality standards and agree to TQM participation.

    d. Capitation is the preferred reimbursement method for most providers, except hospitals, in order to align the incentives of all parties towards the improvement of quality and the reduction of clinical utilization.

    e. The best value integrated health system will be driven by primary care physicians, utilizing a TQM-based seamless flow of information and clinical processes between primary care physicians, specialists, hospitals, and allied providers.

    f. Best value can only be achieved and maintained through the selection of specialists who are most efficient, lowest resource users, and focus on their patients' achievement of highest health status. In addition they must be champions of a continuous improvement methodology.

    g. Overhead inspection rework and waste is a deterrent to maintaining best value. Error-free design is the road to success, using FOCUS-PDCA.

    h. Benchmarking, internal among physicians and external among others, is the primary engine to reduce variation.

    i. Information is the vitamin of continuous improvement and should be widely shared with all partners.

    j. We will seek continuously to manage upstream in the health system as far as possible, drawing an ever larger box around the integrated health system. However, our responsibility for generating measurable benefits to our stockholders will prevent us from expanding the health system beyond our reimbursement boundaries; that is, we will seek to maximize earnings within the reimbursement paradigm accepted by the purchaser of care.

    k. We seek long term partners who share our TQM philosophy. Provider contracts will seek to achieve the gross margin required by each provider while sharing variation in costs within the network so that internal benchmarking will increase the value of the entire MedFirst Health System, while achieving each entity's financial requirements.

    l. Utilization reviews, medical director reviews and other forms of inspection are inherently wasteful to the efficient performance of an integrated health system. Every effort will be made to create error-free clinical processes through the use of internal and external benchmarking selection of efficient specialists by employing FOCUS-PDCA to reduce variation so that inspection and rework are minimized.

Figure 4.11. Integrated health system guiding principles.

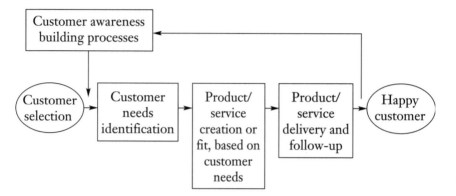

Figure 4.12. Generic customer-product/service development high-level flowchart.

delivery and follow-up," and ending with a "happy customer." Some skill exists in how detailed to make the high-level flowchart. If it is too detailed users cannot visualize the organization as a system. If it is too limited, users do not benefit from the knowledge of all the necessary handoff points creating cost of poor quality.

For additional clarification, a high-level flowchart of West Paces Medical Center is shown in Figure 4.13, and Figure 4.14 shows the same flowchart with the key business process treatment and intervention exploded to reveal additional detail. This convention is helpful to reveal details of one particular key business process without adding the confusing detail that would result if all key business processes were exploded.

These smaller systems or collection of processes inside the organization as a whole are referred to as *key business processes* and the method by which they are improved is called business process quality management. It is at this level that most organizations experience the greatest degree of cost of poor quality and customer dissatisfaction. Remember a fundamental understanding of how the customer experiences the organization is at the heart of TQM strategic deployment. This understanding forms the basis of the strategic deployment road map.

An infrastructure construct suggested earlier in this chapter, BPQM teams, serves as the backbone of most significant breakthroughs in customer service and cost of poor quality. These teams become marketing teams in the purest sense of the term in that they are very close to the customer, involved daily in the performance of

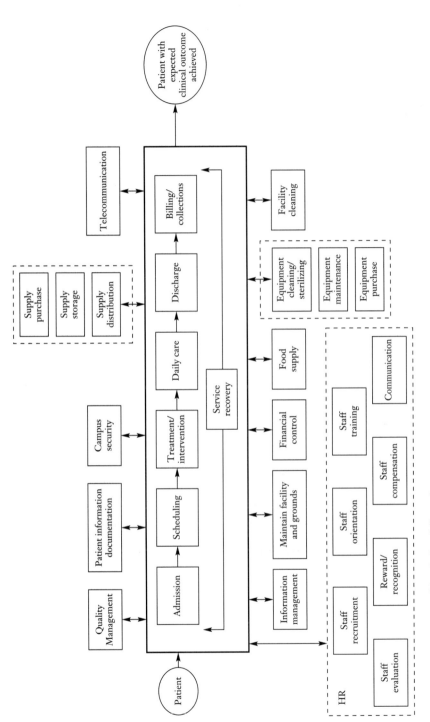

Figure 4.13. Hospital high-level flowchart.

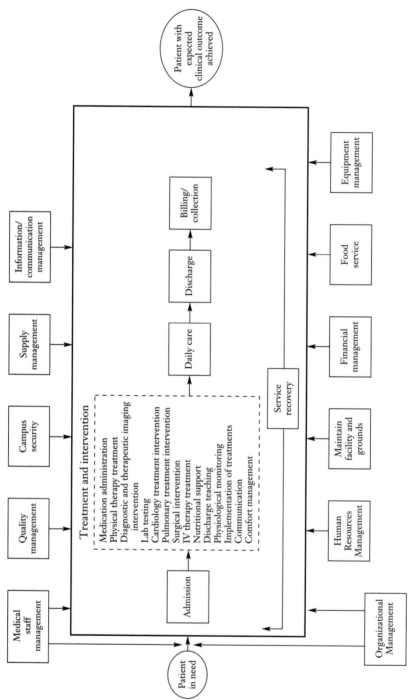

Figure 4.14. Hospital high-level flowchart, with a key business process exploded.

the inclusive processes of the business process quality management activity, and, with adequate training and empowerment, can drive market share and margin growth faster and more effectively than any other organization design vehicle. Some argue that the organization should be totally reorganized around business processes, dismantling the traditional "stovepipe" organizational hierarchy, but this approach requires a significant tolerance for organizational stress. The organization and its culture will be turned upside down and, for this reason, I do not recommend this more radical alternative without first considering the current organization state.

However, BPQM teams or reorganization is a prerequisite to mastering cost of poor quality and customer loyalty failures of the highest order in any company. BPQM teams can be of two different types; product or service BPQM teams, like the clinical teams shown in Figures 4.15, 4.16, and 4.17; or cross-functional teams, like information systems or billing. Examine the two clinical high-level flowcharts in Figure 4.15 and 4.16 in relation to Figure 4.13, the hospital as a whole. Where would you visualize these two clinical paths? Which processes within the hospital as a whole are included in the clinical flowcharts? Which are not? These would take the form of key products, like a laptop computer in a computer company, or frozen desserts in a grocery store, or the engineering college at a university. Now examine the support process of the Health Information Department— Medical Records—in Figure 4.17. Can you locate this department in Figure 4.13, the hospital as a whole?

This exercise of breaking the organization into key business processes will likely produce a large number of processes. In the case of West Paces Medical Center, more than 80 key business processes existed, counting both product processes and functional processes. An attempt to establish BPQM teams or other elaborate methods to manage each of these processes can overwhelm the organization. We learned to use the familiar Pareto principle to establish 10 vital few BPQM teams, which we believed would drive our vision achievement if we could become best-value in each of these processes. The processes were selected on the basis that the seven clinical conditions considered represented approximately 75 percent of the cost of health care to Atlanta employers. Some of these teams were obstetrics, mental health, cancer, diabetes, and orthopedic/workers' compensation. Some of these teams achieved best-value over a period of two to three years, and some were time wasters, but in all, the ability to manage the vital few remained our most important strategic imperative.

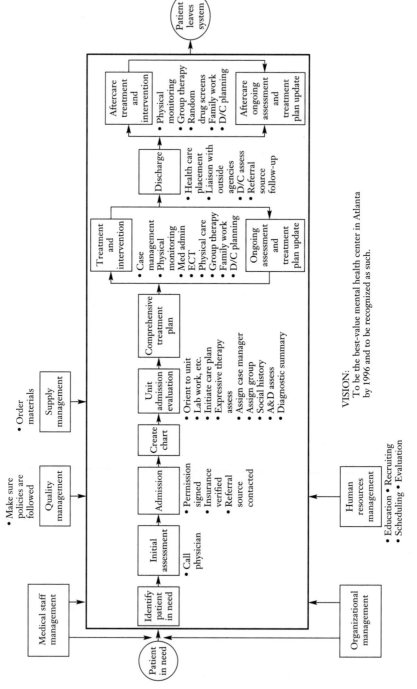

Figure 4.15. Hospital department high-level flowchart—Center for Mental Health.

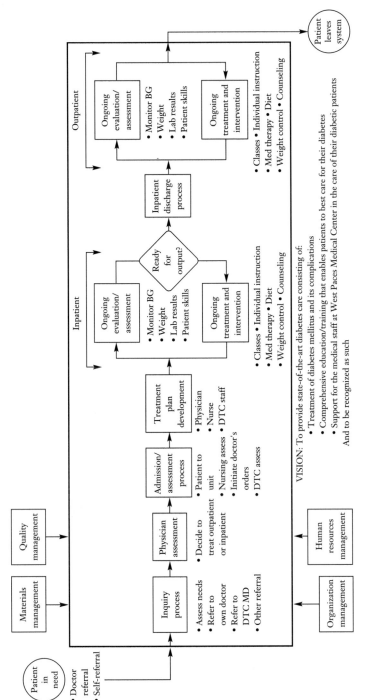

Figure 4.16. Hospital department high-level flowchart—Diabetes Treatment Center.

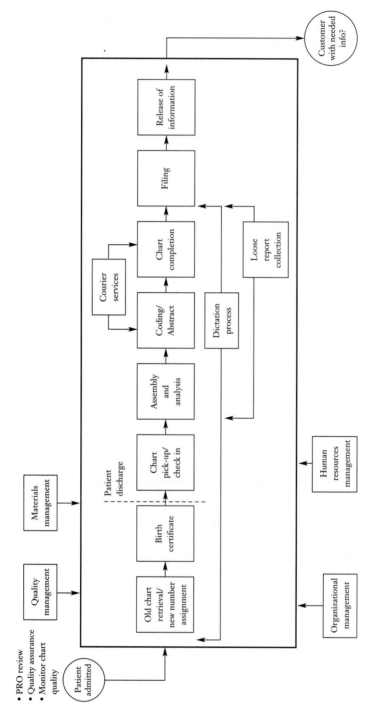

Figure 4.17. Hospital department high-level flowchart—Health Information Department, Medical Records.

Most organizations could stop their TQM strategic deployment at this point and have accomplished much more than they could ever master. The learning that takes place as a result of viewing the organization as the customer experiences it breaks paradigms and opens inter- and intra-department communications in a very profound way.

Strategy Deployment Road Map

The strategic deployment road map is the engine that drives strategy achievement. Expressed in the strategic measurement panel, it is based on the vision and the gap that exists between current outcomes and the level of performance required to achieve the vision on each performance measure. It may be helpful to study Figure 4.1 in detail at this point since we have discussed each of the major components of the transformation model.

Figure 4.18 gives an example of one page of the strategic deployment road map from Suburban Hospital of Bethesda, as created by Brian Grissler, CEO, and the quality council. The road map is the tool that merges the strategic plan and the quality plan. The first page should list all strategic results, with subsequent pages outlining activities for methods and infrastructure, as illustrated in Figure 4.11.

Management Feedback Process

What steps might be followed to generate continuous process improvement of the strategic deployment process? While most organizations are relatively refined in the area of strategic deployment, after years of attempting to link TQM activities and methods with strategic deployment, we came to the realization that most traditional strategic thinking attracts activity along the proper path. These models do not go far enough to capture the ultimate sophistication of a TQM initiative, namely, the collective impact of harnessing the energy and creativity of the entire workforce. Therefore, many strategic thinkers who have learned how to integrate TQM deployment and strategic activities, like Juran and Batalden, have nested steps inside their recommended process improvement models to capture the creative energies of process owners. (See appendix A for Juran's quality improvement model and appendix B for the model Batalden created for HCA.) The following process based on the transformation model can serve as a meaningful

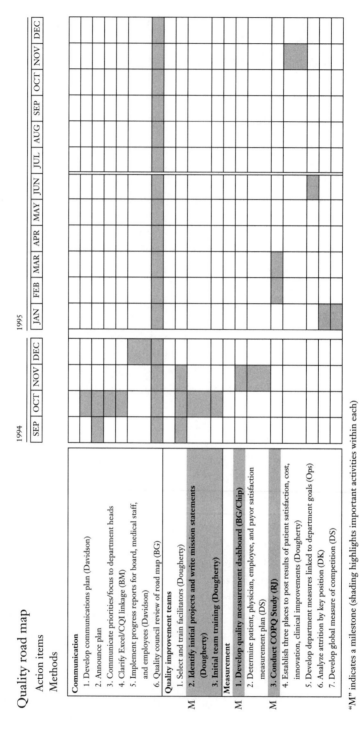

Figure 4.18. Sample strategic deployment road map.

Quality road map

	1994				1995											
	SEP	OCT	NOV	DEC	JAN	FEB	MAR	APR	MAY	JUN	JUL	AUG	SEP	OCT	NOV	DEC
Training and education (QI/QC/QP)																
1. Write training plan—include IS (DK)		▓	▓													
2. Train department managers (Dougherty/Chip)			▓	▓												
3. Educate board (BM)																
4. Assess "lessons learned" from teams (BM)																
5. Orient new medical staff leaders and staff (BM)					▓											
6. Medical staff leaders trained in CQI clinic by Juran (BM)																
7. Develop CQI training process for new managers (Maestri)						▓										
8. Add information to new employee orientation (Maestri)																
9. Train department managers in QC and service recovery (Chip)													▓			
10. Additional training for senior staff																
11. Two-day facility training to 10 emerging leaders (BD)								▓								
12. Train key managers in advanced quality planning tools (Chip)													▓			
13. Human resources development—individual education plans (DK)																
Further team deployment																
1. Create additional QI teams (BG)							▓									
2. Charter clinic lameter teams (begin to) (BM)		▓														
BPQM																
1. Several execs to attend BPQM course							▓									
2. Identify key business processes (BG)					▓	▓										
3. Launch business process redesign teams with measures and sponsors (BG)							▓									
4. Begin to design BPQM initiative for culture										▓						
Align CQI goals with integration partners (BG)																
Intensivists integrated into culture/practice (BM)																▓
Supplier certification program (Ops)																
Audit of quality (Malcolm Baldrige) (Chip)																

Figure 4.18. *continued.*

Quality road map

Infrastructure	1994				1995											
	SEP	OCT	NOV	DEC	JAN	FEB	MAR	APR	MAY	JUN	JUL	AUG	SEP	OCT	NOV	DEC
Quality council and team process																
1. Create project chartering process (Dougherty)			■	■												
2. Create nominating process for ideas (Dougherty)			■	■												
3. Create consistent team reporting form (Dougherty)																
4. Establish team process to present results (Dougherty)																
5. Executives facilitate at least one team (BG)																
6. Develop guidelines for department level teams (Dougherty)			■													
IS system																
1. Audit of measurement and information system (applicability and integrity regarding pursuit of quality) (RJ)						■										
2. Reassess IS ability to meet quality measure needs (RJ)													■			
Committees (medical)																
1. Medical staff committees redesigned (Robertson)			■													
2. Raise medical staff awareness re: meeting effectiveness (Robertson)			■													
3. Raise general awareness of meeting effectiveness (BM)				■												
QA/QI integration plan (BM)						■										
Cost accounting system in place (RJ)										■						
Reward/Recognition																
1. Executive's personal goals are quality goals (BG)										■						
2. Develop recognition program supporting quality goals (DK)									■	■						
3. Develop incentive compensation plan including quality measures (DK)										■						
HR selection																
1. Develop process to identify emerging leaders (DK)									■							
2. Create a plan for developing emerging leaders (DK)										■						
3. Develop a selection process consistent with organization goals (DK)																

Figure 4.18. *continued.*

Barriers to achieving vision for quality

Time (constraints on)
1. Poor time management
2. Perception that team meetings are not "real" work
3. Full executive calendar
4. Twenty-four-hour shifts
5. Current committee structure (ineffective/large number)
6. High demands on front-line employees
7. Lack of priority associated with (team) meetings
8. Too many priorities

Quality system
1. Lack of shared vision
2. Perception that executive staff not on board with quality
3. Minimal participation by executive staff in quality process
4. Perception of "old" teams
5. Prior false starts
6. Internal customer-supplier relationships not understood
7. Converting quality to "bottom-line"—COPQ
8. Lack of outcomes from past efforts

Lack of "data-mindedness"
1. Little or no use of control charts
2. Low comfort level with measurement and data
3. QFD too complex
4. Lots of data, very little information
5. Not enough resources to obtain data (computer)

Human resources
1. Dollar incentives may not support vision
2. No ties of QA/QI to evaluation
3. Managers/employees do not view training/education as essential

Culture/Attitude
1. Level of "fear" of change
   • Middle managers at risk
   • Employees focused on micro changes (e.g. lay-offs, benefits)
2. Turf
3. Functional and departmental thinking; not systems-oriented
4. Focus on bad apples/blame
5. "Arrogance" of the professionals
6. Skepticism
7. Frustration with current system
8. Not living articulated values

Way of work
1. Lack of effective communication (grapevine)
2. Policies are not empowering
3. Middle managers have "control"
4. Fire fighting inhibits innovation

Medical staff
1. Unaware medical staff
2. Medical staff not connected to hospital

Countermeasures

Time
1. Criteria for "need for meetings"
2. Formalized agenda process
3. Showing up and starting on time
4. Criteria for who should attend meetings
5. Consolidating standing committees
6. Stop meeting/committee vehicle to solve accountability issues

Culture
1. Use employee survey results to prioritize
2. Continue to express shared values to department managers
3. Cross-functional team building

"Data-mindedness"
1. Hire management engineer
2. Display key process measures on run/control charts
3. Provide computer training on software
4. As senior managers, ask for data (versus anecdote)
5. Ultimately, deploy measures throughout all departments

Figure 4.18. *continued.*

method for organizations to drive achievement of the strategic deployment road map.

   I. Articulate customer needs in all market segments. Conduct strengths, weaknesses, opportunities, and threats of current market conditions and future estimations.
  II. Discover competitor performance, including best-in-class and world-class performers.
 III. Analyze current outcomes.
  IV. Create a shared vision, based upon mission, market need, and guiding principles with active input and communication from all levels of the organization.
   V. Draw the organization as a system.
  VI. Determine the organization's key business processes, both functional processes, like Figure 4.17, and product or service lines processes, like Figure 4.16. From the sum of processes, identify the *vital* strategic business process quality management processes (for example, chest pain, obstetrics, mental health, scheduling). Effective management of vision achievement presumes that BPQM teams will be established for each key business process.
 VII. Identify infrastructure features and elements that accelerate or support vision achievement and features and elements that inhibit vision achievement.
VIII. Construct a plan to resolve inhibitors and optimize accelerators, including infrastructure reengineering, education and training, and so on.
  IX. Establish a strategic measurement panel (as discussed in the next chapter) and begin weekly, monthly, or quarterly plotting on run charts or SPC charts, as appropriate.
   A. For each CEO-level, VP-level, and business process quality management strategic measure, establish
      1. The Kano Level I threshold, the level below which customers will be repelled or achievement of the vision is in peril.
      2. The Kano Level III threshold, the level above which customers will express delight or achievement of the vision is on track. Create Hoshin targets that must be reached per six-month increment in order to achieve the vision for

each measure at the CEO level, VP level, business process quality management/core process level, and department level. Draw dotted lines on each SPC chart indicating these six-month hoshin target thresholds.

B. Review performance at least monthly.

X. Charter strategic BPQM teams from item VI.

A. Write business process quality management mission statements and construct key strategic measures.

B. Assign a member of the quality council as business process quality management sponsor to assist the team through inhibitors beyond the boundaries of their processes.

XI. Engage the management feedback process by monitoring progress of the strategic measurement panel and strategic deployment road map at least monthly at a quality council meeting. Refer to the strategic deployment process flowchart in Figure 4.19 used by the West Paces Medical Center quality council as a suggested approach.

A. Vice presidents and business process quality management sponsors review the Business Process Quality Management/ Department Monthly Management Feedback Report (see Figure 4.20) monthly, which analyzes each data point.

1. If a data point exceeds targeted performance by three consecutive points, celebrate with owner(s) of the process.

2. If a data point falls below target performance by three consecutive points, the sponsor or owner(s) should present an action plan to the quality council to bring performance to the required Hoshin level.

B. The quality council should review the quality council monthly management feedback report (Figure 4.21) monthly, which summarizes relevant changes in organization data points.

1. If a data point exceeds targeted performance by three consecutive points, celebrate with owner(s) of the process.

2. If a data point falls below target performance by three consecutive points, the sponsor or owner(s) should present an action plan to the quality council to bring performance to the required hoshin level.

XII. Repeat this process annually.

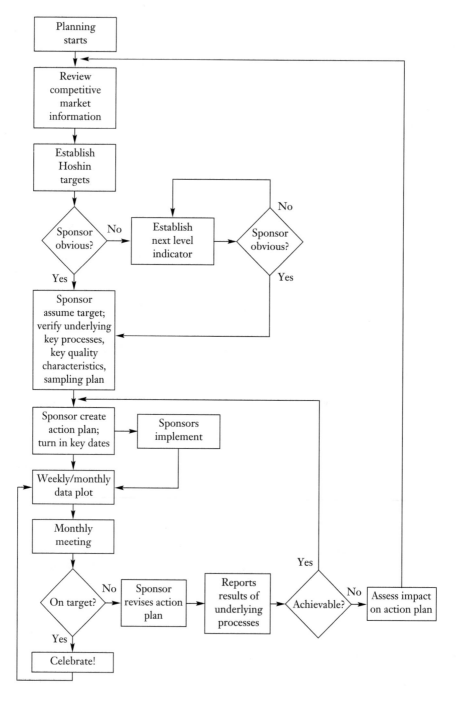

Figure 4.19. Strategic deployment process flowchart.

Department/BPQM team _____ Date _____

Please record the status of your current quality improvement teams.

Quality improvement teams progress	Step	Last meeting	Next meeting

Please record any innovations in your department process this month.

Innovation! Indicator	Old mean or median	New mean or median	Level III delight threshold

Describe change in process _____

_____

_____

Are we meeting or exceeding customer expectations?

Please record any department indicators about Level III, Delight, or below Level I, Repel.

Delighting our customers! Indicator	Status	Delight	Number of periods

Immediate action required! Indicator	Status	Repel	Number of periods

Figure 4.20. BPQM feedback report.

Month:

CEO-level measures							
Exceed Level III, Delight, for six-month threshold for one period				Below Level I, Repel, threshold for one period			
Measure	Actual	Level III Delight	Number of periods	Measure	Actual	Level I Repel	Number of periods
VP-level measures							
Exceed Level III, Delight, for six-month threshold for one period				Below Level I, Repel, for one period			
Measure	Actual	Level III Delight	Number of periods	Measure	Actual	Level I Repel	Number of periods
BPQM or core process measures							
Exceed Level III, Delight, for six-month threshold for three periods				Below Level I, Repel, for three periods			
Measure	Actual	Level III Delight	Number of periods	Measure	Actual	Level I Repel	Number of periods

Figure 4.21. Quality council monthly management feedback report.

This management feedback process is the final touch to be deployed by the quality council to tie the strategic deployment road map and strategic measurement panel monitoring together. This method assures a logical, process-minded, and constructive framework so often missing in otherwise exceptional TQM deployment models.

Department-level measures							
Exceed Level III, Delight, for six-month threshold for three periods				Below Level I, Repel, for three periods			
Measure	Actual	Level III Delight	Number of periods	Measure	Actual	Level I Repel	Number of periods

Figure 4.21. *continued.*

The feedback process provides each leader in the organization with vital progress reporting on the degree to which strategic Hoshin targets are being achieved within the "vital few" strategic business process quality management processes.

As closure on this very busy chapter on strategic visioning and deployment, refer to the transformation model in Figure 4.1. We have now integrated market need, current outcomes, vision, gap, and the strategic deployment road map . Upon this template we have created a management feedback process to track our progress along strategic demands.

Discussion Exercise for the First One-Hour Quality Council Meeting

1. Focus on innovation

   a. What is the average number of days for a quality improvement team to complete a cycle?

    b. How many days did this team trim off the cycle compared to its last cycle?

    c. What is the rate of increase in the number of customer-driven employee suggestions?

    d. How many months does it take us to introduce a new or modified product or service compared to this time last year?

2. Focus on systems integration. Most organizations are aggressively seeking new relationships with customers and suppliers through reorganization and affiliative arrangements. Systems thinking can go a long way toward helping every organization grasp a more reasonable view of the future of its industry.

    a. Draw on a flip chart the boxes that best represent your industry's system as it exists today in your market. Circle your position in the feeding chain.

    b. Draw your best guess of how these entities will be aligned in five years by drawing a box around affiliated entities with a different color marker. Draw boxes around your view in 10 years. Did you include upstream and downstream entities? Suppliers?

    c. Are types of organizations represented that do not exist today? Will any that exist today cease to exist in five years? Ten years?

    d. How can you integrate your existing TQM framework to drive innovation at key strategic interfaces?

3. What additional training will be necessary to support increased innovation? BPQM teams? Cost of poor quality teams?

4. What additional training will new members of partner-integrated health system entities require to understand your vision, strategic deployment road map, and TQM deployment methods?

Discussion Exercise for the Second One-Hour Quality Council Meeting

1. What are your organization's top five strategies (not tactics) for the coming year?

2. Does the strategic plan include increasing the rate of innovation? Decreasing the cost of poor quality? Increasing customer satisfaction? Systems integration? Increasing cash flow?

3. For any of the strategies not listed, are there any reasons to consider them next year? What are the implications for not including them?

4. Do your department managers know your strategy? Vision? Elements of the strategic deployment road map ?

5. Do your employees and other stakeholders know your strategy? Vision? Elements of the strategic deployment road map ?

6. How might your communications plan be modified to ensure the development of a shared vision?

Discussion Exercise for a One-Hour Quality Council Meeting for Health Care Systems

Hospitals and medical centers are up to their hips in reorganization and affiliative arrangements. Systems thinking can go a long way toward helping these organizations grasp a more reasonable view of the integrated health system's future.

1. Draw on a flip chart the boxes that best represent your health care system as it exists today in your market. Circle your position in the feeding chain.

2. Draw your best guess of how these entities will be aligned in five years by drawing a box around affiliated entities with a different color marker. Draw boxes around your view in 10 years. Did you include PHOs? MSOs? IPAs? HMOs? Public Health? Preventive services? Three-day stay surgery centers? Suppliers?

3. Are types of organizations represented that do not exist today? Will any that exist today cease to exist in five years? Ten years?

4. Should a hospital form a PHO? Can the same objectives be achieved without the expensive legal arrangements necessary for the establishment of a PHO? Should specialists be permit-

ted an equal vote in the governance to PCPs? Should PCPs be organized separately from specialists?

5. Should the organization establish an MSO to manage capitation contracting? If so, should we organize our own or bring in an outside firm? What are the advantages and disadvantages of both options?

6. How can you integrate your existing TQM framework to drive innovation at key strategic interfaces?

Discussion Exercise for a One-Hour Department Manager/Team Leader Meeting

One quality council member should serve as facilitator for this session. The facilitator should give a brief overview of the purpose and construction of a high-level flowchart to introduce the session. As with many other department manager learning sessions, the outcome need not be critiqued. The real application of the learning is when managers begin thinking about cost of poor quality and customer satisfaction when relating to other departments.

It is vital that department managers learn to think in terms of systems management as well as the organization's senior leaders. The fully mature organization will be the one in which every manager is aggressively seeking new relationships with customers and suppliers through reorganization and affiliative arrangements. Systems thinking can go a long way toward helping every organization grasp a more reasonable view of the future of its industry. For the purposes of this practice exercise, managers should be divided into groups of eight to 10, with one quality council member serving as a sponsor for each group. Select one department manager and his or her department to serve as the guinea pig for the learning exercises.

1. Getting a hamburger at McDonald's: On a flip chart, draw a large box, framing almost the entire page. Draw a circle at one end of the page and one at the other end. Label the first entry "Customer orders hamburger" and the last "Customer

leaves." Now, with input from the group, draw small boxes inside the larger box to represent the sequential steps to get a hamburger. Upon completion, brainstorm as many ideas as possible of why an order might get delayed. Consider handoff points from one function to the next, supply problems, upstream issues, and so on.

2. Guinea pig department high-level flowchart: On a flip chart, draw a large box, framing almost the entire flipchart page. Draw a circle at one end of the page and one at the other end. Label the first entry "Process begins in my department when _____" and the last "Process is completed in my department when _____." Now, with input from the group, draw small boxes inside the larger box to represent the sequential steps for the department to complete progress through the guinea pig department. Upon completion, brainstorm as many ideas as possible of why an order might get delayed. Consider handoff points from one function to the next, supply problems, upstream issues, and so on.

Discussion Exercise for a Governing Board Meeting

This session should be led by the chairperson of the board quality improvement committee or equivalent, or an interested member. The director of quality should assist by recording responses on a flip chart and engaging facilitation, when needed. The focus of this session is on strategic imperatives.

1. What are your organization's top five strategies for the coming year?

2. Does the strategic plan include increasing the rate of innovation? Decreasing cost of poor quality? Increasing customer satisfaction? Systems integration? Increasing cash flow?

3. For any of the strategies suggested that are not listed, are there any reasons to consider them next year? What are the implications for not including them?

4. Is there evidence that department managers know the strategy? Vision? Elements of the strategic deployment road map ?

5. Is there evidence that employees and other stakeholders know the strategy? Vision? Elements of the strategic deployment road map?

Notes

1. Joseph M. Juran, "The Quality Trilogy: A Universal Approach to Managing for Quality," *Quality Progress* 19 (August 1986): 19–24.

2. Joseph M. Juran, *Juran on Quality by Design* (New York: The Free Press, 1992), 107–114.

3. Donald M. Berwick, A. Blanton Godfrey, and Jane Roessner, *Curing Health Care* (San Francisco: Jossey-Bass, 1990), 35–55.

4. Noriaki Kano, "Attractive Quality and Must-Be Quality," *The Journal of the Japanese Society for Quality Control* 14:2 (April 1984): 39–48.

5. B. Shapiro, V. Rangan, and J. Sviokla, "Staple Yourself to an Order," *Harvard Business Review* 69:6 (Nov.–Dec. 1991): 113.

6. Mary Walton, *Deming Management at Work* (New York: Putnam, 1990), 200–202.

7. Juran, *Quality by Design*, 62.

8. Howland Blackiston, "Quality Measures: The SAS Story," *Quality Minutes Discussion Guide* (Wilton, Conn.: Juran Institute, 1994), 2–5.

9. Peter M. Senge, *The Fifth Discipline*, 205–232.

Chapter 5

Strategic Measures Deployment

The superstructure of any strategy, at least one with any hope of achievement, is the measurement template. Without focus on quantified results, intentional progress simply does not occur. Consider an observation of David Luther, creator of the Corning measurement template, "You get what you measure."[1] In spite of a general agreement by most senior leaders of the critical need for a strategic measurement set, some organizations stop short of establishing quantifiable measures of all dimensions of their strategies, except financial. They would do well to mimic the same logic they follow in their financial accounting system for their strategic requirements. They remain satisfied with simply listing the activities that will occur in their strategic plans and checking off each task as it is accomplished. This approach does not go far enough to quantify the intent of the strategic activity.

Further, most organizations do not merge their financial reporting with the strategic quality reporting. A failure to integrate the two can generate organizational schizophrenia. Leaders do not know which way to turn, toward the budget indicator or the strategic quality indicator. CEOs and CFOs may lose interest with quality initiatives when the two measurement templates are not combined because the financial results, if out of line, require immediate action. Quality initiatives gone astray can be delegated to others to be revisited on another day, unless the quality issue generates a quality alarm, like the Valdez incident.

I feel obligated to add at this juncture that my experiences have not always supported Luther's. You do not always "get what you measure." The achievement of results requires a process of its own. That is the reason the BPQM/department monthly management feedback report and quality council management feedback report were created, found in Figures 4.20 and 4.21. Without ceaseless concentration on regenerative action plans to respond to failure to reach strategic Hoshin targets, the organization may develop degenerative strategic myopia. Simply put, the organization may not have a method to recognize the critical nature of the shortcoming because the vision is a distant view and the hoshin target is only a landmark along the way. The organization has hit this point before, not hitting strategic targets, and everything turned out okay therefore, this shortcoming will be no different. Leaders may think, "We will make it up in the next six months." The management feedback process ensures that you get what you measure.

This chapter focuses on the strategic measurement deployment template intended to measure the effectiveness of the activities discussed in the last chapter. The purpose of the measurement set is to create a quantified, understandable, manageable, and customer-oriented motion picture of the organization as seen through the eyes of its multiple customers. It is, if you will, a clairvoyant view of the organization's past, present, and future.

Berwick has contributed immensely to advancing my thinking in this vital area. He asserts that measurement is effective when two factors are achieved: expectations are made clear by the measurement itself and ownership for improvement rests with the measurer.[2]

He further goes on to classify measurement into two types, measurement for judgment and measurement for improvement. Both types of measurement are necessary in our society, but Americans tend to drive all measurements toward the judgment type. Perhaps it is because from the very first moment we enter the first grade we are ranked by measurement and taught that our entire societal worth is dependent on our results.

Of course, measurement for judgment is a good thing, if it is not carried too far, as it so often is. Regulators need measurement to communicate to the public the degree to which the regulated comply with safety requirements or minimal quality standards. This is the role of the EPA, NRC, JCAHO, ISO 9000, OSHA, FDA, CAP, and so forth.

Unfortunately, our fear of measurement for judgment immobilizes us from effectively using measurement for improvement. We are so accustomed to being judged by measurement, we experience great anxiety when the same methods are applied to measuring current performance of a process with the stated intent to constantly improve it.

Again, Berwick provides an effective discussion paradigm for measurement theory, to which I added a few of my own.[3] See Table 5.1. Berwick further produces a framework of desired characteristics.[4] See Table 5.2.

It is important for leaders to fully appreciate the differences between measurement for improvement and measurement for judgment if their TQM process improvement work is to be fully optimized. Consider the reaction every hospital and its medical staff has to the annual release of the Medicare mortality data. Hours and hours are invested to study each DRG for variation from the expected mortality calculation. For each DRG above the expected mortality figure, all medical records are pulled and scrutinized by medical staff members in an effort to explain away the variation to the community. Answers such as, "Our patients were sicker, and the case mix adjustment protocol possesses too little sensitivity to properly adjust for our sicker patient population." "Our 50 percent mortality rate for DRG 207 does not fairly represent the quality of our care because we only had two patients with this condition last year and one of them was brought by ambulance in critical condition." This reaction to public release of quality data by a regulatory body is understandable, logical, and in the best interest of clarifying a very confusing analysis.

This approach to a quality improvement team database is counterproductive, as illustrated in Tables 5.1 and 5.2. Our purpose is to use data in a nonaccusatory manner to learn, experiment, and drive the process to higher levels of performance. While the audience of

Table 5.1. Measurement paradigm.

Judgment	Improvement
Incentive is to perform	Incentive is for learning
Purpose is for selection and culling	Purpose is to experiment
Mandate is to ensure safety	Mandate is to stabilize and improve
Effect is reward and punishment	Effect is continuous improvement
	Effect is understanding and inventing
Outliers search for excuses	Outliers search to benchmark
Process often punishes copying	Process encourages copying
Process produces fear	Process produces self-esteem
Primary user is external	Primary user is internal

Table 5.2. Measurement of desired characteristics.

Judgment	Improvement
Fairness	Rapid turnaround (more important than accuracy)
Objective measurer	Shows change over time
"Correct" is goal	Locally collected
Easy to interpret	Locally interpreted
Reliable and valid	Reliable and valid
Representative and honest	Complete and honest
Statistically sensitive	Contains lessons about causes
Predictive of the future	Connected to experiments
Elicits fear	Non-accusatory

released regulatory data is external, the audience for quality improvement team data is internal. The data are reserved for ourselves.

Unfortunately, we, as team members, often approach both types of data with the same mind-set. Leaders, facilitators, governing board members, and team leaders equipped with an understanding of how to facilitate the use of quality improvement team data as "measurement for improvement" can greatly accelerate team results.

Luther also provides insights from Corning's experience as we attempt to refine our strategic measurement panel.[5] One principle established at Corning was that measurement should be constructed to reflect the rate of innovation in each vital process with a goal of continuous improvement. Second, all process measures should focus on "customer deliverables" most vital in driving customer loyalty and these deliverables, once understood, should be accurately translated into an internally defined operating statistic. Finally, the organization should avoid percentage measures unless using customer survey results. The measurement system should reflect actual results, like parts per million, reported against performance by a world-class performer.

The structure of the strategic measurement panel begins with the CEO-level spider diagram, which represents those measures determined to be most vital to the organization.[6] The total number of upper-level measures should not number more than 10, but if your organization's CEO follows the same path I did as CEO of West Paces Medical Center, he or she may not be comfortable with less than 16. One of the organizations I mentor currently has 42 CEO-level measures! No organization can stay focused with a measurement panel of this magnitude. Wherever you start, however, it is more important to achieve buy-in from the CEO and CFO than it is to fret over the number of upper-level measures. As the organization and the quality council become more comfortable with the effectiveness of the measurement panel, the volume can be reduced. Once complete, the spider diagram is used to cascade the measurement process throughout the organization to the lowest common job function. A recommended tool to deploy the measurement set is the strategic deployment matrix, or tree diagram.[7]

Strategic Spider Diagram

Figure 5.1 illustrates the layout of a typical strategic spider diagram. The figure reveals several important features of the relationship of the organization's current performance and the expectations of its customers. Try not to become intimately involved with the measures themselves just yet; these will be reviewed in great detail after the spider diagram concepts have been articulated.

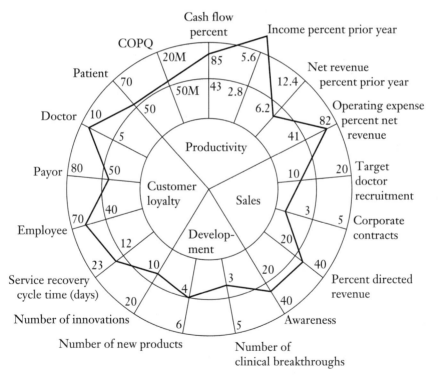

Figure 5.1. Strategic spider diagram.

Take a moment to study the spider diagram. Look at the four categories inside the spider; productivity, sales, development, and customer loyalty. Look at the 17 labels for each measurement. Digest the range of performance for each measure through examination of the inner circle threshold measure and the outer circle threshold. Prior to any explanation, what conclusions can you draw about the patient satisfaction for the organization shown? A review of the overall layout, from the 60,000-foot level, if you will, indicates that senior strategists see the organization's measures fall into the categories of productivity, sales, development, and customer loyalty. These dimensions reflect the thinking from the previous chapter of measuring the best determinants of cash flow, our proxy for ultimate customer loyalty, over a 10-year period. To measure this organization's value today, productivity and sales measures are the best proxies. Measuring customer loyalty today is the best indicator of cash flow generation three years from now; while development, including innovation, serves as the best proxy for cash flow in seven years. Figure 4.2 illustrates this thinking.

Again from the 60,000-foot level another fundamental characteristic of the organization is apparent. The organization is pictured as performing in each of these measures at some level of performance, the thick line, compared to some predefined set of performance thresholds. A review of chapter 3 on paradigms may be appropriate at this point. Paradigm 3, Elements of Customer Judgment, encourages us to think, as Kano suggests, of customer judgments along three dimensions, Level I, Expected Performance, Level II, Requested Performance, and Level III, Delighted Performance. Dropping below Level I performance is a signal that our customers are being repelled by us, while exceeding Level III performance is a signal that our customers are expressing delight about us wherever they go. This fundamental construct of customer judgments is vital enough that every organization should constantly struggle with how best to quantify it, even the elusive Level III indicators.[8] The spider diagram provides an instant picture of how each measure is performing against customer expectations. The outer circle represents Level III performance, the level beyond which we are delighting customers. The inner circle signals Level I performance, the level below which our customers are being repelled. The Level I–Level III construct will appear at each layer of the strategic measurement panel, from CEO level to department level.

As pictured in Figures 5.2 and 5.3, a further review of the overall layout of the spider diagram reveals that the organization exists in some balance, one dimension of performance related to another. The notion that performance along productivity, sales, development, and customer loyalty must be viewed in balance is an important one; it would be foolhardy to consider any dimension in isolation. As exposed in Figure 5.2, this is the picture of an organization that has maximized productivity, but unfortunately at the expense of development and customer satisfaction. The organization has seriously suboptimized development and customer loyalty. This is the picture of an organization that is the cash cow of the moment, but will cease to exist in five years. An unfortunate testimony of the impact of Wall Street on business decision-making is that this is the picture of an organization to appear on this week's *Wall Street Week* as the darling of forecasters.

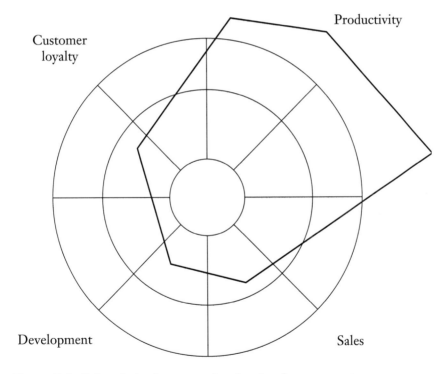

Figure 5.2. Suboptimized customer loyalty signal.

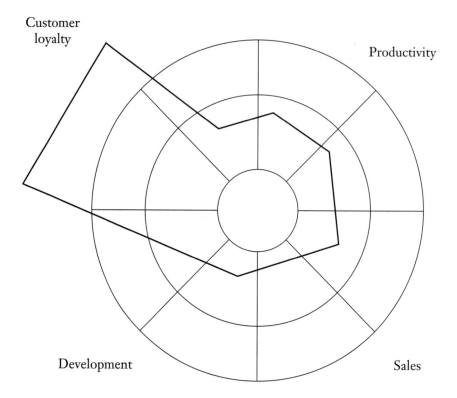

Figure 5.3. Suboptimized productivity signal.

Figure 5.3 exposes the reverse complication. This is the picture of an organization that has maximized customer loyalty through the addition of costly product features not yet appreciated by the customer. Again, the organization has seriously suboptimized its current cash position. This is the picture of an organization that will cease to exist in a year.

The relevance of the spider diagram's portrayal of the organization's performance along all dimensions is that senior strategists and the quality council may view the results of their optimizing efforts.

Figure 5.4 illustrates a sample strategic spider diagram for an integrated health system, defined as a collection of hospitals, specialists, and PCPs. This particular diagram illustrates yet another dimension, prior year historical performance represented by a thick line and current year-to-date performance represented by a dotted line. Again, these are upper-level measures and do not reveal performance of measures subordinate to them; subordinate measures are determined

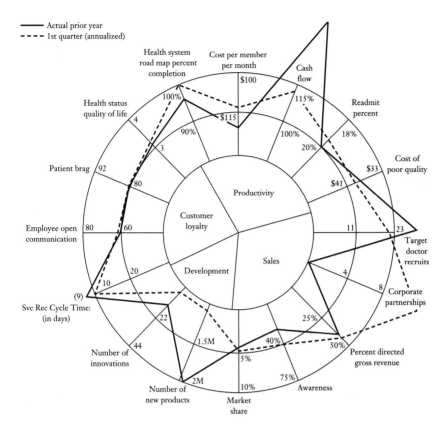

Figure 5.4. Integrated health system strategic spider diagram.

through the strategic deployment matrix, the subject of the next section of this chapter. For dialogue of the logic for selection of these strategic imperatives, refer to chapter 4 on strategy and visioning. Concentration on the top five strategic thrusts focus the organization on innovation, cost of poor quality, customer loyalty, systems integration, and cash flow. In order to reveal the thinking in establishing this particular spider diagram, the logic of each of the 16 measures, progressing clockwise from the top, is as follows:

1. Cost per member per month. The price to the marketplace for an integrated health system is based on a monthly price for each member of a managed care plan or covered by a particular employer. The ability of the sales force to aggressively price the product is, of course, dependent on the cost of providing the service. Subordinate measures would be hospital cost per member per month, further sub-

ordinated to admission rate and average length of stay, primary care cost per member per month, and specialist cost per member per month. Kano Level I, Repelling Quality, is suggested to be $115 per member per month, believed to be that level above which the integrated health system would be uncompetitive and Kano Level III, Delighted Quality, to be $100 per member per month, the market's most aggressive performance. Last year's performance (solid line) fell below the "repel" point at $117 per member per month, but current performance rests at $114.

2. Cash flow percent prior year. Cash flow as a percent of prior year. This measures the growth rate in cash generation, compared to the prior year. Kano Level I is set at 100 percent, the level below which the integrated health system will fail to generate adequate cash to meet strategic objectives and retain stockholder customer loyalty. Currently, the integrated health system is producing 111 percent of prior year, while last year the organization produced a 135 percent growth.

3. Readmit percent. The number one cost of poor quality indicator in an integrated health system is the number of patients readmitted to a hospital for the same condition within 12 months of discharge. For example, on average 20 percent of patients treated for substance abuse are readmitted for treatment within the same year at exorbitant cost to the integrated health system. Presumably, the readmit rate should be nested inside cost of poor quality as a subordinate measure and certainly no error could be charged the integrated health system quality council for subordinating the measure. But the quality council may feel that certain vital few subordinate measures deserve to be followed on the spider diagram, which is the case here. In this example, the readmit rate is 19 percent, with Kano Level I at 20 percent and Level III at 18 percent.

4. Cost of poor quality. Cost of poor quality is the most important productivity indicator, with Level I at $41 million and Level III at $33 million. These figures should be determined from an actual cost-of-poor-quality audit each year. A typical study reveals up to 30 to 40 percent of an organization's costs are cost of poor quality. The illustrated hypothetical spider diagram suggests $38 million in cost of poor quality.

5. Target doctor recruits. A primary sales indicator for an integrated health system is the number of physicians recruited from the target plan. Level I performance must not fall below 11 physicians, with Level III at 23. Last year's performance was 31, with current performance at 21.

6. Corporate partnerships. Another primary sales indicator is the number of corporate contracts for integrated health system services, in this case labeled *partnerships*. Level I is set at four contracts, with Level III at eight. Last year's performance was zero, a danger signal, but current performance is 12.

7. Percent directed gross revenue. One of the greatest threats to an integrated health system or hospital survival at this time, due to shifting physician loyalty and financial pressures, are those physicians, contracts, or patient revenues that are not controlled or directed by the organization. For example, physicians in non–managed care arrangements can admit their patients to any hospital they choose, regardless of the reason. Most often, physicians choose to admit patients to a hospital on a basis other than quality, like convenience to their offices, the hospital purchases the type of equipment the physician desires, and so on. In the current aggressive health care environment, hospitals must partner with physicians and managed care companies to obtain long-term loyalties. One method to achieve this is for the integrated health system to jointly control or direct the patient flow through a contractual relationship with payers and patients, or through the recruitment of patients through sales and marketing. This measure is an indicator of the degree of predictability the integrated health system maintains over hospital admission choice. In this example, Level I is set at 25 percent of revenues and Level III at 50 percent, with current performance (dotted line) at 41 percent, up from 38 percent last year (solid line).

8. Awareness. Awareness measures the degree of "top of mind" market awareness, measured annually by a market research firm. Level I is 40 percent and Level III is 75 percent, established as the highest "top of mind" competitor in the market. The organization has achieved a 41 percent awareness.

9. Market share. No explanation needed.

10. New products. The estimated annualized net revenue produced from any new products introduced in the marketplace during the year.

11. Innovations. Innovation is the number of quality improvement team cycles completed during the year. Innovations, however, as the organization matures in its TQM deployment, would include BPQM team cycles, quality in daily work improvements, employee suggestions, and so on. The rate of growth in this indicator is the most important for the organization to master.

12. Service recovery cycle time. This measures the number of days to resolve a complaint. As the organization becomes more sophisticated in its TQM deployment, quality control and service recovery training should enable the measurement to come down to hours.

13. Employee open communication. The results of the employee satisfaction survey question on open communication.

14. Patient brag. The percentage of patients who indicate they brag about their care, as a proxy for measuring Kano's Level III, Delight performance.

15. Health status quality of life. This is the scoring on patients' degree of return to health status after an integrated health system intervention.

16. Health system road map percent completion. A measurement of the degree of accomplishment of each BPQM team and organizational subsidiary road map or action plan.

These measures, in total, are designed to reflect the degree of achievement of the organization's vision, as discussed in chapter 4. The process to determine the measures that are proper for the organization's current status follows.

1. Revisit the organization or BPQM system map, or high-level flowchart, as instructed in chapter 4.

2. Define all customers, and analyze their needs, both outcome and output.

3. Revisit Kano Level I and Level III requirements for the strategic spider diagram from the activities in chapter 4.

4. Locate target Level I, Repel, performance from competitor data and/or customer surveys. If all else fails, guess. Construct the inner circle of Level I using the data. This inner circle represents the point below which the organization's performance must not fall.

5. Locate target Level III, Delight, performance from competitor data, customer surveys, and/or best-in-class benchmarks from the literature or other information sources. Again, if all else fails, guess. Construct the outer ring of Level III milestones using these data. This outer circle represents the target that must be exceeded for the organization to achieve its vision.

6. Identify the organization's current performance for each of the strategic measures and plot the spider diagram data points.

7. Study the picture of the organization as plotted. Examine Figures 5.2 and 5.3 to compare your current performance against a suboptimized profile. Consider any action plans necessary to bring the organization into balance.

8. Establish a method to collect and display the results on at least a quarterly basis.

Strategic Spider Diagram Run Charts

In order to effectively utilize the management feedback process suggested at the end of chapter 4, the organization must also examine the strategic measures in an analytical format. Plotting and reacting to the spider diagram is a first step in understanding the relationships between the various strategic imperatives facing the organization, however, it is the process of performing analytic functions of these process features over time that produces a level of maturity into the management of the organization. Once the hoshin targets are established for each of the strategic measures in six-month increments, a visualization of performance requirements has been generated. To create these thresholds, begin with the Level III target for each measure. Examine the organization's current performance to get some idea of the gap and the work required to achieve the vision. Following Figure 5.5 as a hypothetical example, it is suggested that "Patient brag about" serve as the CEO-level patient satisfaction proxy. West Paces Medical Center determined in 1988 that one of the 16 strategic measures should be patient delight, following Kano's logic. The hospital plotted from one question in the hospital's 300-question patient satisfaction survey, "Was the care so good at West Paces Medical Center that you have bragged about it to your family and friends?" As Figure 5.5 shows, the percentage of patients who answered "definitely yes" in December 1991 was 64 percent, rising to 65 percent by February 7, 1992. The ultimate Level III achievement to reach the hospital's vision, as charted on the strategic spider diagram, "HQT patient," in Figure 5.1 was 70 percent "definitely yes." In December 1991, the organization is performing at the 65 percent "definitely yes," but must reach 70 percent to achieve this dimension of the organization's vision of being "the best-value Atlanta health system by 1996 and to be recognized as such." Since a gap exists in current performance and the required performance, the strategic run

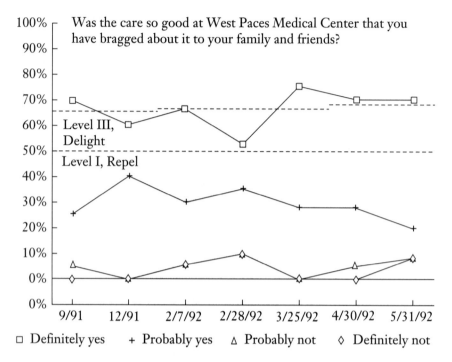

Figure 5.5. Strategic measure run chart—patient brag about.

chart in Figure 5.5 plots the need to hit the hoshin target of 65 percent by September 1991, 68 percent by February 1992, and 70 percent by March 1992. Similarly, Figure 5.6 plots the same strategic process for the employee customer group. To achieve the organization's vision, the strategic spider diagram in Figure 5.1 suggests a need to hit 70 percent "definitely yes" to the question, "Would you work here again?" Performance in December 1991 dropped to the repel point of 40 percent, demanding quality council action. The Level III hoshin target begins at 50 percent in December 1991, climbing to 55 percent in February 1992 for the remainder of the six-month period.

Each month, a quality council meeting begins with the review of the data points from the strategic run charts and the summary level data from the quality council monthly management feedback report (see Figure 4.21). The combined effect of these strategic targeting processes is to establish firm footing for senior management to focus on the vital few strategic processes requiring management attention, without allowing for distractions of less vital ones.

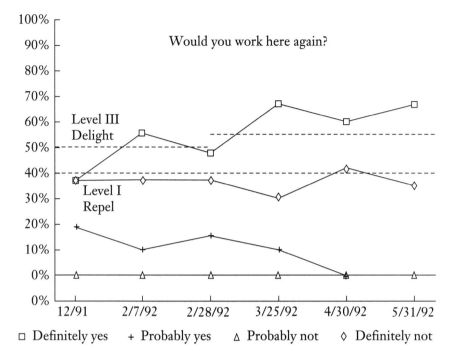

Figure 5.6. Strategic measure run chart—employee brag about.

Strategic Deployment Matrix

Once the strategic spider diagram and a process to manage performance by the quality council is completed, it is necessary to generate the strategic deployment matrix to move the TQM strategy deployment process to the smallest process in the organization.

To visualize the deployment process, examine the logic of the deployment method illustrated in Figure 5.7.

For each of the 16 CEO-level measures suggested in the preceding pages of this chapter, the processes that combine to produce the CEO-level measure must be identified. Generally, three VP-level measures will be identified for each CEO-level measure. At the second tier, the organization does not yet begin to discover BPQM or core processes, defined earlier as the collection of processes that combine to form the macrolevel business processes of the organization. In most cases, the VP-level measures are still management indicators and do not hint at an underlying business process. For example, if the hospital CEO-level measure in question is net revenue as a percent of prior

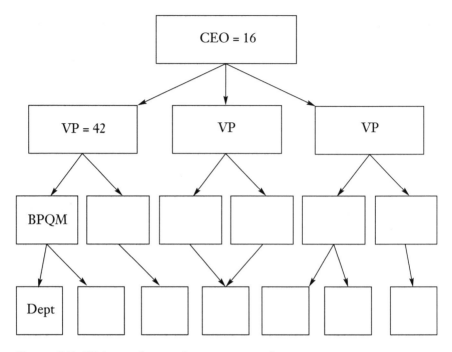

Figure 5.7. Vision and strategic process cascade.

year, then one VP-level indicator might be revenue deductions as a percent of gross revenue. Revenue deductions at the VP-level do not yet suggest a key business process.

The third tier provides key business process identification in most cases. These business process quality management processes become manageable collections of processes at this point. Continuing the earlier example, revenue deductions as a percent of gross revenue cascades to perhaps three business process quality management processes: Medicare contractual adjustments as a percent of Medicare revenue, managed care/HMO policy adjustments as a percent of managed care revenue, and bad debts as a percent of patient portion. These three processes combine to form the collections business process quality management function in a typical hospital and can be viewed, managed, and measured independently.

It is a point worth making during the discussion on strategic measurement deployment that CFOs very often want to divert away from process measures and cascade measures or derivatives of measures based on product operating margin rather than focus on the process.

This tendency has produced a vital flaw in the improvement of processes. Managers simply cannot improve a measure derivative of a measure if a process is not the underlying thesis of the measure. This approach only promotes frustration. Managers require process measures in order to manage. This is not to suggest that operating margin does not enjoy a prominent place in the strategic measurement set, but rather that operating margin is used to help an organization understand and advance the product life cycle and does nothing to help managers understand the behavior of a process under their charge. If a product's operating margin dips below expectations, the organization has several choices. It can raise prices. It can cut costs. It can increase market share, building on production economies of scale. Or, it can combine all of these, which is usually the approach taken, just to make sure all the bases are covered. Process measures as suggested in the cascade help the manager stay focused on the underlying processes producing cost. Customer pricing measures help sales and marketing personnel manage sales and marketing processes. Advertising process effectiveness measures and sales process effectiveness measures help sales personnel evaluate the probability of increasing operating margin given commitment of additional resources. These are three different sets of processes requiring three different management actions. The mixing and production of derivatives of these measures of the different processes thwarts process managers. Each of these three process measures enjoys a prominent place in the strategic measurement set, but it is important to maintain the discipline to stick to process measures. The best method I have found to ensure that a process measure has been created is to ask, "What subprocess of the superior measure does this measure highlight?" Crossing a measure in violation of process logic is voodoo statistics, and voodoo statistics are not manageable.

At the fourth tier department-level process measures surface. These measures are actually the easiest to derive because department managers have a much closer relationship with the processes they manage and the customer's expectations than senior leaders. It can sometimes create a customer paradigm issue when support departments are asked to identify their customers and they claim the external customer instead of the immediate internal customer, but this complexity is easily resolved through analysis of the department high-level flowchart.

Another view of the strategic measurement deployment matrix logic is shown in Figure 5.8. In this view, versus the organizational hier-

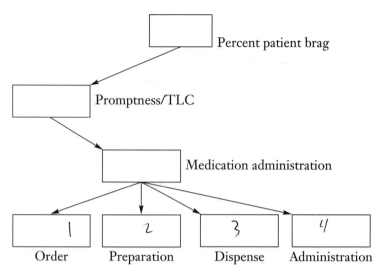

Figure 5.8. System map cascade.

archy model from Figure 5.7, we can follow process logic. In this example, we have again selected the CEO-level measure of Kano Level III, "patient brag." The CEO-level measure is one of the 300 questions in the patient satisfaction survey instrument, which asked, "Was the care so good at West Paces Medical Center that you have bragged about it to your family and friends?" The multivariate analysis against this question revealed that 19.1 percent of the variation in customer expectations was accountable to "promptness." The logic here is that we wished to identify the vital few processes that, if aggressively improved, would likely lead to improved patient satisfaction. Therefore, the second tier was "promptness." Upon identifying the key business processes at the third tier, one of which was the medication administration process, the process characteristic of "medication administration cycle time" was selected because of the importance of "promptness" at the second tier. In other words, if promptness is the most important patient satisfaction requirement, then the logical process characteristic to track is cycle time. The department-level, at tier four, identifies the four department processes that combined form the key business process of medication administration. They are: medication ordering by the nursing unit, drug preparation by the pharmacy, drug dispensing by the pharmacy, and, finally, medication administration to the patient by nursing. We can see that the management, measurement, and continuous improvement of each of the four department-level processes mak-

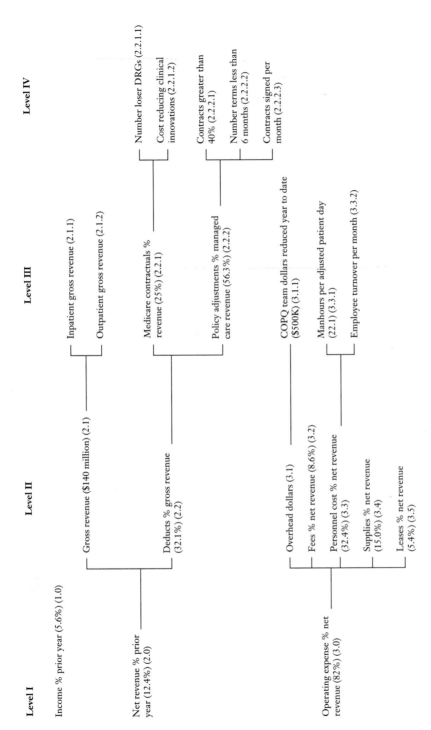

Figure 5.9. West Paces Medical Center strategic deployment matrix.

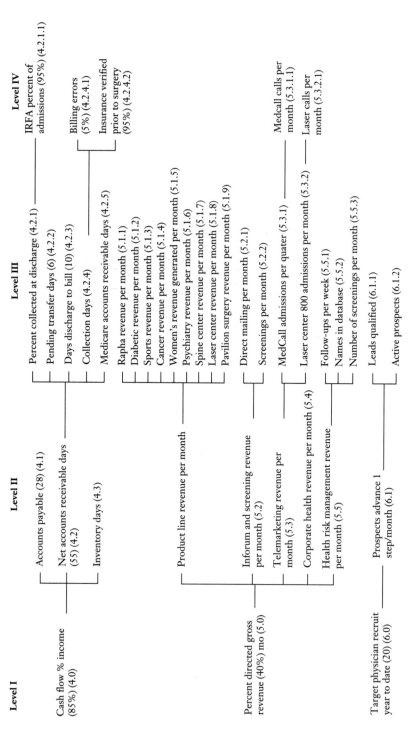

Figure 5.9. *continued.*

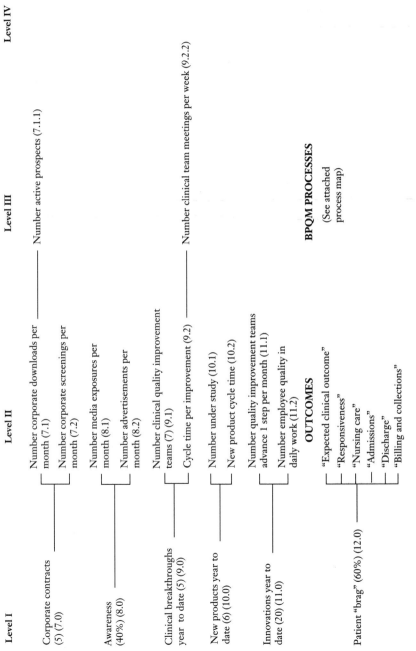

Figure 5.9. *continued.*

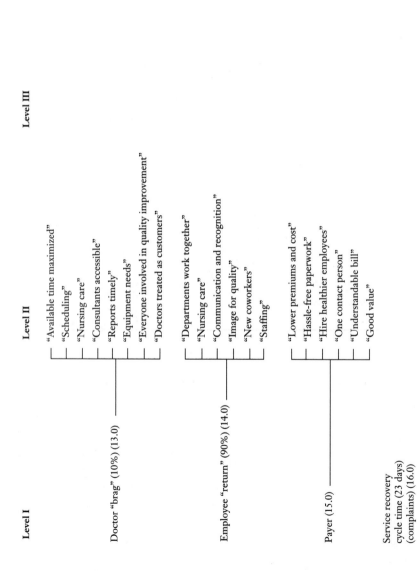

Figure 5.9. *continued.*

ing up the key business process of medication administration will lead to improvement of patient satisfaction.

Now for a look at the structure of the West Paces Medical Center strategic deployment matrix, shown in Figure 5.9. This method of measures deployment allows each measure to be viewed in relation to all others. Figure 5.10 provides examples of department-level measures from West Paces Medical Center. A study of these measures sheds light on how the particular department viewed the relationship of its processes to customer needs.

Finally, Figure 5.11 provides insights into the construction of the strategic deployment matrix for an integrated health system. Note the relationship between the hospital measures matrix and the integrated health system matrix. The health system high-level flowchart contains key business processes for PCPs, specialist care, hospital care, after-care, and administration/inspection. The hospital appears as cost under the medical cost per member per month deployment, the cost of poor quality deployment, and again under member satisfaction.

Department-Level Measures

How does an organization go about discovering the process characteristics most important to customers? The method followed at West Paces Medical Center, illustrated by the Education Department as shown in Figure 5.12, provides a handy method for a department to wrestle with those process characteristics vital to improving customer needs. Adapted from the work we saw upon a visit to Florida Power & Light in 1988 by Davis, the form provides a framework to list the vital few customer expectations as rows, in this case, physician "available time," "scheduling," "nurses," and so on. The second column asks department managers to identify the impact their department processes have on the customer need. As shown, physician "nurses" category holds a dark circle, indicating that the Education Department maintains a heavy impact on this customer expectation. To the right of this indicator are three processes owned by the Education Department that influence the customer characteristic. By following this process and the department high-level flowchart constructed earlier, department managers are able to articulate in statistical terms those vital few process features that must be improved. Figure 5.13 provides an illustration of a typical nursing unit.

Quality Indicators for the Departments

Accounting

1. Days in accounts payable
2. Number of financial statement errors greater than $1,000
3. Invoice discrepancy cycle time
4. STAT errors per week
5. Payroll errors per week
6. Medicare remittance posting cycle time
7. Expense per month

Behavior Medicine

1. Number of PRN's given daily
2. Patient percent compliance with treatment plan
3. Patient beginning assertiveness training within 24 hours after admission
4. Patients instructed in treatment procedures
5. Documentation cycle time
6. Expense per patient day

Business office

1. Time to complete IR/FA form
2. Billing errors
3. Insurance verification on accounts
4. Files forwarded to billing
5. Expense per admission

Cardio-pulmonary

1. Oxygen documentation time
2. Arterial blood gas response time
3. Pulmonary function test report time
4. Electrocardiogram report time
5. Expense per test

Cath lab

1. Cath start time
2. Cath turnaround time
3. Expense per cath

Critical care

1. Number life-threatening conditions per month
2. Lab test ordering/reporting delays
3. Admission assessment within five minutes
4. Monitoring dysrhythmias (telemetry)
5. Medication administration time
6. Expense per patient day

Data processing

1. Generate and distribute daily reports time
2. Data input into distributed system charge data time
3. Data control log balancing errors
4. Master file parameter maintenance behind schedule
5. Expense per month

Education

1. Orientation of patient care employees on schedule
2. Medication administration testing % trained
3. Provision of equipment % requests
4. Education program effectiveness rating
5. Expense per month

Engineering

1. Tube system failures per month
2. Security door checks on schedule
3. Preventive maintenance Bio-Med on schedule
4. Call response time per week
5. Expense per work order

Environmental services

1. Professional building cleaning complaints
2. Patient room discharge cleaning complaints
3. Linen distribution complaints
4. Labor and delivery discharge cleaning complaints
5. Expense per patient day

Food services

1. Nourishment distribution delays
2. Delivery of patient meal trays on schedule
3. Nutritional teaching, instructing, charting, and charging errors
4. Nutritional screening errors
5. Cafeteria serving line average time
6. Expense per meal served

Human resources

1. Number of employees not attending/completing first available orientation
2. Number of payroll action forms received for annual evaluation without proper documentation
3. Number of days from injury before employee incident report received in human resources office
4. Number of payroll action forms returned to department managers for additional information
5. HR expense per employee per month

Lab

1. Turnaround time for charting pathology reports (histology)
2. STAT CBC turnaround time
3. Blood culture contamination rate per week
4. Cardiology blood study delays per week

Figure 5.10. Sample department strategic measures.

5. Delayed or incomplete cultures
6. Expense per test

Labor and delivery
1. Delay time for scheduled procedures
2. Change of shift report within 15 minutes
3. Epidural placement errors
4. Expense per patient day
5. Obstetrics anesthesia complaints
6. Cesarean rate

Materials management
1. Stockouts per week
2. Inventory days
3. Mail delivery time
4. Expense per line item filled

Medical records
1. Coding turnaround time per week
2. STAT chart retrieval time
3. STAT transcription turnaround time
4. Assembly/analysis turnaround time
5. Expense per admission

Neonatal Intensive Care Unit
1. Admission room readiness time per week
2. Admission process culminating in transfer to postnatal unit errors
3. Lab redraws per week
4. Time of physician orders
5. Stabilization of infant's temperature
6. Expense per patient day

Perinatal
1. Change of shift report greater than 15 minutes
2. Call light response time
3. Pediatrician rounds complete on schedule
4. Discharge teaching process errors
5. Expense per patient day

Pharmacy
1. Adverse drug reactions per week
2. Medication delivery turnaround time
3. Medication administration records not reconciled
4. IV waste
5. Order entry request turnaround time
6. Expense per line item filled

Physical therapy
1. Patient procedures delayed
2. Evaluations errors
3. Charges documentation errors
4. Assessments complete within two hours of doctor's order
5. Expense per treatment

Quality management
1. Retrospective reviews demanded by managed care
2. DRG assignment errors
3. Patient stays denied
4. Expense per admission

Radiology
1. Chest X-rays turnaround time
2. Median turnaround time for reports
3. Median turnaround time for transporting patients
4. Median turnaround time for scheduling patients
5. Emergency physicians accuracy of interpretation
6. Appropriateness of exam % total exams (based on clinical indications)
7. Radiologist peer review % total readings (accuracy of interpretation)
8. Expense per exam

RAPHA
1. Admissions process time from admission
2. Patient request response time
3. Daily SHARPS procedure errors
4. Medication teaching completed within 24 hours after admission
5. Expense per patient day

Surgical services
1. Scheduling desired time for doctor as % total requests
2. Preadmission visit % complete
3. Discharge teaching within 15 minutes of schedule time
4. Room turnover time for "to follow" cases
5. Procedure starts as scheduled % total cases
6. Expense per case

Volunteer services
1. Escort services time from request until complete
2. Flower delivery in minutes
3. Number volunteers interviewed for vacancies
4. Expense per month

2 North
1. Pre-operative teaching complete by 10 min. prior to surgery pick-up
2. Discharge process errors
3. Call light response time
4. Expense per patient day

Figure 5.10. *continued.*

3 East
1. Admission assessment time from admission (minutes) per week
2. Patient request response time
3. Daily sharps procedure errors
4. Expense per patient day

3 West
1. Number times IV team called per week
2. Change of shift report total minutes
3. Responsive time to IV alarms
4. Discharge time from doctor's order
5. Expense per patient day

4 West
1. Change of shift report total minutes
2. Treatment response time (patient with hypoglycemia)
3. Peritoneal dialysis completion time
4. Expense per patient day

6 West
1. Lapsed time for change of shift report
2. Lapsed time for administration of pain medication after request

3. Number of second IV attempts by 6 West nurses per week

23 Hour/ER/IV
1. Patient triage time per week
2. Notification of attending physician minutes after intake
3. Peripheral IV starts errors
4. IV team response time
5. Expense per patient

Pavillion surgery center
1. Scheduling requests achieved % total
2. Preadmission visit errors
3. Discharge teaching errors
4. Room turnaround time
5. Procedure starts as scheduled % total cases
6. Expense per case

GI Lab
1. Scheduling requests achieved % total
2. Turnaround time
3. Start delays per week
4. Expense per procedure

Figure 5.10. *continued.*

Managing, measuring, and improving business process quality management and department process measures follows the same method as for CEO-level measures. As suggested in Figure 5.14, the Environmental Services Department run chart teaches us that labor and delivery patients express delight about the cleaning process if completed in 25 minutes or less, but are repelled by the performance of this process if it takes longer than 32 minutes. With this level of customer information, we can manage customer needs very ably.

Pitfalls

No chapter on statistical methods is complete unless it contains a list of pitfalls. So, here they are:

1. Do not allow anyone to discourage you with pitfalls.

2. Ensure all measures are process measures and not derivatives of process measures. To be manageable, managers need information and information comes in the form of process measures, not voodoo numbers.

Strategic deployment matrix

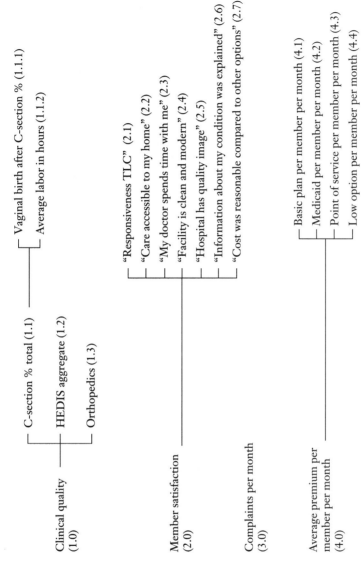

Clinical quality (1.0)
— C-section % total (1.1)
  — Vaginal birth after C-section % (1.1.1)
  — Average labor in hours (1.1.2)
— HEDIS aggregate (1.2)
— Orthopedics (1.3)

Member satisfaction (2.0)
— "Responsiveness TLC" (2.1)
— "Care accessible to my home" (2.2)
— "My doctor spends time with me" (2.3)
— "Facility is clean and modern" (2.4)
— "Hospital has quality image" (2.5)
— "Information about my condition was explained" (2.6)
— "Cost was reasonable compared to other options" (2.7)

Complaints per month (3.0)

Average premium per member per month (4.0)
— Basic plan per member per month (4.1)
— Medicaid per member per month (4.2)
— Point of service per member per month (4.3)
— Low option per member per month (4.4)

Figure 5.11. Integrated health system strategic deployment matrix.

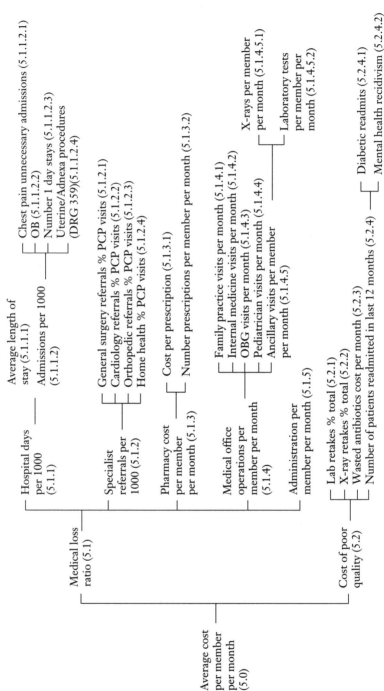

Strategic Deployment Matrix

Figure 5.11. *continued*

Strategic deployment matrix

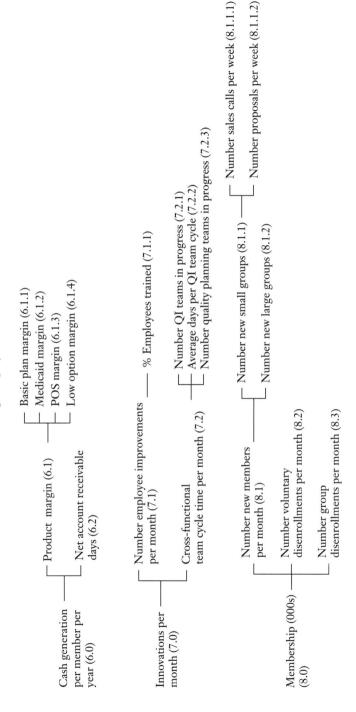

Figure 5.11. *continued*

Departmental matrix Department: ___Education___

Indicators	Impact	Process 1	Process 2	Process 3	Key quality characteristic
Physician					
Available time	◉	AV support	Patient education resources	CPR training	
Scheduling	◯	AV support	CPR training		
Nurses	●	Orientation	Staff development	Patient education resources	
Timely reports					
Accessible consultants	◉	CPR training	Patient education	Office staff training	
Equipment	◉	AV support	CPR, ACLS		
Employee QI	◉	Orientation	Staff development		
Treated as customers	◉	Orientation	Staff development		
Patient					
Clinical outcome	◉	Staff development	Patient education	CPR training	
Response TLC	◉	Orientation	Staff development	CPR training	
Nurses	●	Orientation	Staff development	Patient education	
Living arrangements					
Billing and collections					
Admission	◯	Staff development			
Discharge	◉	Patient education			

Figure 5.12. Sample department strategic deployment template.

Indicators	Impact	Process 1	Process 2	Process 3	Key quality characteristic
Employee					
Nurses	⬤	Orientation	CPR and staff development	Patient education	
Departments work together	◉	Staff development	Division newsletter		
Top leaders understand	◯	Division newsletter	Committee, QIT membership		
Image	◉	Orientation	Staff development	Division newsletter	
Qualified co-workers	◉	Orientation	Staff development	Recruitment, selection, and retention activities	
Efficient processes	⬤	Orientation	Staff development	Patient education resources	
Payers					
Employees brag	◉	CPR and other community programs	Staff development		
Costs less than competitors					
Reduce costs improve quality					

Key for impact symbol

⬤ Heavy   ◉ Moderate   ◯ Slight   None

Instructions: Review list of hospital quality indicators listed by customer group (physician, patient, employee, and payer). Indicate the degree of impact your department has on each quality indicator by entering the appropriate symbol in the impact column.

List three processes that directly relate to the outcome of customer satisfaction for each indicator. Choose a *total* of three processes that relate to a "heavy" impact indicator from which the QIC will select one as your next opportunity for improvement.

1. Providing employee development opportunities
2. Coordinating patient education resources
3. Orienting new patient care employees

Figure 5.12. *continued.*

Department: 3 West   ● Heavy   ■ Moderate   ▲ Slight

Indicators	Impact	Process 1	Process 2	Process 3
Available time	●	Doctor rounds update	Chart procure	Procedure assistance
Scheduling	▲	Requisition process		
Nurses	●	Doctor rounds update	Procedure assistance	Complications notification
Timely reports	■	Filing	Abnormal result notification	Requisition process
Consultation access	▲	Order notification		
Equipment				
Clinical outcome	●	Acute myocardial infarction	Bronchitis	Heart failure
Response TLC	●	Pain medication	Nourishment	Call light response
Nurses	●	Patient condition information	RN skills assessment	Complaint notification
Living arrangement	■	Complaint notification	Discharge cleaning	Diet order
Admission	▲	DC cleaning		
Discharge	●	Discharge notification	Discharge instructions	

Figure 5.13. Sample nursing department strategic deployment template.

3. Keep the number of measures manageable—not too many, not too few. For the CEO-level strategic spider diagram and run charts, 10 measures should be adequate, but more than 15 becomes weighty. Aggregate most current CEO-level measures into a superior level measure, then include the remainder at the VP level. In this way, the organization can stay focused on the vital few strategic measures.

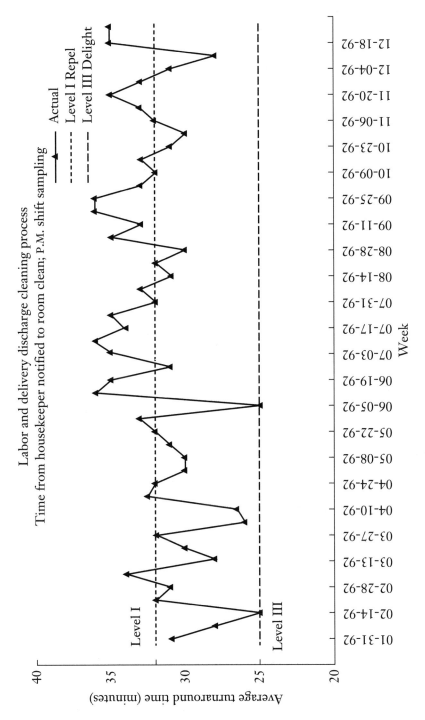

Figure 5.14. Sample run chart for Environmental Services Department.

4. Focus on customer measures, not just volume.

5. Insist that process owners plot their own data and keep run charts in their departments for employees and customers to see. The best place to place customer measures is on the department storyboard, which is hung in common corridors.

6. Maintain the discipline to utilize the management feedback report and run charts.

Congratulations! You have just completed the most challenging chapter of this text. Statistical methods are rarely easy to express and even more difficult to read and understand. I encourage the use of the quality council and department manager exercises at the end of the chapter to internalize the most important features of the strategic deployment matrix process.

Discussion Exercise for a One-Hour Quality Council Meeting

1. Create a strategic spider diagram. First, review Figures 5.1 through Figure 5.4. Then, draw a blank spider diagram on a flip chart and post it on the wall in preparation of your own rough draft model. Consider this first round a very rough draft and do not be concerned with accuracy at this point.

   A. Using measures generated from exercises from a previous chapter or other activities, identify and list the top three to four measures in each of the following categories.

      1. Productivity

      2. Sales

      3. Development (include rate of innovation/quality improvement team cycle time)

      4. Customer satisfaction (key customers who drive revenue)

   B. If your organization is like most organizations, you now have 20 to 40 measures. This is too many. For each category, using nominal group technique, identify two to three measures that can be followed at either the VP level or in some other format. Repeat this process until no more than four measures exist for each category.

    C. For each measure, identify your best guess for Level I
       Repel performance and Level III Delight performance

2. Plotting the spider diagram.

    A. For the inner circle, Level I Repel, write the number in the
       proper location. Note that for some measures the desired
       direction is ascending while for others it is descending, so
       the order of Level I and Level III is reversed.

    B. For the outer circle, Level III Delight, write the number in
       the proper location.

    C. Given the range between Level I and Level III, plot your
       current performance for each measure.

3. Current status analysis.

    A. Where do you fall below Level I? For these dimensions,
       you are currently repelling your customers. For some
       measures, particularly those that anticipate cash flow five
       years from today, the impact of this performance may not
       seem threatening, but do not allow yourself to be lulled
       into complacency. For a discussion of what is meant by
       that remark, review chapters 3 and 4 and see if you resem-
       ble this remark. Action plans are required for these
       processes.

    B. Where do you exceed Level III? For this dimension, you
       have achieved your vision. Celebrate !

4. Evaluate the meeting on flip chart paper.

    A. What did you like about this session?

    B. What could be improved for future sessions?

Discussion Exercise for a One-Hour Department Manager/Team Leader Meeting

For this meeting, managers will complete their key process measures, using Figure 5.13 as a guide. Again, a quality council member should facilitate the session. Before this exercise can be conducted, a list of organization-wide customer needs must be generated to fill the rows of the deployment template. The quality council facilitator, with help from other council members, should complete a sample deployment template to serve as an example. Organize participants in tables of eight. A quality council member should be assigned to each table to assist. Provide enough copies for each department manager and team leader attending.

1. The quality council facilitator explains that the purpose of the session is to begin thinking about which process measures at the department level are linked to the organization's quality measures. Show the sample deployment template created to explain this form on an overhead projector and ask if participants have questions.

2. Hand out one deployment for each participant and allow 20 minutes for completion.

3. With assistance from the quality council member at each table, each member should discuss two or three entries. Allow 20 minutes for this segment.

4. Each table should select one participant to explain two or three entries to the group as a whole, if time allows. Allow 15 minutes for this segment.

5. A quality council member evaluates the meeting on flip chart paper by asking

   A. What did you like about this session?

   B. What could be improved for future sessions?

Discussion Exercise for a Governing Board Meeting

This discussion should be lead by the CEO, or designee, with a board member facilitating at the flip chart. In this session, board members will be asked to reflect on quality from a personal perspective; therefore, the leaders of this session should review the tool of affinitization before conducting this meeting, but do not become overly concerned with perfection. For a description of the rules for affinitization, ask your quality director or simply follow the process prescribed. For this portion of the exercise, you will need to supply two 3 × 5 Post-It pads of two different colors for each member and a transparency pen. Transparency pens or markers are important because members will stand at a distance to review responses. In advance of the session, tape four blank flip chart pages to a wall: Label them, "patient good surprises," "patient bad surprises," "payor good surprises," and "payor bad surprises." Also, members will review some of the organization's data on run charts or SPC charts. If the organization does not currently produce financial or customer satisfaction measures in run chart format, create a 12-month history using a format like the one found in Figure 5.5. Alternatively, you may use examples from the text.

1. Explain the process to members and assure they understand what the output will look like. For large boards of more than 10 members, feel free to break the group into teams of two or three.

2. Patient judgments.

   a. All members (or teams) should be asked to reflect on a recent hospital experience by themselves or a close associate, or, in the absence of a personal experience, to attempt to envision a four-day stay. Silently, using one color Post-It pad as a personal brainstorming device, each person (or team) should record one response per note in answer to the question, "What good surprises did you experience during your stay?" Ask members to write large enough so that responses can be seen from several feet from the flip chart. Likely responses might be, "quick admission," "The nurses kept me informed of my test results," "The nurses answered my call light promptly," or "The OR staff place a warmed blanket over me as I came out of anesthesia and spoke reassuringly to me."

   b. Ask each member (or team) to go to the "patient good surprises" flip chart all together and place their notes in common groupings. Dialogue is encouraged, but do not allow the group to get bogged down in commentary over individual events; storytelling time comes later in the exercise. All members should feel comfortable to move the notes from other members so that four or five common groupings begin to emerge. For example, "The nurses kept me informed" and "The radiologist explained what he was going to do and when I might be told of the results" might be grouped under a common heading of "information." "The nurses answered my call light very promptly" and "I received pain medications as soon as I asked" might be grouped under the common heading of "quick response to requests."

c. All members (or teams) should be asked to reflect on the same recent hospital experience. Again using the same color Post-It pad as a personal brainstorming device, each person (or team) should record one response per note in answer to the question, "What bad surprises did you experience during your stay?" Likely responses might be, "I was awakened every day before 7 A.M. with someone carrying by breakfast tray, but they left it in the corner until someone came to feed me, which was usually 30 minutes later, and the eggs were ice cold," or, "The doctors and nurses never took the time to explain what was going on."

d. Ask each member (or team) to go to the "patient bad surprises" flip chart together and place their notes in common groupings, following the same process as before.

3. Payor judgments (employers, HMOs, PPOs)

a. All members (or teams) should be asked to reflect on the payor as customer. Using the second color notepad, follow the same process as in section 2 for "from the payor's perspective, what good surprises have you experienced with a hospital and its physicians during the last year?" Again, group these responses in common categories on the "payor good surprises" flip chart.

b. Repeat the process for "payor bad surprises."

4. The entire group should stand near the flip charts. Informally, ask for commentary about commonalities and differences between the two customer groups (in different colors) for both "good surprises" and "bad surprises."

5. In a future meeting, bring typed versions of the flip charts and discuss how the organization might measure the degree of

achievement in each of the broad categories, using the strategic measurement concepts presented in this chapter.

Notes

1. David Luther, "Advanced TQM: Measurements, Missteps, Progress Through Key Result Indicators at Corning," *National Productivity Review* (winter 1992/93): 25.

2. Donald M. Berwick, "Current Trends" (presentation at George Washington Medical Center Conference, Washington, D.C., February 28, 1994).

3. Ibid.

4. Ibid.

5. Luther, "Advanced TQM," 23–36.

6. Takashi Kanatsu, *TQC for Accounting: A New Role in Companywide Improvement* (Cambridge, Mass.: Productivity Press, 1990), 187–192.

7. Ibid., 190–191.

8. Noriaki Kano, "Attractive Quality and Must-Be Quality," *The Journal of the Japanese Society for Quality Control* 14:2 (April 1984): 39–48.

Chapter 6

Evidences of Readiness

In addition to relating our status along TQM transformation paradigm lines, it is also helpful to make observations of department manager and employee attitudes and behavior in order to fully analyze the organization posture, maturity, and weaknesses. As the Lewin model suggests, changing from one paradigm to another involves unfreezing from the present state and proceeding through some unknown and unknowable transition stage to arrive at the future state. Along these three dimensions in the paradigm shift, everyone involved in the transition experiences discomfort, and this discomfort is manifest in behaviors at all levels of the organization.

The emotions and behaviors that occur at these three different points in a paradigm are complicated by the fact, as we reviewed in chapter 2, that we are unfreezing and refreezing several different paradigms simultaneously and are at different points in the paradigms' transitions. The purpose of the following dialogue is not to help TQM practitioners avoid these attitudes and behaviors, because I am not certain it would be constructive or possible to avoid the organizational learning that occurs as a result of working through these issues. Rather, it is hoped that TQM practitioners will be able to draw observations during their own organization TQM transitions and place them in a framework for discussion and ultimate growth.

Present-State Behaviors

High Uncertainty

As it becomes apparent that current notions are changing, many have found that uncertainty runs high. It goes without saying that we grow comfortable with our paradigms, and, when we see them changing, we become uncomfortable. Employees have never been asked to participate in quality improvement teams before; what are the new expectations of us and how will we be dealt with if we fail? What if we make a foolhardy recommendation? When we began preparing for our triennial accreditation survey, more than 50 percent of the nursing units were very anxious over their strategic indicators. These managers immediately pulled out the quality assurance steps and ensured that they inspected certain events, that had always been required of them, but were no longer required under TQM. These managers were frightful that if they abandoned the old way of quality control they would be out of compliance.

Curiosity and Skepticism

In addition to high uncertainty, any change brings with it curiosity and skepticism. In fact, as we began transition of each new paradigm, it has appeared that approximately 25 percent of all individuals involved in the transition would fall into the class of skeptics. Those individuals who enjoy change and challenges will exhibit curiosity and may begin experimenting with TQM tools in advance of the organization's deployment. Others may be intimidated by change in a general sense by some component of the TQM model that threatens a current paradigm, or from fear of failure. Regardless of the source of intimidation, the result is the same—expression of skepticism. As the gap between champions and skeptics grows, the organizational culture experiences discomfort. I believe this discomfort is not destructive and may be necessary for the organization to grow. An effective TQM rollout can be made more effective by the constructive use of skeptics. Many believe that skeptics are counterproductive, but skeptics can become a powerful force in the organization if their skepticism can be harnessed to raise organizational awareness to a new level of understanding.

Lack of Stability

Change brings with it not only uncertainty but also the inability to predict future events because TQM is designed to change processes. The transformation into a mature TQM state creates a certain amount of instability that appears to manifest itself at all levels of the organization as the expectations of various roles emerge and evolve. Most individuals are uncomfortable with ambiguity, yet ambiguity is what TQM is all about. Widespread innovation, the inverse of certainty, is the engine that drives improvement. Developing a comfort level for ambiguity requires an organization culture that has grown well past criticizing mistakes and failures. One of the most difficult transitions for me and our senior management team was the realization and practice of patience. It is far easier to step in at the department level and direct the efforts of quality improvement teams than it is to mentor improvement. Yet, patience as a management talent may well be the most vital, if widespread innovation is to occur. Mentoring and coaching individuals and teams to feel comfortable with ambiguity requires an acknowledgment that lack of stability is uncomfortable for most people. Peters said, in *Thriving on Chaos*, that "one could identify a mature organization because it was always in chaos."[1] Those corporations that are advanced in TQM can certainly grin at this statement.

Emotions Running High

One certain characteristic of TQM introduction into an organization is that emotions will run high, particularly if the quality council is aggressive in the introduction of internal customer identification and strategic measures deployment. It is interesting to me that a management process that is designed to reduce variation in process performance has the inverse effect on organizational emotions. As improvement efforts intensify, emotions run wild. Successes drive everyone to a higher sense of purpose, of growing closer to realizing achievement of the organization's vision and well-being. The following month the organization may experience a significant setback or reduction of improvement initiatives and everyone feels defeated. We have grown to expect the highs and lows associated with an evolving culture. In fact, I grow nervous that we have become complacent if emotional stability occurs.

Unclear Direction of Focus

Unless the organization is able to perfectly match its mission statement, vision, and measures of quality and productivity with the introduction of the TQM model, use of tools, and deployment to the entire workforce, the direction and purpose of the organization will seem fuzzy to many people. Almost every organization I have mentioned, including our own, showed that the vision and measures cannot be firmly established at initiation because deeper process knowledge, customer focus, and identification of cost of poor quality results in restructuring the organization. In our case, two layers of nursing management were removed because the deployment of measurement to the department removed the need for these two levels of supervision. The result was that many managers and employees felt a change in direction.

Increased Need for Power, Control, and Dependence

A different set of managerial behaviors are required in a TQM environment. Managers begin to see department teams formed around a team mission statement, and they collect data, analyze root causes of variation and cost of poor quality , and generate testable theories to remedy these causes. To a large degree the authority and power base, which for some managers is the very reason they entered management in the first place, is being eroded. TQM can be seen as a management process that is governed by a higher authority—customer data. Therefore, managers can become testy during the introductory phase.

Similarly, employees, many who might state that the organization has never asked their opinions about anything important for 20 years, are placed in the position of analyzing customer data and making improvements. The old quality thief, fear, produces certain anxiety in many employees. They become uncertain what is expected of them. Many will become even more dependent upon their supervisors. This is why facilitators enjoy such an important role in every TQM deployment. They are charged, along with the team leader, with creating a safe environment for employees to express their knowledge of process cost of poor quality and opportunities to exceed customer expectations.

Old Ways Become Cherished and Threatened

Of course, much of what we are currently doing is good and, therefore, the old way may be the best way. But, in an environment in which every process comes under scrutiny, many will feel threatened that even effective processes will be altered. The need for data is ever more compelling to ensure that we change those things that ought to be changed and have the data to provide the wisdom of those processes that ought not be changed. It might be discovered that even obviously contradictory policies, attitudes, and habits bring the comfort of stability. Every paradigm comes under scrutiny. Methods to evaluate employees, to interview and select new employees, to achieve rapid results, to obtain capital for replacement or new equipment, to discipline employee behavioral problems, in short, everything the organization has done in the past is opened to scrutiny. This fact is not to suggest that every policy followed by the organization must change, but rather that the very nature of a TQM deployment opens everything to judgment and analysis, and the result is a threatening feeling by almost everyone in the organization over one issue or another.

Self-Esteem and Self-Confidence Are Questioned and Reassessed

This observation is perhaps the most complicated in my experience of mentoring others in deploying a TQM transition.

First, TQM deployments create a new infrastructure. A quality council emerges. Facilitators are selected and given special training and attention. Pilot teams are formed and given special training and assistance. Physicians and suppliers are brought together to receive training. Even new employees at orientation are equipped with new words and ideas. The focus of department manager meetings takes on a different flavor. Managers are stuck in a tough place. They ask themselves, "I wasn't selected to be a facilitator, but I always thought I was one of the strongest managers. Have I slipped in my importance here without knowing it?" Or, "My department wasn't picked to participate in a pilot study. Does this mean my department is not as important as it used to be? Will my department be closed or merged with another department?" These questions of anxiety are logical and understandable, but perhaps more important, they again raise the head of the quality thief, fear.

Transition State

As individuals proceed from the present state through the transition state, a different set of attitudes and behaviors becomes evident.

New External Allies

Suppliers, vendors, customers, and networking opportunists are all very eager to assist most organizations that demonstrate a genuine thirst to improve customer loyalty through continuous improvement. Taking advantage of this opportunity can become a great accelerator.

Mixed Signals Everywhere

Old ways. New ways. Everything comes under scrutiny. Policies regarding purchasing on the basis of raw cost versus total cost versus cost of poor quality. Short-term versus long-term. Policies regarding capital allocation. Performance appraisal and compensation strategies. Physician relationships. Strategic planning. Capital building programs. Operations budgeting. Growing comfortable with the discomfort of recognizing that the organization and its leaders, managers, suppliers, and employees have a lot to learn. Many policies and methods to accomplish organization requirements are not in need of revamping, while many must be redesigned because they contradict the strategic logic of TQM.

Short-Term, Long-Term Focuses

The recognition that the strategic visioning required to generate long-standing market need for the organization and the certainty that full maturity of TQM deployment to the employee level may take 10 years does not neutralize the fact that the competitive environment is unforgiving and cannot wait for market innovation.

Unbelievably Strong Commitment to Status Quo

Everyone is comfortable with certainty, even when the certainty is not pleasant. Some TQM theorists believe that an organization cannot make the TQM transition without facing an organizational crisis. As Deming advised the auto manufacturers, many observed that the only way they could drive change was to be faced with certain bankruptcy. Others, however, believe that change is possible short of catastrophe, but expert application of accelerator and inhibitor management must be exerted. Regardless, the organization will show signs of cherishing the status quo. Open and honest communication about the organization's vision and strategic deployment road map will be helpful to work through unfreezing and refreezing activities.

Confused and Resisting Employees

It should go without saying that employees begin to experience anxiety at the equivalent or greater level than managers. The organization has gone berserk. Employees are being asked for the first time to serve on teams, and some evidence begins to surface that TQM is not just another program of the month or employee suggestion program. The organization is committing resources to training employees and team members. The CEO and other senior leaders are visiting team meetings and asking questions about needed support to make improvements more rapid.

Tired Leaders

A TQM deployment is hard work. The tools and techniques are not as easily understood as other management training programs. The required mentoring management style takes practice, practice, and still more practice. Yet, the current strategic initiatives do not go on hold while the transition is occurring. Results are still necessary while the transition takes place.

New Missions/Purpose Identified

The transformation model activities drive a deeper understanding of customers, both internal and external, their needs and expectations, and the processes producing these needs. Long-term and short-term strategic targets refocus not only the organization, but also the ways in which departments work together. Business process quality management improvement, formerly without owners, emerges as a new organizational imperative, and new relationships emerge from these revelations.

Champions of the Change Come Forward

Unexpected champions begin to use TQM tools and techniques outside of formal structures to improve process performance against customer expectations. Some employees begin to use training to advance the processes they own. Maureen Bisognano, senior VP of Juran Institute, tells the story of a linen worker at Massachusetts Respiratory Hospital who began to utilize Ishikawa principles and Pareto analysis to uncover root causes of linen cost of poor quality without a formalized structure.

Some People Leave

It is an unfortunate fact, but some managers feel uncomfortable with a mentoring management style that requires sharing decision-making with employees and posting of customer measures in visible locations.

At West Paces Medical Center, two department managers found jobs in other hospitals because their discomfort of posting storyboards became so burdensome. Both were strong managers, but could not embrace a mentoring style.

Confusion over Roles Begins to Clear

Upon introduction of new roles for facilitators, quality council members, team leaders, and team members, great confusion develops over the new hierarchy. Managers have asked, "To be recognized, should I become a facilitator?" As the transition stage proceeds, these new roles begin to become clearer.

Mature State

Once the paradigm shift achieves refreezing, an entirely different set of behaviors becomes apparent.

Work More Efficiently Together

One of the many positive results of teams is that departments, which in a traditional hierarchy become compartmentalized, begin to work together to identify wait loops, waste, and cost of poor quality at handoff points between and within departments. This occurs because theories of group behavior suggest that, given a common mission, people tend to work constructively together even if they were adversaries previously.

Common Language Evolves

The TQM deployment generates a language unto itself, most of which is intended to express relationships between process performance and customer needs. TQM. CQI. Benchmarking. Vision. Quality improvement. Quality planning and reengineering. Quality control and service recovery. Ishikawa diagram. Strategic spider diagram. Business process quality management. These and other terms begin to surface as a new language.

Listening to Customers Drives the Organization

Lessons from customer focus groups, multivariate regression analysis against customer surveys, and process output measures at the department level become methods engaged by the organization to better understand the customer. At West Paces Medical Center, Allen, the service recovery expert, affinitized patient responses to the patient survey question, "What bad surprises did you experience during your stay?" and "What good surprises did you experience during your stay?" Upon deriving the top categories, she placed responses on a storyboard and placed the board in visible spots in the hospital, like the cafeteria, physician lounge, and entrance corridor.

Productivity Continues to Increase

As process improvement identifies cost of poor quality, needless waste, rework, and inspection, unnecessary steps are identified in processes and eliminated, which results not only in less customer dissatisfaction but decreased cost of poor quality.

Every Worker Is Important

One of the most touching observations I have made regarding TQM deployments involved an engineering department employee. The pharmacy team was looking to reduce the variation in the delivery of medications and discovered that the greatest root cause was the consistent failure of the pneumatic tube system. Instead of asking for a new system as it might have done before learning Ishikawa's technique of asking *why* five times, the team members invited the engineering employee to become part of the team. To their surprise they discovered through data collection that the greatest reason for breakdown was misplacement of the tube in the carrier. The team created an insert inside the tubes that directed its proper insertion into the carrier and almost totally eliminated breakdowns. Upon presenting results at a storyboard review session, the engineering employee had tears in his eyes. Later he confided to me that he never knew his job was important to the care of patients. This building of self-esteem and importance of everyone in the organization becomes an everyday occurrence and drives the rate of innovation.

Mentoring Becomes a Continual Learning Opportunity

Mentoring skills—like listening skills—are hard to acquire. Managers are so accustomed to observing a process failure, pulling the employee performing the process aside, and instructing the employee in proper procedures, that mentoring is difficult to practice. Taught so well by Batalden, a mentor would inquire of the employee, "What would happen if . . . ?" and walk away. The learning that takes place by the employees in a mentoring environment gives not only widespread results, but a great deal of satisfaction that individuals are learning and growing in their work.

For those who have drawn comfort in the notion that there may actually be a mature state, the general consensus among those mentors with whom I associate is that there may not be, in fact, a mature state. Refer again to Figure 2.3 on page 15 illustrating that paradigm revolution requires the management of ever more complex changes. Just when we begin to feel we have matured, we discover another conceptual hurdle to jump. This, in fact, fairly represents our progression over seven years at West Paces Medical Center. Upon completion of the cross-functional team structure and rollout of functional teams in each of our 54 departments, we realized that we had just begun to apply supplier certification and benchmarking processes. And the cycle of maturation goes on and on. Do draw comfort, however, in the notion that change begets change. As the organization grows comfortable with a data-driven customer-focused strategy and the rapid production of quality improvement team cycles, change in all forms becomes less and less threatening.

In all, behavior modification, whether our own or someone else's, requires patience, careful observation, and recognition of the current state, introduction, transition, or maturation, to be effective. Attention to the organizational signs and symptoms manifest during the TQM deployment will enable quality councils and managers to effectively manage the accelerators and inhibitors discussed in the next chapter.

Discussion Exercise for a One-Hour Quality Council Meeting

1. Brainstorm, clarify, and nominally group responses to the question, "What present state behaviors may prevent us from achieving our strategic vision?"

2. Brainstorm, clarify, and nominally group responses to the question, "What present state behaviors may accelerate the achievement of our strategic vision?"

3. Brainstorm, clarify, and nominally group responses to the question, "What future state behaviors might accelerate the achievement of our strategic vision?"

4. Report and test these presumptions among department managers and board members as they generate their own lists.

Discussion Exercise for a One-Hour Department Manager/Team Leader Meeting

1. Brainstorm, clarify, and nominally group responses to the question, "What present state behaviors may prevent us from achieving our strategic vision?"

2. Brainstorm, clarify, and nominally group responses to the question, "What present state behaviors may accelerate the achievement of our strategic vision?"

3. Brainstorm, clarify, and nominally group responses to the question, "What future state behaviors might accelerate the achievement our strategic vision?"

4. Review the list from the quality council and ask for feedback about commonalities and differences. Point out that differences should be accepted as what they are. Opinions from different vantage points are not necessarily barriers to progress.

Discussion Exercise for a Governing Board Meeting

1. Brainstorm, clarify, and nominally group responses to the question, "What present state behaviors may prevent us from achieving our strategic vision?"

2. Brainstorm, clarify, and nominally group responses to the question, "What present state behaviors may accelerate the achievement of our strategic vision?"

3. Brainstorm, clarify, and nominally group responses to the question, "What future state behaviors might accelerate the achievement of our strategic vision?"

4. Review the lists from the quality council and department managers and discuss relevant differences. Do not become immersed in problems; the purpose of this exercise is to simply become educated about the vantage points of varying groups.

Note

1. Thomas J. Peters, *Thriving on Chaos*.

Chapter 7

Accelerators and Inhibitors

Managing accelerators and inhibitors is perhaps the hardest work of mentors and quality council members. Mentoring requires a totally different set of skills than traditional forms of management behavior and most of us must unlearn many behaviors in order to master mentoring. Still others confuse mentoring with "soft" management, preferring to continue management behaviors that they believe generate greater and faster results. Still others, even champions of TQM, feel more comfortable in advancing new tools and techniques rather than the roll up your sleeves approach to successfully attend to accelerators and inhibitors. Yet, for the disciplined, these efforts produce by far the most astounding results, far greater than the use of a new technique like reengineering or benchmarking. These efforts, in fact, convert the organization into a learning organization, the one that others visit to benchmark and to learn. Optimizing organizational learning through the advancement of accelerators and the neutralization of inhibitors fosters an environment characterized by widespread creativity, enthusiasm, and innovation.

Again relying on the transformation model (see Figure 7.1) to identify where, in the big scheme of deployment, accelerators and inhibitors reside, we can see a relationship between the strategic deployment road map and the organization as a system. In our model, we are attempting to exert radical change on the organization through achievement of the road map.

The notion of accelerators and inhibitors has been framed for us through Senge's reinforcing model.[1] We may introduce many accelerators into the organization, and most quality councils are prone to invest significant energy toward this end. However, as we discussed in

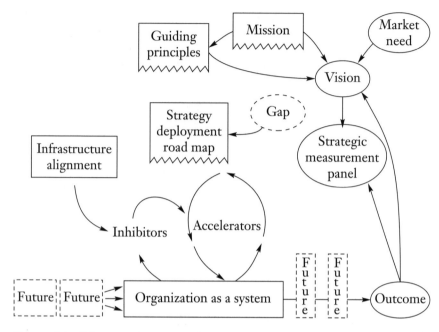

Figure 7.1. The transformation model.

chapter 2, Lewin noted that for each accelerator introduced an equal force is generated that exerts an offsetting effect on the accelerator. We may conceptualize this notion in terms of physics laws, for every action there is an equal and opposite reaction. Therefore, quality councils must invest an equal, if not greater, amount of time and resources to neutralize inhibitors. Introducing accelerator on top of accelerator on top of accelerator, without attention to inhibitors, may, in fact, be harmful to the organization.

In order to successfully transition from one paradigm to another, TQM leaders must look for conventions to accelerate the process and promulgate their use while at the same time look for and resolve inhibitors that exist in the organization.

It was the failure to recognize the importance of inhibitors that caused several setbacks at West Paces Medical Center during 1988 and 1989. It was not until Batalden began to help us recognize the importance of inhibitors, how to recognize them, and how to manage their resolution that our accelerators became maximally effective. While accelerator development tends to involve creation of new processes and structures, inhibitors generally take the form of policies, procedures, and requirements that make innovation difficult. In other words, in the absence of effective resolution of inhibitors, increasing the number of accelerators will not achieve a paradigm transition.

Accelerators and Inhibitors

The framing of conventions into the broad conceptional topics has proven invaluable in accelerating the transformation. While many conventions are suitable for some organizations, others may be ineffective. For example, one organization with which we networked found the widespread use of storyboards resisted by team leaders for reasons they did not fully understand. Storyboards were, however, remarkably successful in our transformation, both as an accelerator and as a communication device. This particular convention may not be effective in every organization, but the accelerators of celebration, visibility, and momentum deserve creative solutions if storyboards are not used. In any event, the organization's speed to TQM maturity will be served if it innovates conventions within each accelerator. I suggest that a leader in the organization be assigned the task of sponsoring development of these conventions. It would be best to assign someone who is closest to the organization's team leaders and facilitators. Involving team leaders and facilitators in the development of accelerators and overcoming inhibitors has the added benefit of sending the signal throughout the organization that the success of the transition is broadly owned and not just the duty of the CEO, senior management, or the quality manager. Plus, since innovations and solutions are being developed where they will be applied, team leaders and facilitators are constantly learning to continuously improve and evaluate the effectiveness of changes they make to the environment.

The following list of accelerators is suggested as a good place to start, but is by no means intended to be an all-inclusive effort.

1. Make heroes of champions and producers.
2. Link the TQM quality plan to the accomplishment of strategic plans.
3. Promote a shared vision.
4. Focus on measurement.

5. Assign meaningful work.

6. Create constant discomfort with the present state.

7. Make sure senior management is visible.

8. Maintain momentum (for example storyboards, storyboard reviews, team road maps).

9. Network with other TQM organizations.

10. Build the self-esteem of every employee and manager to participate in vision achievement.

11. Remember the quality council accelerators.

   a. Spend at least 50 percent of quality council's time on the achievement of results.

   b. Spend at least 40 percent of quality council's time on resolving infrastructure issues like the performance appraisal process, organizational structure, and so on.

   c. Adopt a mental model like the transformation model in Figure 7.1 and communicate it widely.

   d. Conduct an annual Baldrige Award-type self-assessment like the one offered by SunHealth Alliance in appendix E and revise the strategic deployment road map to include recommendations.

   e. Assign a sponsor from the quality council to each quality improvement team, quality planning team, and BPQM team.

   f. Conduct an annual cost-of-poor-quality study and use the results to drive team chartering.

   g. Use TQM tools and methods, such as flowcharts, to draw policies and procedures.

While development and enhancement of accelerator conventions speeds the transformation, recognition of inhibitors cannot be overlooked. The following categories, if neutralized, will enable the accelerators to achieve maximum effectiveness.

1. Lack of employee empowerment

2. Socializing champions

3. Paradigm lock (or inability to innovate)

4. Lack of structure

5. Organizational design flaws

6. Constantly changing TQM policy

7. Proceeding without evidences of readiness

8. Senior management impatience with department managers

9. Failure to recognize and confront failures

10. Variation in skills and leadership abilities of facilitators

11. Focusing improvement initiatives on "bad apples"

12. Time constraints

Accelerators

Make Heroes of Champions and Producers

One of the most effective accelerators, if not the most effective, is to capitalize on the energies of champions as they emerge from education and team meeting opportunities. By paying close attention to who within the organization is investing time to learn more about TQM and is trying new tools to improve, the organization can advance the transformation exponentially. The quality management director at West Paces Medical Center, Vicki Davis, fell into this category. Previously the materials manager, Davis saw the use of TQM tools as an effective aid to her goals of improving purchasing and receiving processes. Visible results became apparent as she applied TQM tools to dramatically reduce invoice discrepancies. She also invested time to read more about Deming, Juran, and others. After several months, she was appointed as the full-time quality director. Al Hallum, M.D., team leader of the pregnancy/childbirth team, was initially trained along with 12 other physicians in October 1989; his persistent inquisitiveness made it apparent that he possessed the energy and foresight to champion his colleagues to success. Within two years, his team's efforts had improved patient satisfaction significantly while saving the Atlanta business community more than $500,000. Oscar Cogan, M.D., the chest pain team leader, also instantly recognized the power of using process improvement tools and championed savings of more than $330,000; he engaged the use of TQM tools into his large group practice to improve the process of patient scheduling. Leo Tyler and

Gina Harris in the pharmacy began using TQM tools to reduce the medication delivery time and reduce antibiotic waste long before their colleagues attempted applications. Many of these individuals were not formal leaders in the organization before their efforts and our recognition of them occurred.

Often champions can come from unexpected sources within the organization, so careful observation is important. Likewise, trying to guess who the champions will be in advance proved to be hazardous to our efforts early in the transformation. Just because someone talks about use of tools or has become an informal leader in the organization under the previous management paradigm will not ensure that any given individual can serve as champion. Simply stated, an effective champion is a producer. Look for evidence of the champion's results before getting the individual deeply involved in leadership activities.

Link the TQM Strategic Deployment Road Map to the Strategic Plan

Significant portions of chapters 4 and 5 were devoted to the need and methods to link the organization's TQM efforts to the achievement of strategic imperatives.

Grow a Shared Vision

Successful companies, whether they follow a TQM discipline or not, share at least one common ingredient. Everyone in the organization—the CEO, VPs, board, medical staff, and employees—has become passionate about identifying and exceeding customer expectations. A TQM rollout can be accelerated when team leaders and department managers enjoy the freedom to establish their own independent departmental visions as opposed to a mandated set of measures and indicators from senior management. Of course, TQM initiatives would become undisciplined unless some mechanism ensured that departmental TQM objectives link with organizational policy. The feature of linking department objectives to organization-wide measures can be achieved by incorporating the Florida Power & Light matrix approach, as shown in the chapter 5. Each department articulated its role in the quality improvement effort by indicating which of the hospitalwide quality measures were impacted by its work. Once the department managers have labeled those areas in which they have organizational influence, they are free to choose within those areas any opportunity they wish. In other words, since we statistically validated that "maximizing available time" for physician customers was an important organization-wide imperative, the OR's quality matrix suggested employees maintained a significant impact over this area and hence worked to reduce OR turnover time. Every department within the organization was able to establish its own vision.

Focus on Measurement

It was also helpful to post hospitalwide and department-level quality indicators prominently. While other accelerators and structures enable teams to move through the quality improvement cycle, focus on improvement through measurement heightens awareness throughout the organization of the importance of improvement and process variables and how the teams have performed in the past. Extensive use of run charts is a major accelerator. Another accelerator is the effective use of data. Many organizations have struggled with this skill, and, as suggested in Appendix I, a preprinted data collection form can greatly aid managers at all levels to address the key questions necessary to construct a viable run chart.

Meaningful Work

It is also accelerating if TQM team leaders and members invest time and energy in the TQM process. They must recognize their efforts are meaningful and understand how team successes are interpreted into organizational success. This accelerator is usually handled through the articulation of TQM policy, vision, or strategic stages, as provided for in most TQM models. At West Paces Medical Center, our TQM policy stressed and communicated: (1) the mission of the hospital; (2) its definition of quality; and (3) statistically determined hospitalwide measures of quality. Some of these measures of quality were: maximizing physician available time, meeting physician scheduling needs, timeliness of physician reports, promptness of fulfilling patient requests, and nursing skills and responsiveness. The communication of customer expectations to everyone in the organization is not only a helpful method to ensure that the organization understands customers, but it also helps them relate the importance of their processes to customers. West Paces Medical Center wished to ensure that each new employee understood vital customer expectations and, as illustrated in Figure 7.2, presented all employees with pocket cards containing its 24 customer expectations. This link is often neglected. Ernst and Young discovered in its *International Quality Study* in 1992 that only 1 percent of U.S. hospitals communicated their strategic issues beyond senior management.[2] While the importance of customer measures such as these seems common sense, ensuring that employees and physicians understand that their quality improvement team work is meaningful can be easily overlooked. It is an accelerator to link a quality improvement team success directly to one of the hospitalwide quality indicators.

Create Constant Discomfort with the Present State

As with any organization change, the amount of attention by everyone in the organization governs the amount of intensity devoted within any given area. For this reason, we encouraged visitors from throughout the world to visit on our Quality Improvement Forum Day and hosted the National Demonstration Project, National Baldrige Committee, Veterans Administration, Institute of Medicine, JCAHO, and numerous other organizations. The organizational inquisitiveness resulting from these activities proved extremely beneficial. Not only did the organization receive a well-deserved national reputation for its efforts, more importantly, the physicians and employees became more interested in participating and learning about their roles in the TQM deployment.

Another key accelerator to generate discomfort with the current state is education and training. Continuously enhanced training at all levels is a strong conveyor of learning about what the organization should look like if its vision is to be accomplished. Every department manager, facilitator, and senior manager received extensive training, and every employee benefitted from a TQM orientation. A sample of the curriculum held for these programs can be found in appendix D.

Visibility of Senior Management

It goes without saying that an area of significant importance to senior management will receive greater attention than those that are not evidently important. One convention to attend to this accelerator is the presence of senior management at the head table during the monthly

Hospitalwide
Customer Expectations

"A PHYSICIAN BRAGS ABOUT WEST PACES MEDICAL CENTER WHEN . . ."

- Available time is maximized.
- Scheduling needs are met.
- Nurses are responsive, informing, and accessible.
- Reports are timely.
- High-quality consultants are accessible.
- State-of-the-art equipment is available.
- Every employee is involved in quality improvement.
- Physicians are treated as valued customers by everyone.

"A PATIENT BRAGS ABOUT WEST PACES MEDICAL CENTER WHEN . . ."

- The expected clinical outcome is achieved.
- Requests are responded to promptly and with TLC.
- Nurses are responsive, skilled, caring, and informative.
- Living arrangement needs are met.
- Billing and collections procedures are understandable, accurate, and efficient.
- Discharge procedures are understandable, quick, and efficient.

"AN EMPLOYEE BRAGS ABOUT WEST PACES MEDICAL CENTER WHEN . . ."

- Nurses are skilled, concerned, and caring.
- All departments work together to improve quality.
- Top leaders understand employee issues, communicate regularly, and recognize employee contributions.
- HCA and West Paces Medical Center have an image of high quality.
- New coworkers are highly qualified and will be long-term employees.
- Processes are sufficiently efficient to allow requirements to be met with budgeted staffing.

"A PAYER BRAGS ABOUT WEST PACES MEDICAL CENTER WHEN . . ."

- Employees brag about their care.
- His/her health costs are less than the competitors'.
- The hospital demonstrates efforts to reduce cost while improving quality.

Figure 7.2. Customer expectations pocket card.

quality improvement team reviews, to be detailed in the next paragraph. Additionally, approximately every three weeks, I, as the CEO, conducted an informal tour of the departments, asking employees to explain items on the department storyboard and to openly celebrate successes and to discuss inhibitors. In addition, hospitalwide quality indicators as referenced earlier and in chapter 5 were linked together through every department in the hospital to department quality measures. These measures were discussed each month between VPs and department managers, using the department monthly feedback report.

Momentum

Conventions to maintain momentum have perhaps proven the most valuable in mature TQM deployments. Momentum strikes at the heart of the most important strategic imperative, as discussed in chapters 3 and 4. The absence of momentum is the single largest complaint I receive from those with whom I have discussed accelerators and inhibitors. Several conventions to drive momentum are discussed here.

Team Road Map. A major acceleration convention is the use of a team road map for each department, similar in structure and intent to the organization's strategic deployment road map. The road map's purpose is to sketch, for the upcoming six months, the activities. During the work of one of the first quality improvement teams at West Paces Medical Center during 1988, it became apparent after the team concluded the quality improvement cycle that a tremendous loss of momentum occurred because the team had no idea what its quality improvement activities might be in the future. It was disheartening to see the team flounder without a vision of the future. For this reason, the team road map concept was established to ensure and foster team momentum, and it has proven very effective for those organizations deploying the concept.

Quality Improvement Storyboard. Many organizations have successfully relied heavily on the use of storyboards. At West Paces Medical Center we almost became dependent on them as communication devices, progress tracking, and storytelling. Storyboards hung prominently in every department in the hospital. An example of the storyboard layout can be seen in Figure 7.3.

What to Look for on a Storyboard

F • Who is the customer? • What is the name of the process? • What are the process boundaries? • Is the opportunity statement there? Is it clear? • Who will benefit from the improvement? • How is the process tied to the hospital as a system and its priorities?	**C** • Is the process presented at a level of detail that identifies possible causes of variation? • Is there evidence of agreement on a best method as represented by a single flow diagram? • Do the boundaries of the flow diagram align with the opportunity statement and the team? • Were there quick and easy improvements made in the C phase using PDCA? Did the team defer any improvements to the S phase? • Is there evidence that the actual flow of the process was documented rather than some perceived flow?
O • How big is the team? • Did the members represent people who work in the process or did the "organizational chart" show up? • Does the team's knowledge of the process align with the boundaries in the opportunity statement?	**U** • How did the team identify the KQC and potential KPVs? • Is there an operational definition for the KQC and the potential KPV? • Is there a data collection plan? Is it clear how the data will be collected? Who will collect them? • Does the team understand how long it will take to collect enough data to make a decision? • How does the performance of the process vary over time? • Can the team show a relationship between the KQC and the KPV?
Road map • Does the road map indicate key actions that the team is likely to take? • What is the time frame? • Is the team on track? • Is there evidence of updating or reviewing the roadmap? • Where is the team on the road map? **A** • Did the team act to implement the process gain beyond the pilot? • Did the team act to generalize the lessons learned from the pilot? Or did the team act to discard the planned improvement? • Can the team find another opportunity for improvement within this process? • What did the team learn from the effort?	**S** • How did the team select the opportunity for improvement? • Are there any data or other evidence to support the selection? • What were the criteria for making the decision? **P** • Does the team have a plan for piloting the improvement and collecting data? • Does the pilot plan indicate dates, communications, and ownership of specific steps? • What training was necessary?
Diary • What previous improvements have been realized after completing the FOCUS PDCA cycle? **C** • Do the data on the run chart suggest that the process changed? • How did the data change? • Does the team know anything that helps explain any evident change? • Is the team comfortable that enough data are present to support an action? • If the team is not comfortable with the amount of data or the knowledge provided by the data, what is the plan for obtaining more?	**D** • How was the plan executed? • Did any contingencies arise? • Were dates on the data collection met?
QI process measures • What process measures are being trended by the department? • Are the data displayed on a run chart?	

Figure 7.3. Sample storyboard layout and review questions.

Sections contained on the storyboards include the department's key quality measures, a diary of team quality improvement successes over the history of the TQM deployment, a road map of the department's activities to occur over the next six months, and a display of statistical tools from the current quality improvement opportunity. Storyboards should be visible to visitors, patients, physicians, employees, and volunteers who travel throughout the organization.

Storyboard Review. Perhaps one of the most effective accelerators is the constant use of celebrations. A convention heavily utilized at West Paces Medical Center was the storyboard review. Each month a quality improvement team review was conducted using the very positive approach crafted by Masao Nemoto.[3] This method includes a 10-minute overview by each presenting team followed by a five-minute section in which the CEO notes areas for celebration and suggested next steps.

At West Paces Medical Center, the storyboard review was typically held on the third Tuesday of each month from 9:00 A.M. to 11:00 A.M.. Often, however, additional reviews were scheduled to accommodate presentations when there were more than eight in line to present. The room was set up with two flip charts on opposite sides of the room with an overhead projector in the center to accommodate transparencies. The quality council, including the CEO, sat at the first table in a long row of tables. Behind the quality council sat the teams scheduled to present. At the back of the room, employees, department managers, and other visitors were crowded behind team tables.

At one review, the OR turnover team, invoice discrepancy team, physical therapy treatment interruption team, and charting time of Accuchecks team were scheduled to present. The OR supervisor stood before an audience of approximately 50 to relate the results of the OR turnover team's work. She indicated that the opportunity for the OR turnover team was to reduce total operating room turnover time by improving the efficiency of the preoperative and postoperative processes.

West Paces Medical Center used the FOCUS-PDCA model created by Batalden, which is highlighted in appendix B. It can be contrasted to the Juran method found in appendix A and the StorageTek approach found in appendix C.

As the OR supervisor presented the C step, the team's flowchart was shown, and she pointed out that there were eight times from the time a patient was admitted to the hospital until the patient was placed on the operating room table that the medical record was inspected for the presence of lab, X-ray, and EKG reports. The team learned that three persons conducted these eight different inspections yet no one person knew the degree of inspection conducted by the other inspectors. This revelation of cost of poor quality and the ramifications to organizations is discussed in detail in chapters 3 and 4.

As the team studied delays at various stages in the preoperative process, it was noted that significant time was devoted in the holding area to gather preadmission work. The holding area is a small cubicle where presurgical patients are housed until the OR is ready to receive them and its entire existence and cost can be thought of as cost of poor quality. Upon further investigation, it was discovered that only 17 percent of patients had been preadmitted. That is, of all surgery patients scheduled for surgery, less than one in five had received advance diagnostic processing. Benchmarking with the outpatient surgery center, the team discovered that more than 80 percent of its outpatients were preadmitted for advance diagnostic work. Therefore, the team redefined the opportunity statement to "increase the preadmission rate in an effort to reduce the length of time in the holding area."

At its first remedial theory implementation, the team decided to pilot three improvements. First, a process was created to schedule patients for preadmission appointments at least two days prior to surgery. Second, the team noted that no one person owned the process of routing the patient to the various ancillary departments for preadmission testing. Therefore, the nurses in the ambulatory surgery unit were designated as owners for the preadmission testing process, thus becoming the focal point for the patient routing through the system. Finally, the team noted that physician offices were rarely supportive of the hospital's preadmission scheduling efforts primarily because surgeons did not recognize the relationship between OR efficiency and the preadmission process. After an extensive education effort tailored to surgeons and their offices on the benefits of preadmission testing was conducted, the preadmission rate rose from 17 percent to 80 percent. This significant increase led to a reduction in the average length of time in the holding area from 23 minutes per case to 16 minutes per case.

At the conclusion of her 10-minute presentation, the OR supervisor presented two suggestions team members recommended for improving the use of the FOCUS-PDCA cycle. This important step is often overlooked by organizations. The role of team members is to constantly improve the "process of improvement." In order to accelerate the rate of innovation, an organization's number one strategic imperative, each team, team member, and facilitator must practice the role of improving the use of TQM tools to benefit everyone in the organization.

Following the OR supervisor's presentation, I stepped before the room and asked the audience for questions. Hearing none, I initiated Nemoto's review process by placing a transparency on the overhead illustrating a smiley face, at the top, below which appeared three hand-written comments. "We can all celebrate with this team the tremendous success in increasing the rate of preadmissions," I remarked. "And we should also recognize the effective use of a flowchart to determine needless waste and rework present in the lab, X-ray, and EKG inspections processes. And finally the team's diligent efforts to tie its specific improvement efforts to a statistically determined calculation of preadmission rate and reduction in holding area times strikes at the heart of the reason we use statistical tools. Before we move to 'next steps,' does anyone have any other observations for celebration?"

Several positive remarks were solicited from various members of the audience.

Next, I revealed on the transparency the symbol of the "sweaty man," a notorious symbol for all at West Paces Medical Center, "that we all could do a little more." Below the symbol appeared two hand-written comments. One suggested to the team that the use of average time in the various areas in the preoperative process was indeed helpful but, variation in the process was unknown since all values were not posted on the run chart. The team was encouraged to consider using a run chart or control chart of turnover values to gain additional insight into the performance of this process from case to case. It was also suggested that the team update its road map so that it would be obvious for team members and others reviewing the OR turnover storyboard the precise future activities for the next six months.

"Are there any other observations for next steps for the OR turnover team?" Hearing none, I concluded, "I think our OR turnover team deserves a special round of applause and encouragement for its future work."

At the conclusion of the review, I asked the audience to conduct a Nemoto review on the day's session. Upon drawing a smiley face on a flip chart page, the audience was asked, "What did you like about today's session?" After several minutes of recording observations, they were asked, "And how can this session be improved?"

It was obvious that the culture at West Paces Medical Center was truly encouraging continuous improvement.

This session was not random, but was conducted on a rather careful-ly constructed dialogue based on Nemoto's technique. Each audience—the OR turnover team members, other team leaders and members, attending employees, and the general public—was carefully considered as separate audiences with differing needs.

For the specific OR turnover team members, it was a time for great celebration as the team concluded a significant accomplishment, and precise comments of celebration were offered. It was also important for the team to recognize that continuous improvement requires careful planning.

For team leaders and members of other teams, the review takes on different meaning. In the review section for celebration, the reviewer is careful to point out to other quality improvement practitioners that the presentation suggests several items of which all teams should be mind-ful. For example, the OR turnover team's use of a flowchart to uncover numerous wasteful inspection points was discussed at length. Also, in the could-I-ask-you-to-do-more section, other team leaders were cau-tioned to avoid the pitfalls faced by the presenting team.

And finally, the review was intended for the general public, as a customer. The hospital wished to celebrate with the community that a significant improvement had occurred. But also it was pointed out to the general public that the hospital's culture of continuous improve-ment demands that this team come back in three months with a fur-ther improvement in quality.

How does the quality council prepare its remarks and what ques-tions are typically addressed? The following questions form a good, but not all-inclusive, basis for a pre–storyboard review:

Find Step
1. Is the opportunity statement written?
2. How does this opportunity link with hospitalwide measures of quality? (Is it meaningful?)
3. Does it describe the process?
4. Are the boundaries of the process identified?

5. Is the process too large—or too small—to study effectively?

6. Was the process flowchart completed identifying the supplier customer connection?

7. Are known customer needs clearly stated?

8. Is a clear owner or coowners of the process identified?

Organize step

1. Does the team representation include those knowledgeable of the process?

2. Is the size of the group appropriate to the size of the process?

3. Did the team make the mistake of placing customers or suppliers of the process on the team who do not have knowledge of the process? If yes, suggest that team meetings are perhaps not the best vehicle to gain customer or supplier knowledge and that focus groups can provide valuable customer or supplier knowledge, reserving team meetings to examine the process by those who know how the process works. It seems to be a great temptation of teams to include customers and suppliers in meetings because the team wishes to ensure that these individuals are represented. The pitfall is that decisions are made by those who know nothing of the internal workings of the process.

Clarify step

1. Are the boundaries of the flowchart consistent with the boundaries of the opportunity statement?

2. Is the flowchart technically accurate?

3. Are wait loops present and identified?

Uncover step

1. Did the team follow logical steps to uncover root causes of variation?

2. Has the vital customer measure characteristic, measuring the output of the process, been identified?

3. Does the customer measure link with the process described in the opportunity statement, and does it measure the stated customer expectation?

4. Are appropriate statistical tools present (run chart, control chart, Ishikawa diagram, Pareto, scatter plots)?

5. Are the tools technically accurate?

6. Were enough levels of root causes identified? (Did the team ask "Why, why, why, why, why?")

7. Are operational definitions clear?

8. Did arbitrary standards (for example, JCAHO nursing standards) drive the analysis or did the team uncover root causes of variation? Teams are often tempted to use arbitrary standards, like "30 minutes to chart an Accucheck" or "15 minutes to administer medication after delivery from pharmacy." They then wish to concentrate on the question "yes or no" to the arbitrary standard. It takes great discipline to concentrate on the raw measure and use standards as benchmarks.

9. Did data collection use available existing or modified data or did the team create additional work? Teams should be encouraged to use as much existing data as possible, from the medical record or elsewhere, rather than create additional work. Often, existing charting can be tailored to fit data collection needs.

10. Are root causes specified in the flowchart? If not, did the team go back to C and modify the flowchart when appropriate? Frequently, the Pareto diagram revealing root causes of variation can be used to check the accuracy of the flowchart and vice versa.

11. Were any special causes identified? If present, were they acted upon?

Start step

1. Is there evidence that the team brainstormed possible improvements or did the team think of a solution before U? In other words, did the team let the data talk to them or did it construct the statistical measures around a preconceived improvement? Obviously, this is a very sensitive area and the way the reviewer approaches discussion of the issue can be constructive or destructive. The reviewer, of course, does not wish to discourage any improvement initiative, even if it was predetermined. At the same time, the reviewer maintains an

obligation to look for evidence that the team is using continuous improvement tools to identify true root causes of variation and brainstorming potential improvement ideas. Evidence should be present that these ideas were recorded and rank ordered, and discussion of effective piloting occurred in team meetings.

2. Was the selected improvement the best choice?

Plan step

1. Did the run chart or control chart show improvement?

2. Was the data collection plan clearly stated and logical?

Do step

1. Did the pilot reveal enough data points to make the analysis valid?

Check step

1. Did the run chart or control chart show an improvement?

2. Did the team use other methods to show the effect of the pilot?

Act step

1. Did the team modify the flowchart to reflect the improvement?

2. Was it mentioned that the team intends to review the run chart or control chart at some future time to ensure that the improvement is stable?

3. Did the team suggest ways to improve the use of FOCUS-PDCA and the statistical tools?

Storyboard Review Success Factors

1. All reviews should be on a regular schedule to ensure the organization has knowledge of the storyboard review.

2. Ensure a majority of department managers are present at each session.

3. Permit attendance by as many employees as possible on a voluntary basis.

4. Merge storyboard reviews with routine department manager meetings, if possible.

5. Hold reviews in a convenient onsite location.

6. Conduct a storyboard review every month, even if only two teams can present.

Storyboard Review Failure Factors

1. Concentrating on the use of tools instead of focusing on the process and its improvement.

2. Lack of preparation and the prereview of a team's work.

3. Failing to allow a department manager input on how to structure storyboard reviews.

4. Failure to keep each team on a preset storyboard review schedule. (For example, if the pharmacy team is scheduled to present in three months, ask it to present even if it is not fully ready.)

5. Outside visitors, who are often distracting. If visitors become a problem, it might be best to hold a special session every four to six weeks.

6. Lack of consistent presentation format, such as storyboards and FOCUS-PDCA.

7. Allowing more than 10 minutes for each presentation. (Observers become bored during lengthy presentations.)

Team Status Worksheet. A very common complaint by quality council members is that teams take too long. Many of the conventions discussed thus far are intended to help increase the rate of innovation. The team status worksheet, Figure 7.4, was created by Davis to help team leaders, facilitators, and quality council members focus on the rate of team progress.

Other Momentum Conventions. Other conventions used to drive momentum through celebrating TQM successes are stories in publications and informal acknowledgments. West Florida Regional Hospital in Pensacola found it useful to award graduates of its quality course with a graduation pin.

Networking with Other TQM Organizations

HCA and others recognized the importance of networking in accelerating TQM development and innovation. Not only does networking

TRENDS REPORT

STATUS OF QIT CYCLES: MONTH OF ___ June 25, 1992

#	STATUS	DIV MG	TEAM	START DATE	FACILI-TATOR	TEAM LEADER	01 JUN	01 JUL	01 AUG	01 SEP	01 OCT	01 NOV	01 DEC	02 JAN	02 FEB	02 MAR	02 APR	02 MAY	02 JUN	02 JUL
1	Clinical		Back Pain		Ed McEachern	Richard Moore														
2	Active	CC	Administration	1/90	Jim Browne	Mitch Mitchell														
3	Active	CC	Quality Management	9/90	Lorraine Schiff	Lorraine Schiff	⋮													
4	Clinical	EM	Nosocomial Infections	9/90	Ed McEachern	Dr. Marlowe	⋮													
5	Active	EM	SHS Scheduling	10/90	Ed McEachern	Oscar Cogan, M.D.	U	S	PID	CA	S	PDCA2		P	DC	A1				
6	Clinical	EM	DTC		Ed McEachern	P. Davidson, M.D.	U	U	S	PD	CA	A	S	P	DC	A2				
7	Active	EM	Chest Pain	1/90	Lorraine Schiff	Ed Mosachem								U2	U2	U2				
8	Clinical	EM	C-Section	2/90	Lorraine Schiff	Dr. Hallum														
9	Clinical	EM	Clinical Research		Ed McEachern	Dr. Marlowe						S	P3			P4				
10	Active	AJ	Food Service Deli Line	11/90	Julie Flegal	William Turner														
11	Active	AJ	Dietary Issues to Units	1/91	Julie Flegal	Carla Rapp														
12	Active	JB	TAT of Lab Tests Accery	11/90		Marilyn Porter	P			P	P			C	C	C	C	F		
13	Active	AJ	Waste	12/90	Jim Browne	Curtis Miller	P			P	P									
14	Active	JB	Engineering	2/90	Debbie Snell	David Thornton			U	F	C	C	C	C	C	C	C	C		
15	Active	AJ	Food Service–Trayline	2/90	Julie Flegal	Dick Watts														
16	Active	JB	Respiratory Care Charges	8/90	Lorraine Schiff															
17	Active	JB	Pharmacy	5/90	Carol Allen	Gina Harris	F		E	E	F	F		F	A3					
18	Active	JB	Cath Lab	3/90	Rodney Ray	Betty Potarus	C2	C2	C3	C3	A3			A3	A3					
19	Active	JB	Paces Pavillion		Rodney Ray		U		U	U										
20	Active	JB	TATOR	4/90?	Rodney Ray	Lisa Catall	⋮													
21	Past Opp.	JB	Antibiotic Waste	2/90		Mike Langley				S	S			PDCA				PDCA	PDCA	
22	Past Opp.	JB	Radiology	1/90	Rodney Ray	Roberta Shoup	A			C	A									
23	Active	AJ	Volunteer Services Awareness	10/90	Lorraine Schiff	Mike Francisco		A		A	A									
24	Active	JC	Check Request	2/90	Rodney Ray	John Slate				A	A	A	A	A	A	A	A	S		
25	Active	JC	Bus. Off. Pt. of Svc. Blng	12/88	Carol Allen	David Traupeur		C2		A	A	A	A	A	A	A	A	A		
26	Active	JC	Data Processing	10/88	Vicki Davis	Debbie Baker	⋮			⋮			⋮			A	A	A		
27	Active	JC	Invoice Discrepancy	9/87	Rodney Ray	Susan Asire				⋮	C2		⋮		C2	C2	C2	C2	C2	
28	Active	MM	Treatment Delay	12/90	Julie Flegal	Debbie Baker	⋮													
29	Past Opp.	PH	NICU Stim	2/91	Julie Flegal	Cathy Abrams			U	U	C	C								
30	Active	PH	Perinatal Cost Reduction	8/90	Edward	Susan Asire			U	U	C	C		C2	C2					
31	Active	PH	Antibiotic Appropriateness	1/91	Lisa Catell	Cathy Abrams	C1			C1	P1	C1		C2		P1				
32	X-Fat. Cl	EM	MAR Documentation	8/90	Edward	Lisa Catell	C1	C2							C2	A2				
33	Active	PH	CCU	1/91	Karen Schmidt	Karen Schmidt	⋮				⋮	C								
34	Inactive	PH	Competence Assessment	11/89	Carol Allen	Kay Moffit						C	CU	CU	CU	CU		CU	CU	
35	Active	PH	4W	7/90	Debbie Snell	Sharon Nelson				FINISHED										
36	Past Opp.	PH	PeriNatal Discharge Teaching	12/89	Julie Flegal	Leslie Kitchen			⋮	P2	A	A				C3				
37	Active	PH	3W Medication Administration	9/89	Julie Flegal	Eva Weaver	⋮										A	A		

Figure 7.4. Sample team status worksheet.

aid continued learning, but it also enables senior leaders and department managers to benchmark conventions and techniques and to aid one another during the transformation. In addition to HCA's network, Quorum in Nashville, the Healthcare Forum in California, Juran's annual IMPRO convention, SunHealth, and the Institute for Healthcare Improvement in Boston are effective networking and educational opportunities.

Build Everyone's Self-Esteem to Participate in Vision Achievement

As Batalden noted so often, fear is a major quality thief. It not only robs individuals of freedom to express their creative insights, it destroys their self-esteem. Any effort to elevate the self-esteem of a team, department, or individual will produce a tenfold return on investment of time and effort. One team during a storyboard review session presented what was perhaps the worst example of use of tools I ever witnessed. Davis; Jim Browne, the chief operating officer; and I struggled for days before the session to come up with one good remark to make about the team's work. We identified at least 200 things that were wrong about the team's TQM application, but we simply could not find one redeeming quality about its efforts. As the day of the review approached, we were nervous about destroying the team's self-esteem. At the conclusion of the team's 10-minute synopsis, I rose to conduct the Nemoto review. We had agreed that I would celebrate with the team that they had been diligent in meeting every week, that they stayed focused on the team's mission statement, and that each member attended every meeting. That was the only good we could say about the team.

When identifying the "do more" tasks, we reported only three suggestions. At the conclusion of their presentation, any observer could see the pride of the team members about their celebration. They were overjoyed to be positively recognized. Two weeks later the team leader asked if the team could present its next improvement. We were astounded. Not only did they move through the next cycle faster than any other team members in our history, they were eager to do more. The next improvement was not much more impressive than the first, but it was an advancement. They came back again three or four weeks later with a slightly better use of tools. The quality council learned an important lesson in all of this. It is more important to build the self-esteem of teams and individuals than it is to aggressively critique a single improvement cycle. Senior leaders are so tempted to try to drive perfection in every team presentation, however, the cost to the team's self-esteem prevents them from becoming a learning team.

Quality Council Accelerators

1. Spend at least 50 percent of each quality council meeting on degree of achievement of results.

2. Spend at least 40 percent of each quality council meeting on resolving infrastructure issues.

3. Adopt a mental model like the transformation model in Figure 7.1 and communicate it widely.

4. Conduct periodic assessments, like the annual Baldrige Award-type self-assessment offered by SunHealth Alliance in appendix E and internal quality audit in appendix H. Revise the strategic deployment road map to include recommendations.

5. Assign a sponsor from the quality council to each quality improvement team, quality planning team, and BPQM team.

6. Conduct an annual cost-of-poor-quality study and use results to drive team chartering.

7. Use TQM tools and methods, such as flowcharts, to draw policies and procedures.

Inhibitors

Lack of Empowerment

It is an understandable point of reservation that senior management withhold a certain amount of power from teams for fear that unchecked teams will increase operating costs or make changes impacting other departments. The failure to offer teams empowerment, however, can become a disastrous inhibitor for the effective establishment of a TQM environment. It is vital that management not create barriers to the effective rollout of TQM, but rather innovate conventions to ensure organizational objectives are met while empowering teams. The fear of rampant cost increases also concerned senior management of West Paces Medical Center, when our first teams were formed.

To ensure that the teams did not indiscriminately increase costs, we initially required teams to include the phrase "at the same or reduced cost" in every team mission statement. We were pleasantly surprised to find that employees clearly understood the importance of cost, and we were later almost embarrassed to admit we had so little confidence in their abilities during our initial efforts. Every team that completed the improvement cycle considered cost when appropriate.

One team, looking to improve the process to repair damaged walls, suggested that a full-time painter be added to the staff, which would reduce the length of time to repair walls and at the same time reduce the cost of the hospital's existing contract service. A nursing team, wishing to reduce the length of time to administer medications to HIV patients, recommended the purchase of a capital item. Before making its final decision, the team embarked upon a three-month pilot to document the cost benefit to patient care, nursing, labor expense, and expenditure of supplies.

Our experiences illustrate that, once employees are educated about organizational issues and are empowered to innovate, they demonstrate a deeper knowledge of process and process variation than senior management comprehends. They are, after all, closer to the processes than anyone else in the organization.

However the organization decides to control for its concerns, withdrawing empowerment from quality improvement teams can become a serious inhibitor to success. It is possible to construct other controls without withdrawing empowerment.

Socialization of Champions

Great fanfare surrounds those who become visible TQM leaders in the organization. These individuals are called upon by senior management and colleagues to present their views on the use of tools, how to organize and structure TQM efforts, how to train employees in the use of tools, and how to overcome common organization barriers to making TQM most effective at the team level. The result of this special attention from others, particularly senior leaders, can be that the organization's key movers and shakers take their eyes off the ball and fumble.

It is far too easy for the champion to relish in the glory of telling the team's past successes than to systematically achieve new heights of accomplishment, and, yet, continuous innovation is what transforms the organization. If the organization's efforts result in any degree of notoriety due to TQM success and visitors frequent the organization to study techniques employed by TQM leaders, there is an even greater danger that champions will become socialized. Symptoms to signal an impending socialization of key champions include observations that the organization's leaders are spending a significant amount of time making presentations to those within and outside the organization, spending significant time helping other team leaders, taking on increasing burdens of facilitating other teams, taking increasingly lengthy absences from the department, a decrease in the number of team meetings being conducted, and a decrease in the rate of innovations by teams.

An organization can avoid socialization of its champions by being sensitized to the phenomenon, conducting open and honest dialogue within the organization, and by maintaining the focus of rewards and recognition on the increasing effectiveness in use of tools and specific process improvement successes. In most cases, an organization can assure it does not take its eye off the ball by simply managing its conventions of acceleration and do not allow unintended reinforcers to enter the organization culture.

Of course, balance is required in this area; no one wishes to imply that it is a bad thing for champions to take a leadership role in aiding their colleagues, but rather that assistance cannot take precedence over ever-increasing innovation.

Paradigm Lock (or inability to innovate)

When one examines the effect of following the ritual of a TQM model, it becomes apparent that the organization is achieving a marriage of right-brain and left-brain thinking. Following the discipline of flowcharting a process, and then systematically uncovering failures to meet customer expectations and root causes of variation in the process is distinctly a left brain pursuit; piloting redesign innovations to reduce the greatest source of customer dissatisfaction is distinctly a right brain initiative. My observations of TQM work suggest that an area of greatest difficulty is applying creativity to improve the process of improving, that is, improving the use of tools and the model itself.

It is for this reason that we invest so much time discussing paradigm shift management. It does little good to uncover the sources of variation if creativity cannot be unleashed to remove them. The importance of resolving paradigm lock is not immediately apparent as an organization begins the TQM transformation because paradigm lock does not manifest itself as a significant inhibitor until three or four years into the transformation. But, since solving paradigm lock takes a long time, beginning the resolution process must begin relatively soon in the transformation or the organization will stall.

Kent Sterett, TQM mentor for Southern Pacific Railroad, formerly at Florida Power & Light, enlightened me about the importance of paradigm lock in 1989. He described the rigors of innovation during the transformation by drawing the parallel of "picking the loose change from the ground" when the organization is in years one and two. The sources of variation during this stage are easy to spot, and innovation is not particularly hard to come by. During years three through five, however, the most obvious innovations have been implemented and creativity becomes more difficult. Sterett refers to this stage as "picking the low-hanging fruit." The final stage of maturity comes during years six through 10. Sensitive statistical tools are required to detect process variation and innovation brings chaos and migranes. He refers to this stage as "picking the high-hanging fruit."

An organization can "pick up the loose change" without devoting serious thought to paradigm lock, but it can never mature. While knowledge of and sensitivity to paradigm lock is the greatest defense against it, education in creativity and fostering an environment in which team leaders learn from the creativity of their colleagues is the required solution. There are several signs of paradigm lock. My favorite sign is listening to the comments made during the idea evaluation stage of team meetings. If you hear the statement, "Oh, we just can't do it that way!" it is a safe bet that this team must dig itself out of paradigm lock before it can become productive again. I refer to this statement as the Medusa effect; as soon as it is spoken, every team member turns to stone. The first time I heard this kiss of death statement was when I asked a nurse manager, "Why do we have eight inspections for lab and EKG work at different points along the surgery preparation process?" and received the answer, "We must make sure that we have performed these tests before we place a patient under anesthesia."

"I can certainly appreciate the importance of these tests, but it seems that designing an error-free process would ensure patient safety while providing this service faster and less expensively," I replied.

Self-assuredly she responded, "Oh, honey, we just must do it this way."

Another symptom in teams can be detected when the team enters the process improvement pilot phase, but can only generate one potential improvement idea for discussion. It was obvious that several of our department managers and team leaders decided long before the team's first meeting what improvement they wished to implement and constructed the team's work to support the preconceived improvement. While I would never suggest criticizing a team's improvements, even if they were predetermined, proliferation of this method of improvement is counterproductive to process knowledge discovery and true TQM maturity.

It is useful to create conventions to discourage paradigm lock and encourage invigorating brainstorming. Two helpful methods to employ are to ask teams to place the entire listing of all improvement ideas discussed during team meetings on the storyboard and to ask team leaders to show this listing during their presentations. By simply asking for evidence that the team did create a list of alternative improvement ideas, members are forced to brainstorm. The ultimate solution, however, is intensive education and training for everyone in the organization regarding creativity tools and techniques.

Lack of Structure

Many of the setbacks I have observed over the years can be attributed to failure of senior management to properly set up the necessary organization and structure to accomplish a particular phase. For example, upon initiation of the effort to measure department quality indicators, many managers become confused as to the purpose of the measurement, how their measures would contribute to the overall hospital vision accomplishment, and how they could best set up a sampling process. The complication in this phase of our TQM rollout was ultimately resolved by a group of five department managers, who developed easily understood forms for completion by department managers. These user-friendly forms removed the mystique of the data sampling and plotting process until managers could grow comfortable without the use of standard forms. In fact, very often the design and use of forms for completion by managers was all that was needed to move beyond a point of confusion. Also, we found the use of small pilot groups of department managers to identify possible areas of confusion before entering a new phase of our deployment very effective (for example, vendor certification, creation of the first storyboard, establishment of the first physician teams).

Organization Design Flaws

In 1989 I met a very enlightened leader of McDonnell Douglas Fighter Aircraft Division at a TQM dinner in Nashville. He not only displayed a deep understanding of the importance of employee empowerment, he had determined that the traditional organizational design impedes TQM effectiveness. He showed me an organization chart in which the organization had determined its business process quality management functions and had systematically reengineered the customer interface at all points. He was at the bottom, with several VP-level persons above his position; the third level (from the bottom) revealed several circles that he said represented major processes needed to produce a fighter aircraft. Assigned to each team was an accounting person, a purchasing person, and a few other functional types. At the top of the chart was the designation "customer." Each team was responsible for not only managing the processes within its areas, but also to improve these processes. These individuals were also charged with identifying internal and external customers and knowing the degree to which the team was meeting the customers' needs. More importantly, they were empowered to improve processes without several layers of management. This company had reorganized itself into several interrelating self-directed work teams. By contrast, reporting relationships in most organizations are crafted along job class lines. We tend to set up our organizations so that everyone with similar jobs works together and shares the same supervisor. Supervisors of employees with similar jobs then report to managers, and so on, until we create layer upon layer of bureaucracy to ensure control. These layers then require sophisticated coordination and internal communication processes to maintain them. It should be evident that these added processes of coordination, communication, and control, complete with several layers of management, add a massive overhead burden to the organization. It goes without saying that competitiveness becomes increasingly more difficult as organizational layers are added.

Process thinkers get all tangled up when working in these organizations because process improvement opportunities with this kind of hierarchy require many special maneuverings to generate innovations. We hear them refer to "managing the white spaces" and persist in asking, "Who is the owner of this process?" They are then told that no one owns the entire process, so often a process sponsor is assigned, or, in many cases, cross-functional teams are charted to improve these organization-wide processes. The complexity grows more pronounced as the organization gains greater effectiveness in uncovering the needs of customers and identifies wait loops, needless inspection, and ineffective communication processes between departments as they hand off their part of the process to the next department.

A growing innovation in many American hospitals is the complete redesign of inpatient care processes by assigning individuals to admit and perform X-rays, other diagnostic and therapeutic services, and most other direct patient care processes on the same floor. In this way, every patient floor is responsible for almost all patient care services for its customers instead of transporting the customer throughout the organization to receive services by individuals over which the nursing personnel maintain no direct connection.

Constantly Changing TQM Policy

One of the dangers that TQM consultants continued to present to the senior leadership at West Paces Medical Center was constantly changing their minds on how to structure and format the articulation of TQM policy, the process to articulate the organization's vision, the process to form teams, and teaching new statistical tools before old ones were commonly used. No less than four different concepts were implemented at the top level in less than two years, which then required communication, understanding, and internalization throughout the organization. These changes required months of committed communication and were always at the expense of key elements of the transformation.

This is not to say that a change in TQM policy direction is not appropriate, but rather it is imperative that senior management critically access the cost benefit to the organization's deployment timetable. Most consultants are exceedingly knowledgeable about TQM models, measurement of variation, and TQM's technical requirements, but are often naive regarding organization management and transformation. This is particularly true within your organization. Consultants should be constantly challenged to defend any change in TQM policy. Further, TQM consultants should be selected after careful reference checks.

Proceeding Without Evidences of Readiness

This is one of the more important inhibitors and was taught to us after our mentor recognized we had stumbled. Our first implementation road map included major topic areas for the organization to address (For example, physician teams, quality assurance–TQM integration, rollout of department teams) with a date of initiation for each phase. We found that without considering the concept of evidences of readiness we were often ill-prepared to enter a critical phase. For example, we began training physicians in October 1988 and quickly found that many physician champions were emerging, expecting to lead clinical teams, and yet our organization was totally unprepared to enter this phase. We simply did not have enough facilators capable of managing clinical teams at the point of physician education. The concept of evidences of readiness would have suggested that, rather than simply designating physician rollout to occur in October 1988 on our road map, we would have identified the major steps required to happen prior to physician involvement. While resolution of this inhibitor appears simple enough, TQM has created many unexpected surprises in the absence of consideration of evidences of readiness.

Impatience with Department Managers

If one management trait is consistent among American managers, it is a drive for results. This characteristic can be held up as a vital need in the chaotic world of management. As mentors, however, this trait is a two-edged sword. The tool that saves us in a traumatic situation causes much harm in other situations. The situation to which I am referring here is the impatience with managers as they learn to apply TQM methods. Embarking on an organizational transformation requires transition through several paradigms and that transition requires time, patience, learning, and teaching by senior management.

Failure to Recognize and Confront Barriers

Perhaps this inhibitor could go without saying, but on more than one occasion at West Paces Medical Center we decided to postpone conceptualizing an issue like quality assurance-TQM integration, performance appraisal redesign, human resource involvement, and understanding the needs of the business community. Yet failure to assign responsibility of these areas to key managers responsible for understanding the issues and questions surrounding these issues has the negative effect of distracting vital issues of the deployment.

Variation in Skills and Leadership Abilities of Facilitators

The process of organizational transformation is inhibited unless the organization facilitators, those individuals trained in statistical measures and group leadership techniques, are all teaching the same methods. Our rollout of the first department teams in 1988, more than 35 in total, was done after 14 facilitators had completed a three-day training program. The variability in use of tools and methods by these facilitators varied so greatly that one department might be proceeding along a totally different path than another. To avoid this inhibitor, Davis established a six-month Facilitator Certification Program, in which every facilitator was required to demonstrate skills and uses of statistical tools. The certification was not a typical U.S. classroom model in which extensive testing and grading occurs. Rather, she followed the Japanese Deming Prize approach in which facilitators entered the program and emerged upon successfully demonstrating requisite skills. As a result, facilitators were very consistent in their language, use of tools, and suggestions for resolving team issues.

Focusing on "Bad Apples"

Berwick, president of the Institute for Healthcare Improvement, popularized this inhibitor several years ago. He observed while at the Harvard Community Health Plan that the traditional approach to quality management in health care was to use data to identify those physicians and health care providers who failed to provide care at a certain threshold. This approach was even the central feature of accrediting bodies. We began to recognize the phenomenon discussed in chapter 3 on paradigms that the use of data for judgment drove the level of fear and defensiveness so high that there was no room for improvement work. Data were not viewed for improvement or learning, they were viewed as a judgment tool.

The complexity of attempting a TQM deployment at a time when its most effective weapon, data, is viewed as the enemy, is a major inhibitor.

Time Constraints

In March 1993, the department managers at West Paces Medical Center were asked to identify their accelerators and inhibitors. The number one inhibitor was time constraints. Eighteen months later, I conducted a similar session for the senior leaders of Suburban Hospital of Bethesda. Again, time constraints won as the number one inhibitor. Countermeasures must be adopted by every organization to make the TQM strategic deployment road map and subsequent strategic improvement measures the top priority in the organization. Opportunities to merge existing meetings, eliminate others, shave minutes off current meetings using efficient meeting techniques, and reduce members of committees, are all important activities to drive the organization vision.

In summary, the feeding of accelerators and the starvation of inhibitors is a vital management activity. Engaging all audiences (senior leaders, managers, employees, physicians), in an effort to identify and generate countermeasures to inhibitors is the basic blocking and tackling of TQM deployments. It is not as glamourous as reengineering, benchmarking, or other newer TQM buzzwords, but its payoff provides a richer return on investment than any other management endeavor. The satisfaction as well as the results achieved from advancing accelerators and thwarting inhibitors should enjoy a prominent place on the quality council agenda.

Discussion Exercise for a One-Hour Quality Council Meeting

1. List the accelerators identified in this chapter on a flip chart in advance of the meeting.
2. Engage quality council members to brainstorm additional ones.
3. Nominally group the top five supporting your organization at this moment.
4. List the inhibitors identified in this chapter on a flip chart in advance of the meeting.

5. Engage quality council members to brainstorm additional ones.

6. Nominally group the top five facing your organization at this moment.

7. Select several inhibitors to place on future quality council meeting agendas and assign a discussion leader for each one to research how other organizations manage the accelerator or inhibitor.

8. Evaluate the meeting on flip chart paper.

   A. What did you like about this session?

   B. What could be improved for future sessions?

Discussion Exercise for a One-Hour Department Manager/Team Leader Meeting

Assign a quality council member to facilitate this session. Other council members should be available at each table to help in group discussion. Organize participants in tables of eight and provide a flip chart to each table. Conduct the following activities.

1. The facilitator should discuss on transparencies and an overhead projector the accelerator and inhibitor concepts discussed in this chapter (but not the specific accelerators and inhibitors). The facilitator should feel free to also address the paradigms discussed in chapter 3, if desired.

2. List the accelerators relevant to department managers and team leaders identified in this chapter on a flip chart at the front of the room. Appropriately label them A through Z so that table members can nominally group them later.

3. Each table should be engaged to brainstorm additional ones.

4. Nominally group the top five accelerators supporting your organization at this moment.

5. List the inhibitors relevant to department managers and team leaders identified in this chapter on a flip chart at the front of the room. Appropriately label them A through Z so that table members can nominally group them later.

6. Each table should be engaged to brainstorm additional ones.

7. Nominally group the top five inhibitors facing your organization at this moment.

8. Each table should select one inhibitor and brainstorm countermeasures to neutralize the inhibitor.

9. Each table should present its countermeasures to the whole group.

10. Evaluate the meeting on flip chart paper.

    A. What did you like about this session?

    B. What could be improved for future sessions?

Discussion Exercise for a Governing Board Meeting

1. Review results of the quality council session.

2. Review results of the department manager/team leader session.

3. Advise the board of the selection and timetable to implement selected accelerators and the plan to address vital inhibitors.

4. Discuss implications from the board's perspective.

5. Brainstorm, clarify, and nominally group responses to the question, "What role does the board play in the maintenance of accelerators and inhibitors?"

Notes

1. Peter. M. Senge, *The Fifth Discipline: The Art and Practice of the Learning Organization* (New York: Doubleday, 1990), 97.

2. Ernst & Young and the American Quality Foundation, *International Quality Study: Health Industry Report* (Cleveland: Ernst & Young, 1992).

3. Masao Nemoto, *Total Quality Control for Management: Strategies and Techniques from Toyota and Toyoda Gosei*, trans. David Lu (Englewood Cliffs, N.J.: Prentice-Hall, 1984), 77–99.

Chapter 8

Putting it All Together

Many are thinking, like I often do, that the last chapter is simply a rehash of previous material. That is true, of course, but it is often the revisitation of previous concepts after having internalized others that brings richness to new learning. Do not deprive yourself of the learning that takes place through the progressive struggling with new material built upon the old.

Our goal in a TQM deployment is simple. To achieve strategic results faster than our competitors. To do this we create a vision. This vision is grounded on our firm understanding of market needs, both now and in the future. Upon creating the vision, everything we do, every activity we undertake, every dollar we spend, every meeting we attend, every policy we write, and every employee we hire is done with one thing in mind—results. Too often quality councils become immersed in their TQM deployments, advancing new techniques like business process quality management reengineering or merging with another organization, and they take their eyes off the ball. This is certainly easy to do in an environment fraught with competitive pressures. But the outcome is predictable. Organizations do not achieve the results specified in their visions.

For the purposes of this summary, we will start with the transformation model. We will relook at the paradigms that confront our organizations, the five strategic necessities, and, finally, the quality council time allocation table.

As we again examine the transformation model, Figure 8.1, look at it as if for the first time. What key observations can you make about the interrelationships between its components? What is the single most important one? Is one component most important? What would

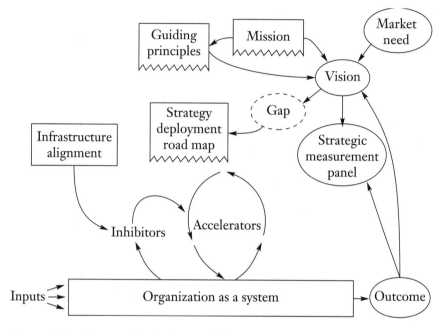

Figure 8.1. The transformation model.

be the result of elimination of one of the components? Which components are strong and effective currently in your organization? Which components are lacking? Does the absence of lacking components cause any organizational dysfunction? If so, in what ways? How would the introduction of a completed model remedy these dysfunctions? And, where would organizational resistance (an inhibitor) surface to thwart your efforts to become more effective in the marketplace?

In chapter 3, we discovered in detail many of the market paradigms that confront our organization in our efforts to drive results. Examine these paradigms again.

1. Importance of velocity of innovation

2. Reduction of cost of poor quality

3. Elements of customer judgment

4. Progressive systems integration

5. Alignment of support infrastructure

6. Understanding the cycle of continuous improvement

7. Reduction of variation

8. Employee empowerment

Have any of these paradigms been mastered by your organization? Is there one or two that seem to strike at your heart? Are there others not listed that cause you more difficulty? How does your organization manage paradigm issues? Does it just plow ahead, taking whatever casualties it feels it must in the name of progress? Or, does your quality council invest time to fully understand what it is like to work in your organization and create action plans to make accomplishing the vision as smooth as possible? Has your organization discovered effective methods at resolving one or more of these? If so, are you willing to write about it? Literature is full of stories about teams; it is very lacking in management of accelerators and inhibitors. Have you made mistakes that you are willing to share?

This book suggests that, based on the paradigms discussed earlier and in chapter 3, it is possible to create a 500-year strategic plan. The following represents this thinking.

1. Increase the rate of innovation 20 percent per year.

2. Reduce cost of poor quality 20 percent per year.

3. Increase customer satisfaction 20 percent per year.

4. Progressively integrate the organization as a system.

5. Exceed stakeholder cash flow expectations 20 percent per year.

Do these strategies have meaning to your current situation? Can you think of other organizations no longer in existence that might have survived if they had followed one or more of these? Which ones? Why these particular strategies instead of the others? What about your organization prevents you from becoming better than your competitors in all of these? For those who feel you have achieved Kano Level III, which competitors are silently gaining on you? How are they able to innovate in this area faster than you? What about your organization prevents you from gaining more ground on your competitors?

Finally, study the time allocation table again, Table 8.1, as first discussed in chapter 4. In the last chapter on inhibitors, we discovered that at every level in most organizations, time is listed as the greatest inhibitor.

Table 8.1. Time allocation chart.

Time allocation	Results	Methods	Infrastructure
I. Quality council	50%	10%	40%
II. Quality management director	10%	70%	20%
III. Facilitators	10%	90%	0%
IV. BPQM teams	20%	70%	10%
V. Cost-of-poor-quality teams	20%	70%	10%
VI. Cross-functional teams	20%	70%	10%
VII. Department teams	20%	70%	10%

Results include: 1. Rate of innovation   2. Cost of poor quality
3. Customer satisfaction   4. Systems integration   5. Cash flow
Methods include: 1. QI Teams   2. Quality planning teams   3. BPQM
teams   4. Cost-of-poor-quality teams   5. Benchmarking   6. Networking
7. Education
Infrastructure includes: 1. Organizing design   2. Compensation
3. Performance appraisal   4. Capital allocation   5. Legal structure
6. Supplier relations   7. Facilities

How are key players in your organization currently investing their time? From your recollection of the last three or four quality council meetings, what percent of time was devoted to reviewing statistical measures of the vision or strategic deployment road map progress? What was the majority of time spent on? What are the reasons that the quality council does not focus on statistical expressions of results? Does the CEO chair the council? If not, why do you think the CEO does not? What would the CEO say? What changes could be made to the quality council focus to be more appealing to senior leaders?

In all, if we look from the 60,000-foot level our task is simple enough. It is important to return to this level from time to time. It is refreshing up here. We can see our vision and our identified market need. And, we can see all of the organization-as-a-system processes that come together to make it all happen. It is important, too, to drive to a spot in the transformation model and generate improvement, and it is important to invest most of our time here, but continuously grounding ourselves in measurable results as an expression of our vision accomplishment helps us stay focused and communicate our focus to others.

Introduction to Appendices

These appendices have been assembled from various quality resources and companies deploying TQM to highlight and illustrate several concepts contained in the book.

Appendix A: The Juran Quality Improvement Process. The six-step problem-solving process taught by the Juran Institute is highlighted in this appendix. This model is probably the most widely used throughout the United States, Canada, Australia, United Kingdom, and Europe. It is distinguished by its recognition that cultural resistance must be resolved before effective implementation and replication can occur.

Appendix B: The HCA FOCUS-PDCA Model. The HCA (now Columbia HCA) FOCUS-PDCA model, crafted by Batalden, VP of quality for HCA from 1987 through 1994, is provided in this appendix. This model is probably the second most widely used in the United States. It is distinguished by the ease with which team members can recall the sequential flow of the process improvement logic.

Appendix C: The StorageTek Model and Ft. Sanders Health System Policy. The StorageTek continuous improvement model, a nine-step repeating cycle of improvement, is shown in this appendix. This model is an illustration of how a company can craft its own unique approach, while maintaining the integrity of the process improvement logic. This approach permits local management and local teams to progress through identification of key customer requirements, quantify quality costs, prioritize improvement opportunities, and celebrate improved performance in an ever-repeating cycle. The Ft. Sanders Health System Employee Involvement Policy suggests a straightforward approach to guide the selection of teams and employee involvement.

Appendix D: Employee TQM Orientation and Department TQM Orientation. Two sample orientation sessions are highlighted in this appendix. The first is an example of a two-hour CEO and senior management-led employee orientation session providing a basic understanding of common quality requirements, importance of process variation, the supplier-action-customer chain, and storyboarding. The second is a 90-minute CEO or senior management-led department orientation imparting the notions of cost of poor quality (waste, rework, unnecessary complexity) and the importance of department visioning.

Appendix E: Self-Assessment. A sample annual self-assessment, jointly created by the SunHealth Alliance and Johnson & Johnson, illustrates a standardized scored approach for a health care organization assessment utilizing the Baldrige Award section heads as a baseline criterion set.

Appendix F: Capital Budget Flowchart and Product Development Flowchart. This appendix contains two flowcharts, capital allocation process and product development flowchart, illustrating how one organization, West Paces Medical Center, revised its approach for the prioritization of capital allocation and product development. The first provides a flowchart of the converted capital allocation philosophy to support the organization's vision. The flowchart and accompanying Department Capital Expenditure Request Form guide department managers through a process to analyze the degree to which capital equipment acquisition supports the organization's vision. The second illustrates how quality planning tools reformed the manner in which product development work progressed.

Appendix G: MedFirst Integrated Health System Quality Improvement Plan. An example of an integrated health system quality improvement plan is highlighted in this appendix. The plan provides a sample vision, guiding principles, methods, and infrastructure.

Appendix H: Sample Quality Audit Plan. This appendix illustrates an organization-wide quality audit and assessment plan

Appendix I: Sample Data Collection Plans. Two sample department process data collection plans are provided in this appendix.

Appendix A

The Juran Quality Improvement Process

THE JURAN QUALITY IMPROVEMENT PROCESS

1 Identify a Project

2 Establish the Project

3 Diagnose the Cause

4 Remedy the Cause

5 Hold the Gains

6 Replicate Results and Nominate New Projects

THE JURAN QUALITY IMPROVEMENT PROCESS

1 Identify a Project
- Nominate projects.
- Evaluate projects.
- Select a project.
- Ask: Is it quality improvement?

2 Establish the Project

3 Diagnose the Cause

4 Remedy the Cause

5 Hold the Gains

6 Replicate Results and Nominate New Projects

THE JURAN QUALITY IMPROVEMENT PROCESS

1 Identify a Project

2 Establish the Project
- Prepare a mission statement.
- Select a team.
- Verify the mission.

3 Diagnose the Cause

4 Remedy the Cause

5 Hold the Gains

6 Replicate Results and Nominate New Projects

THE JURAN QUALITY IMPROVEMENT PROCESS

1 Identify a Project

2 Establish the Project

3 Diagnose the Cause
- Analyze symptoms.
- Confirm or modify the mission.
- Formulate theories.
- Test theories.
- Identify root cause(s).

4 Remedy the Cause

5 Hold the Gains

6 Replicate Results and Nominate New Projects

THE JURAN QUALITY IMPROVEMENT PROCESS

1 Identify a Project

2 Establish the Project

3 Diagnose the Cause

4 Remedy the Cause
- Evaluate alternatives.
- Design remedy.
- Design controls.
- Design for culture.
- Prove effectiveness.
- Implement.

5 Hold the Gains

6 Replicate Results and Nominate New Projects

THE JURAN QUALITY IMPROVEMENT PROCESS

1 Identify a Project

2 Establish the Project

3 Diagnose the Cause

4 Remedy the Cause

5 Hold the Gains
- Design effective quality controls.
- Foolproof the remedy.
- Audit the controls.

6 Replicate Results and Nominate New Projects

THE JURAN QUALITY IMPROVEMENT PROCESS

1 Identify a Project

2 Establish the Project

3 Diagnose the Cause

4 Remedy the Cause

5 Hold the Gains

6 Replicate Results and Nominate New Projects
- Replicate the project results.
- Nominate new projects.

Appendix B

The HCA FOCUS-PDCA Model

Find a process to improve

1. State the process that constitutes an opportunity for improvement and tell why that is so.

2. Indicate the current owner of the process.

3. Explain how the suppliers and customers, including the ultimate external customers, are related to the process.

Organize a team that knows the process

1. Attach individual photos of team members large enough for the people to be recognized from at least six feet away. (Individual photos will allow for any later changes in team composition.)

2. List each team member's name, title or job description, and team role, such as process owner, team leader, facilitator, and so on.

Clarify current knowledge of the process

1. Describe the detailed steps of the process using a flowchart. Indicate the boundaries within which this improvement effort is focused.

2. If necessary redundancy or complexity was identified that should be eliminated before proceeding, then display how the PDCA cycle was used to make the process change.

3. If steps in the process were being performed differently, then display how the PDCA cycle was used to change the process based on the agreed-upon current best method.

HOSPITALWIDE QUALITY IMPROVEMENT PROCESS^{SM}
STRATEGY FOR IMPROVEMENT

FOCUS-PDCA^{SM}

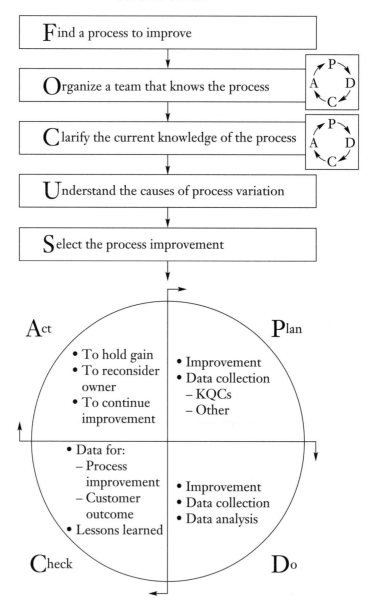

4. If available, display data over time on the results of the process performance as viewed by the customer of the process, using a time plot or run chart.

Understand causes of process variation

1. State the operational definition(s) of the KQC(s) of the process. Describe how you involved the customers of the process to determine the KQC(s).

2. Describe the data collection plan developed to obtain measurements of the KQC(s).

3. Display the KQC(s) of the process over time using a control chart or run chart.

4. If special causes are indicated, then describe how they were eliminated. (A cause-and-effect chart may be a helpful starting point.) Display how the PDCA cycle was used to eliminate the special causes and prevent them from recurring.

5. Display the cause-and-effect chart used to describe the common sources or causes of variation in the process under study.

6. Describe the data collection methods used to gather information about the relationship between the common sources of variation and the KQC(s).

7. Display the results of the data collection graphically using a Pareto diagram or other appropriate displays.

Select the process improvement

1. State a clear, simple description of the proposed process improvement.

2. Describe the criteria and methods used to help you select the process improvement.

Plan the improvement and continued data collection

1. Summarize the planned improvement to be introduced in the process.

2. Explain how the planned improvements will be made.

3. State what data will be collected, indicating how the data relate to the KQC(s).

4. If possible, state how the planned improvement in the process will relate to the ultimate external customer.

Do the improvement, data collection, and analysis

1. Describe the improvement steps that were actually taken. Include any changes from the original plan.

2. Display the instrument used to collect the information.

3. Display the summarized and analyzed data using the appropriate graphical format, such as a run chart, pre-post Pareto diagram, and so on.

4. State what was learned by the improvement effort.

Check and study the results

1. Reproduce the displays generated in the "U" step using data gathered after the process change was made.

2. State how the improvement affects the larger context of the process, the hospital, and its external customers.

3. Describe the major lessons learned in the process of working together as a team to make the improvement.

4. If known savings have been identified as a result of the improvement efforts, state what they are and how you know they exist. List some of the less apparent savings attributable to the process change.

Act to hold the gain and to continue to improve the process

1. Describe the steps taken to hold the gain being made. Include a new flowchart to illustrate process changes.

2. Indicate if the process ownership should be changed.

3. Tell how the KQC(s) will continue to be monitored.

4. Explain how the process improvement is being moved from the pilot stage to more widespread implementation.

5. Describe briefly the next steps for the continuous improvement of the process, possibly using a Pareto diagram or other graphical tools.

Appendix C

The StorageTek Model and Ft. Sanders Health System Policy

QUALITY IMPROVEMENT PROCESS

9. Recognize and reward

1. Document process flows and identify process ownership

2. Identify customer requirements and establish effective measurements

8. Maintain the solution(s)

7. Implement plans and monitor/measure results

CONTINUOUS PROCESS IMPROVEMENT

3. Identify quality costs

6. Present improvement plans to management

4. Identify and prioritize improvement opportunities

5. Organize a team(s) and develop improvement plans

Continuous Improvement

Continuous improvement is the third quality concept pictured in our Excellence Through Quality triangle. A belief in continuous improvement means we cannot be satisfied with just meeting current customer requirements. In order to survive in a competitive marketplace we must strive to continuously and relentlessly improve products and services. The method StorageTek has chosen for accomplishing this ideal is the use of the Quality Improvement Process.

Quality Improvement Process Overview

In steps 1–3, we become intimately familiar with our current process. The activities to accomplish this and why they are done is summarized below.

Step 1:
Activities
- Documenting process flows
- Identifying process ownership

Purpose and Value
- Understand how our process currently operates
- Identify customers and suppliers

Step 2:
Activities
- Determining customer requirements
- Establishing effective measures

Purpose and Value
- Communication
- Establish objective way to evaluate your process

Step 3:
Activities
- Identifying quality costs

Purpose and Value
- Understand the magnitude of nonvalue-added activities

Upon completion of Step 3, we have a great deal of information which we can use to proceed with the Quality Improvement Process. In Steps 4–6 we use that information to plan our involvement activities.

Step 4:
Activities
- Identifying improvement opportunities
- Prioritizing improvement opportunities

Purpose and Value
- Determine where to direct limited resources

Step 5:
Activities
- Developing improvement plans to address opportunities

Purpose and Value
- Ensure use of a systematic approach

Step 6: (as necessary)
>   **Activities**
>   - Presenting plans to management
>
>   **Purpose and Value**
>   - Obtain necessary buy-in and resources
>   - Allow management to ensure this plan fits in with business objectives

Once the planning is done and resources are obtained, it is time to implement.

Step 7:
>   **Activities**
>   - Implementing solutions
>   - Measuring effectiveness of solution
>
>   **Purpose and Value**
>   - Effect change by implementing improvement plans
>   - Determine effectiveness of changes in an objective manner

To ensure solutions remain effective over time:

Step 8:
>   **Activities**
>   - Standardizing the improved process
>
>   **Purpose and Value**
>   - Maintain gains in performance

In Step 9, both team and individual contributions to quality improvement should be recognized and rewarded as appropriate.

Step 9:
>   **Activities**
>   - Management providing recognition and/or rewards
>
>   **Purpose and Value**
>   - Reinforce the behavior you want repeated
>   - Improve morale and trust in the system

As you can see, the Quality Improvement Process gives us a common process and language for continuous quality improvement.

Fort Sanders Health System
CQI Policy
Team Formation/Employee Involvement

System leadership within the Fort Sanders Health System must be committed to creating an organizational culture that empowers employees. Together, we can meet and exceed the clinical and service quality expectations of our customers, while creating an ideal environment in which to work and grow. Managers are leaders—identifying goals, then guiding and inspiring empowered employees who develop creative strategies to accomplish quality goals.

The following CQI principles and quality guidelines are intended to ensure that every employee is encouraged and empowered with opportunities to contribute to the CQI process.

- Every employee has the right to participate.
- It is the responsibility of leadership to assure that this right is supported—that the path is clear.
- CQI participants in defined roles will be allocated two hours of work time per week for project involvement.
- Team facilitators will be included in extensive training as well as team support. Their need for leadership access to resolve barriers and communicate system goals is fundamental.
- It is understood that trainers will be allowed adequate preparation time for a class and may require up to eight hours of teaching time per module, per class, in addition to Train the Trainer sessions of two days.
- The role of Quality Councils at both system and facility levels is to support the CQI process, not to control it. Quality Councils will support resource allocation in conjunction with team formation.

We anticipate that team projects will be generated as a result of:

a) CSI results

b) spontaneous employee identification

c) leadership commissions

d) clinical quality indicators

e) the Tennessee Quality Award feedback report

In all cases, we recognize that any process improvements ultimately impact customer satisfaction.

This policy was approved by the
System Quality Council on May 19, 1992
Revised-November 24, 1992
Revised-November 15, 1994

Appendix D

Employee TQM Orientation and Department TQM Orientation

I. Introduction   10 minutes

—Deming plan

—History of West Paces quality improvement process

II. What is quality?   15 minutes

Flip chart: "What brand names do you associate with quality?"

After: "What features of these companies caused you to identify them?" (look for consistency, dependability...

Teaching point: Why is it that we do not measure the consistency or the dependability of major processes within the hospital such as the medication administration system?

Deming points out to us that reducing variation (i.e., dependability) is a major factor in quality improvement.

III. Deming cycle of continuous improvement versus traditional western management   10 minutes

—22 ways to get a Coke

—Eight times we inspect the presence of lab, X-ray, and EKG reports in our OR process

IV.   Quality improvement policy   20 minutes
V.   List of quality improvement teams   5 minutes
VI.   Customer-mindedness   10 minutes
       Process-mindedness
       Statistical-mindedness
       Create supplier-input-action-output-customer chart
       for cholecystectomy on flip chart
VII.   FOCUS-PDCA: group exercise   20 minutes
       With group input, work with the seven statistical
       tools to reduce the length of time of the medication
       administration process
VIII. Introduction of the storyboard   5 minutes
IX.   Question and answer   5 minutes
       Total

Focus on Continuous Improvement
Department-Specific Orientation

Agenda

15 minutes	I.	Introduction
		Summary: mission, vision, and road map
30 minutes	II.	Exercise: Who are your customers?
15 minutes	III.	Exercise: Where is there waste, rework, and unnecessary complication?
15 minutes	IV.	What is your department's purpose?
		Exercise: key words, concepts, phrases
15 minutes	V.	Success stories
		Quality improvement teams with examples of flowcharts, control charts, FOCUS-PDCA

Appendix E

Self-Assessment

Created by SunHealth Alliance, with assistance from Juran Institute and Johnson & Johnson.

Self-Assessment of Healthcare Organizational Performance

This survey is based on the Malcolm Baldrige National Quality Award. It is designed to assist healthcare organizations in an assessment of their implementation of total quality management and its effects on organizational performance. It will allow leadership to identify strengths and areas for improvement in the seven major categories relating to quality management: leadership, information and analysis, strategic quality planning, human resource development and management, quality assessment of products and services, quality and operational results, and customer focus and satisfaction. Vignettes or brief case studies are provided to highlight excellence in a healthcare setting for each category. You may use the vignettes to gain a better understanding of how the criteria are put into action. These profiles were designed to highlight some of the important characteristics of a successful total quality management implementation.

How to Use This Survey. This survey was developed for use as a consensus building tool regarding total quality management and organizational performance. It can be used as a barometer of current status and as a vehicle for realignment and/or change. Following is a recommended strategy for using this survey:

ACTION	DATE	RESPONSIBLE
1. CEO decides to conduct an organizational assessment.		CEO
2. CEO decides who to include on the 'assessment team.' *Include all direct reports.*		CEO
3. CEO sends memo and/or meets with assessment team to participate in self-assessment process. *See sample memo on page 210.*		CEO
4. Meeting with the assessment team is scheduled to discuss the process, the survey and how it will be used.		CEO
5. Date is set for assessment team to review survey results.		
6. Person is designated to collect tally sheets from each respondent and average the scores for the group.		
7. Team members submit scores to designated person.		
8. Designated person presents scores in meeting with assessment team.		
9. Assessment team identifies organizational strengths and areas for improvement based on scores.		
10. A short- and/or long-term plan is developed based on the team's assessment.		
11. The assessment team meets to follow up on action plans.		

Additional Instructions

- Each member of the assessment team completes the survey individually.

- Identify any relevant key facts, strengths, and areas for improvement and write them in the comments section after each category. These notes will be helpful in the group discussion.

- To ensure that the latter categories are given ample attention, please complete the survey in two sittings.

- Tally your scores for each category after you have completed the entire survey and enter them in the grid on page 230.

- A designated person will then average the scores for the assessment team.

How to Interpret the Scores

- You may use these scores to compare one another's perceptions of current organizational performance as a place to begin your discussion and action plan. Remember, the discussion is what is important, not the scores.

- The assessment team should address those categories that were disparately scored or received low scores compared to the possible scores. Providing data and information to substantiate your perceptions will help facilitate consensus building.

- Recognition of organizational strengths should also be a part of the assessment.

- Short- and long-term plans may be developed to include actions that will address areas for improvement while reinforcing existing strengths.

Sample Memorandum Announcing the Process

TO: (List of Assessment Team Members)
FROM: (CEO Name)
DATE: (Date)
SUBJ: Self-assessment of organizational performance

For the last (___ months/years) we have been actively involved in developing a quality-based organization. SunHealth has developed a tool that will be useful in our evaluation of our quality management process to date. Attached is a copy of the survey that I hope will provide us with useful information about where we stand today and guide us in planning for the future.

Please complete the questionnaire individually and note any thoughts or comments you have about each section. (Name of coordinator) will collect your scoring grid and average the scores for the group. We will then meet to discuss our perceptions and develop an action plan to move forward. In addition to our internal analysis, our organization's data will be compiled with that received from others in The SunHealth Alliance.

Your input is valuable to the continued success of our organization. Please give your score grid to (name of coordinator) by (date). Our meeting to discuss the results has been scheduled for (date) and will be held in the (location).

Please contact me if you have any questions or comments.

Self-Rating Scale

0   NOT SURE how my organization compares to this statement.

1   STRONGLY DISAGREE: This statement DOES NOT DESCRIBE my organization AT ALL. There is no evidence of this activity in our facility.

2   DISAGREE: This statement generally DOES NOT DESCRIBE my organization. There is little evidence of this activity in our organization.

3   AGREE: This statement GENERALLY DESCRIBES my organization. There is a great deal of evidence of this activity in our organization.

4   STRONGLY AGREE: This statement DEFINITELY DESCRIBES my organization. This activity pervades our organization.

I. Leadership

The Leadership category examines how senior executives create and sustain a clear vision and visible quality values, along with a management system to guide all activities of the organization toward quality excellence. Also examined are the senior executives' and the organization's commitment to cooperative structures in fostering excellence.

Vignette for Leadership. Deborah Dodson, CEO of Southwood Health System, invited the quality management team to perform a total quality fitness audit on her executive office. Ms. Dodson is known for walking around at all hours and asking employees how she can help them. The first four hours of the monthly senior leadership team meeting are devoted to quality improvement. Through quality improvement efforts, length of stay for 10 selected DRGs has decreased by 40 percent, while improvements in outcomes and customer satisfaction have been noted. Ms. Dodson holds all management accountable for having a people-first attitude, displaying impeccable service to internal and external customers while keeping costs down and revenue up. All employees have been given a wallet-sized card printed with their quality policy: total customer satisfaction. Ms. Dodson holds regular meetings with her management team regarding ways to demonstrate the hospital's vision and values. Southwood reduced the number of managers by 45 percent and gave them more contact with their customers on a daily basis. Employees are encouraged to borrow good ideas from other healthcare systems and replicate them at Southwood. The attitude that personal success is derived from team success permeates all areas of the organization. Administration has a positive and active working relationship with physicians and the board of directors.

Please use the self-rating scale to indicate the extent to which you believe each statement describes your organization.

Evaluation Statements

1. Senior executives and medical staff leaders provide leadership and are personally involved in quality-related activities (for example, goal setting, planning, reviewing organization quality performance, communicating with employees and physicians and recognizing employee contributions).

   Circle one: 0   1   2   3   4

2. Overall leadership of the quality effort is clearly defined, has multi-disciplinary representation and includes the senior leaders in nursing, medical staff, general administration and the board of directors.

   Circle one: 0   1   2   3   4

3. Senior executives and medical staff leaders communicate quality achievements and goals outside the organization to such groups as national, state, community, professional, education, government and other healthcare organizations.

   Circle one: 0   1   2   3   4

4. Our organization has a written vision, policy, mission or guidelines that demonstrate its quality values.

   Circle one: 0   1   2   3   4

5. We have a clearly defined communication system to project the organization's vision and quality values both internally and externally.

   Circle one: 0   1   2   3   4

6. Leadership and medical staff leaders regularly evaluate how well the vision and quality values have been adopted throughout the organization and continuously find ways to reinforce management, employee and physician adoption of these values.

   Circle one: 0   1   2   3   4

7. Senior executives involve and encourage leadership throughout the organization.

   Circle one: 0   1   2   3   4

8. Our organization provides ways for promoting cooperation between various professional disciplines and among all levels of management across different functions.

   Circle one: 0   1   2   3   4

Self-Rating Scale

0   NOT SURE how my organization compares to this statement.

1   STRONGLY DISAGREE: This statement DOES NOT DESCRIBE my organization AT ALL. There is no evidence of this activity in our facility.

2   DISAGREE: This statement generally DOES NOT DESCRIBE my organization. There is little evidence of this activity in our organization.

3   AGREE: This statement GENERALLY DESCRIBES my organization. There is a great deal of evidence of this activity in our organization.

4   STRONGLY AGREE: This statement DEFINITELY DESCRIBES my organization. This activity pervades our organization.

9. Leadership regularly reviews key quality indicators to assess organizational performance.

   Circle one: 0   1   2   3   4

10. Actions are taken to assist areas not performing according to quality plans or goals.

   Circle one: 0   1   2   3   4

11. Our policies and practices reflect sound business ethics, waste management, environmental protection, and public health and safety.

   Circle one: 0   1   2   3   4

12. Employees are encouraged to become involved in quality activities outside of the organization.

   Circle one: 0   1   2   3   4

Comments regarding key facts, strengths and areas for improvement:

_____

_____

_____

_____

_____

II. Information and Analysis

The Information and Analysis category examines the scope, validity, use and management of data and information that underlie the organization's overall quality management system. Also examined is the adequacy of the data, information and analysis to support a responsive, prevention-based approach to quality and customer satisfaction built upon action based on facts, data and analysis.

Vignette for Information and Analysis. The CEO, board members, medical staff leaders and all managers at MacInnes Healthcare System received training on how to use statistical tools to support their quality efforts. Organizational leaders and employees are expected to use quality data to track progress and identify problems and solutions. Fifteen key quality indicators that correlate the highest with customer satisfaction were identified and each component is measured, documented and reported to the board by each of the system's six hospitals (examples: number of delighted patients and post-operative rate of return to work). External customer focus groups are conducted to validate the components that are measured and to determine if the efforts are having an impact on customer satisfaction. An ongoing process determines the usefulness of the data that are collected and the reports generated.

Evaluation Statements

13. Our organization has selected key quality indicators that correlate the highest with internal and external customer satisfaction.

    Circle one: 0   1   2   3   4

14. Challenging benchmarks have been selected to support quality planning, evaluation and improvement. (For example, competitive and benchmark data are used on patient outcomes, service quality, customer satisfaction, supplier performance, employee data, business processes and support services.)

    Circle one: 0   1   2   3   4

15. Our organization uses clearly defined processes to ensure reliability, consistency, standardization, review and timely update of quality-related information.

    Circle one: 0   1   2   3   4

Self-Rating Scale
0   NOT SURE how my organization compares to this statement.

1   STRONGLY DISAGREE: This statement DOES NOT DESCRIBE my organization AT ALL. There is no evidence of this activity in our facility.

2   DISAGREE: This statement generally DOES NOT DESCRIBE my organization. There is little evidence of this activity in our organization.

3   AGREE: This statement GENERALLY DESCRIBES my organization. There is a great deal of evidence of this activity in our organization.

4   STRONGLY AGREE: This statement DEFINITELY DESCRIBES my organization. This activity pervades our organization.

16. Meaningful data are collected, analyzed and used to support planning and operational priorities, review overall quality performance and improve clinical outcomes, business processes and support services.

    Circle one: 0   1   2   3   4

17. Leaders ensure that effective mechanisms exist to communicate and coordinate quality improvement priorities and activities across functional lines.

    Circle one: 0   1   2   3   4

Comments regarding key facts, strengths and areas of improvement:

_____

_____

_____

_____

_____

_____

_____

_____

_____

_____

_____

III. Strategic Quality Planning

The Strategic Quality Planning category examines the organization's planning process for achieving or retaining a quality leadership position and how the organization integrates quality improvement planning into overall organizational planning. Also examined are the organization's short-term and longer-term plans to achieve and/or sustain a quality leadership position.

Vignette for Strategic Quality Planning. Saranac Regional Medical Center has so tightly integrated its quality planning and business planning processes that the hospital now has only one plan that links all business and quality initiatives. The hospital's benchmarking process has been deployed to the work unit level. They benchmark performance for 55 processes in 10 critical clinical and non-clinical areas. Customer satisfaction is central to all short- and long-term goal setting throughout the hospital. Processes chosen for project teams are directly tied to strategic goals.

Evaluation Statements

18. Our organization has established short-term and long-term plans to achieve and maintain a quality leadership position in target markets.

    Circle one: 0   1   2   3   4

19. We use customer requirements, process capabilities, competitive data and supplier abilities to develop overall strategic plans.

    Circle one: 0   1   2   3   4

20. Strategic plans and goals are implemented and reviewed among all areas of the organization and with external suppliers.

    Circle one: 0   1   2   3   4

21. There is a direct link between strategic goals and objectives and departmental/service line goals and objectives throughout the organization.

    Circle one: 0   1   2   3   4

Self-Rating Scale
  0 NOT SURE how my organization compares to this statement.

  1 STRONGLY DISAGREE: This statement DOES NOT DESCRIBE my organization AT ALL. There is no evidence of this activity in our facility.

  2 DISAGREE: This statement generally DOES NOT DESCRIBE my organization. There is little evidence of this activity in our organization.

  3 AGREE: This statement GENERALLY DESCRIBES my organization. There is a great deal of evidence of this activity in our organization.

  4 STRONGLY AGREE: This statement DEFINITELY DESCRIBES my organization. This activity pervades our organization.

22. Goal setting and strategic planning processes are evaluated and improved.

    Circle one: 0   1   2   3   4

23. Our organization has established major quality goals and strategies to achieve these goals.

    Circle one: 0   1   2   3   4

Comments regarding key facts, strengths and areas of improvement:

_____

_____

_____

_____

_____

_____

_____

_____

_____

_____

_____

IV. Human Resource Development and Management

The Human Resource Development and Management category examines the effectiveness of the organization's efforts to develop and realize the full potential of the work force, including management and physicians, and to maintain a work environment conducive to full participation, empowerment, quality leadership, and personal and organizational growth.

Vignette for Human Resource Development and Management. Stamper General Hospital developed a comprehensive program to measure all of its customers' expectations including internal customers (i.e., employees). If employees do not rate management leadership at least as high this year as last year on the organization's annual employee survey, no one in management receives any bonus money for the entire fiscal year. In addition, the process includes peer evaluation and "one-up" evaluations whereby everyone provides feedback to the person two levels above regarding his or her immediate supervisor. All managers and employees receive a minimum of two weeks of training a year in quality management tools, techniques and principles. Stamper General has adopted a "Power Down" concept which empowers employees with decision rights. Key criteria are: (1) Is it good for the customer? (2) Is it good for the organization? (3) If yes to both, then do it. Exemplary individual and team performance is recognized on a quarterly basis. Patients are contacted by their primary, in-hospital caregiver after they return home to determine the status of the patients and to receive feedback about their experience while in the hospital. Turnover for nurses and other professionals decreased from 20 percent to 9.4 percent while employee absenteeism went from 5 percent to 1.9 percent since 1989. In addition, the hospital has a leading edge benefits and wellness program. The program provides incentives to employees who improve their personal health status. Stamper General is considered an "employer of choice" in its region.

Evaluation Statements

24. Our human resource plans (including training, development, hiring, employee involvement, empowerment and recognition) are derived from our quality goals, strategies and plans.

   Circle one: 0   1   2   3   4

Self-Rating Scale

0   NOT SURE how my organization compares to this statement.

1   STRONGLY DISAGREE: This statement DOES NOT DESCRIBE my organization AT ALL. There is no evidence of this activity in our facility.

2   DISAGREE: This statement generally DOES NOT DESCRIBE my organization. There is little evidence of this activity in our organization.

3   AGREE: This statement GENERALLY DESCRIBES my organization. There is a great deal of evidence of this activity in our organization.

4   STRONGLY AGREE: This statement DEFINITELY DESCRIBES my organization. This activity pervades our organization.

25. We have an effective system to assess and monitor the need for quality education and training for physicians and various types of employees.

   Circle one: 0   1   2   3   4

26. The amount of quality education and training received by physicians and employees has increased substantially over time.

   Circle one: 0   1   2   3   4

27. Our organization has useful measures to evaluate and improve the effectiveness of quality education and training activities.

   Circle one: 0   1   2   3   4

28. Support for the organization's quality objectives is achieved through employee and physician recognition, reward and performance measurement systems.

   Circle one: 0   1   2   3   4

29. Individual and group contributions to quality are recognized and rewarded.

   Circle one: 0   1   2   3   4

30. We consistently inform staff of quality improvement activities and how those activities support our quality vision and goals.

   Circle one: 0   1   2   3   4

31. Middle managers are provided training on how to encourage continuous quality improvement.

   Circle one: 0   1   2   3   4

32. We use key indicators to evaluate and improve our reward and performance systems.

   Circle one: 0   1   2   3   4

33. Factors contributing to employee and physician satisfaction are considered in quality improvement activities.

   Circle one: 0   1   2   3   4

34 Employee development is supported through mobility, flexibility and retraining.

   Circle one: 0   1   2   3   4

35. Special services and facilities such as fitness, counseling and recreational or cultural opportunities are available to employees.

   Circle one: 0   1   2   3   4

Comments regarding key facts, strengths and areas of improvement:

_____

_____

_____

_____

_____

_____

_____

_____

_____

_____

Self-Rating Scale

  0   NOT SURE how my organization compares to this statement.

  1   STRONGLY DISAGREE: This statement DOES NOT DESCRIBE my organiza-
       tion AT ALL. There is no evidence of this activity in our facility.

  2   DISAGREE: This statement generally DOES NOT DESCRIBE my organization.
       There is little evidence of this activity in our organization.

  3   AGREE: This statement GENERALLY DESCRIBES my organization. There is a
       great deal of evidence of this activity in our organization.

  4   STRONGLY AGREE: This statement DEFINITELY DESCRIBES my organiza-
       tion. This activity pervades our organization.

V. Quality Assessment of Products and Services

Categories V and VI are very closely related; therefore, they will be
explained together. Category V, the Quality Assessment of Products
and Services category, examines the systematic processes used by the
organization for assuring quality of products, initiatives and services.
Also examined is the integration of process control with continuous
quality improvement of services. Category VI, Quality and
Operational Results, is outcome oriented and examines quality levels
and quality improvement based upon objective measures derived from
analyses of customer requirements/expectations and of the organization's operations. Also examined are current quality levels in relation
to other healthcare organizations.

Vignette for Quality Assessment of Products and Services.
James Wood Memorial Hospital implemented a quality review system
which measures and monitors quality for all areas of the hospital. The
emphasis of the system is on quality improvement rather than traditional quality assurance. Each service line defines its services and customer needs and measures its performance frequently relative to the
criteria outlined in the quality review system. Data are assessed using
internal and external databases. The organization has an integrated
quality information system that tracks relevant data on patient,
employee, physician, patient families, payors and community satisfaction, outcomes of care, suppliers and key process characteristics. Data
are actively used by quality planning and quality improvement teams
throughout the hospital. Currently, James Wood Memorial has 50
project teams that are focused on designing key organizational
processes; the goal is to have every employee and physician participate
on at least one project team every two years. Suppliers' quality guide-

lines have been developed and are monitored on a regular basis. Supplier representatives are also active on project teams to ensure product and process improvements.

Evaluation Statements

36. Our organization effectively measures the quality of its systems, processes, practices, products and services.

    Circle one: 0   1   2   3   4

37. When we design new services and processes, we select key process performance characteristics based on customer requirements.

    Circle one: 0   1   2   3   4

38. When we design new services and processes, we determine appropriate performance levels and measure our performance relative to these levels.

    Circle one: 0   1   2   3   4

39. We review and validate new product, service and process designs by considering current and future processes and supplier capabilities and requirements.

    Circle one: 0   1   2   3   4

40. We have identified key indicators of quality and operational performance and have an effective mechanism to monitor in-process and end-of-process measurements.

    Circle one: 0   1   2   3   4

41. We have a specific mechanism to identify significant variations in processes and outputs and a methodology to define and correct root causes.

    Circle one: 0   1   2   3   4

42. We use benchmarking information, research, technology, information from customers and challenging goals to improve the quality of our services, business processes, suppliers and overall operational performance.

    Circle one: 0   1   2   3   4

43. We design our key business processes and support services to meet customer and operational performance requirements.

    Circle one: 0   1   2   3   4

Self-Rating Scale

0   NOT SURE how my organization compares to this statement.

1   STRONGLY DISAGREE: This statement DOES NOT DESCRIBE my organization AT ALL. There is no evidence of this activity in our facility.

2   DISAGREE: This statement generally DOES NOT DESCRIBE my organization. There is little evidence of this activity in our organization.

3   AGREE: This statement GENERALLY DESCRIBES my organization. There is a great deal of evidence of this activity in our organization.

4   STRONGLY AGREE: This statement DEFINITELY DESCRIBES my organization. This activity pervades our organization.

44. Processes are continuously improved. Opportunities for improvement are identified from day-to-day process control, patient outcomes, competitive data, evaluation of all process steps, process benchmark data and other sources.

Circle one: 0   1   2   3   4

45. We define and communicate the organization's specific quality requirements to suppliers.

Circle one: 0   1   2   3   4

46. Through appropriate mechanisms (audits, etc.) we ensure that our suppliers meet our quality requirements.

Circle one: 0   1   2   3   4

47. We have an active, current strategy to improve the quality and responsiveness of external suppliers through partnerships, training, incentives, recognition and/or supplier selection.

Circle one: 0   1   2   3   4

Comments regarding key facts, strengths and areas of improvement:

_____

_____

_____

_____

_____

_____

_____

VI. Quality and Operational Results

See explanation under Category V.

Vignette for Quality and Operational Results. Idylwild Park Rehabilitation Center monitors its service through a variety of key measures that relate to customer requirements. It has a clearly defined strategy to compare itself with major competitors in its area, other caregivers and non-healthcare organizations throughout the world. Employees use quality management statistical methods and tools every day to measure and monitor their processes. All employees know who their internal and external suppliers are and how their external suppliers compare to other potential suppliers.

Evaluation Statements

48. We monitor trends in service quality through key measures derived from customer requirements and process analysis.

    Circle one: 0   1   2   3   4

49. We compare our current product and service quality levels with principal competitors in our key markets, healthcare industry averages, industry leaders and national leaders.

    Circle one: 0   1   2   3   4

50. We monitor trends and current levels of key quality measures for our processes, operations and support services.

    Circle one: 0   1   2   3   4

51. We compare our measures of quality for processes, operations and support services with industry averages, industry leaders and national leaders.

    Circle one: 0   1   2   3   4

52. We measure trends and current levels of external supplier quality.

    Circle one: 0   1   2   3   4

53. We compare our external supplier quality with that of competitors and/or with other appropriate benchmarks.

    Circle one: 0   1   2   3   4

Self-Rating Scale

0   NOT SURE how my organization compares to this statement.

1   STRONGLY DISAGREE: This statement DOES NOT DESCRIBE my organization AT ALL. There is no evidence of this activity in our facility.

2   DISAGREE: This statement generally DOES NOT DESCRIBE my organization.
There is little evidence of this activity in our organization.

3   AGREE: This statement GENERALLY DESCRIBES my organization. There is a
great deal of evidence of this activity in our organization.

4   STRONGLY AGREE: This statement DEFINITELY DESCRIBES my organization. This activity pervades our organization.

54. Every employee can suggest a quality improvement study
based on comparative data.

Circle one: 0   1   2   3   4

Comments regarding key facts, strengths and areas of improvement:

_____

_____

_____

_____

_____

_____

_____

_____

VII.   Customer Focus and Satisfaction

The Customer Focus and Satisfaction category examines the organization's knowledge of, responsiveness to and ability to meet the requirements and expectations of its customers. Also examined are current levels and trends in customer satisfaction and community perception.

Vignette for Customer Focus and Satisfaction. McLean Health System instituted an extensive customer feedback strategy that includes surveying more than half of all patients discharged from its facilities. In one year alone, it queried more than 20,000 patients. When 70 percent of the respondents indicated a need for more health information, McLean introduced a free, 24-hour Ask-A-Nurse telephone line to answer questions and provide referrals to other community health resources. The service responds to over 800 calls per day. Seven percent of the patients surveyed indicated that they would not return to McLean again. The majority cited problems with admitting procedures. A quality improvement team was established to refine the admitting process to make it a less stressful experience for everyone. Customer focus groups are also conducted on a quarterly basis to obtain feedback, determine the effectiveness of process improvements, share ideas about clinical process design and learn more about future customer expectations in a variety of service areas. All employees are given the authority, responsibility and training to handle customer complaints in a timely way. Employees also use a system that allows them to record customer feedback immediately. These data are monitored along with other data to determine performance to short- and long- term goals. A component of the recognition and reward system includes acknowledgment of employees who go out of their way to make a customer happy. Customer service standards are developed by teams of employees and physicians and are constantly updated according to customer feedback. Customer complaints are treated as opportunities for improvement rather than inconveniences. Last year, over 93 percent of all customers polled said they believed that McLean health System delivered above average to excellent patient care.

Self-Rating Scale

  0   NOT SURE how my organization compares to this statement.

  1   STRONGLY DISAGREE: This statement DOES NOT DESCRIBE my organization AT ALL. There is no evidence of this activity in our facility.

  2   DISAGREE: This statement generally DOES NOT DESCRIBE my organization. There is little evidence of this activity in our organization.

  3   AGREE: This statement GENERALLY DESCRIBES my organization. There is a great deal of evidence of this activity in our organization.

  4   STRONGLY AGREE: This statement DEFINITELY DESCRIBES my organization. This activity pervades our organization.

Evaluation Statements

55. We determine current and future requirements and expectations of customers through objective surveys, interviews or other appropriate mechanisms.

    Circle one: 0   1   2   3   4

56. We have a process in place to identify and prioritize the importance of service offerings and features to our customers.

    Circle one: 0   1   2   3   4

57. We evaluate and improve our processes for identifying customer requirements and expectations.

    Circle one: 0   1   2   3   4

58. Our customers have easy access to the organization to comment or seek assistance.

    Circle one: 0   1   2   3   4

59. We follow up with customers to assess their satisfaction with services or recent experiences.

    Circle one: 0   1   2   3   4

60. Our employees are specially trained, empowered with decision-making authority, recognized and rewarded for excellent customer service.

    Circle one: 0   1   2   3   4

61. Our technology and logistics support enables customer-contact personnel to provide reliable and responsive service.

    Circle one: 0   1   2   3   4

62. We assess our customer relationship management through such factors as accuracy, timeliness and customer satisfaction and use this information to improve training, technology or business practices.

    Circle one: 0   1   2   3   4

63. We have established well-defined service standards on an organizational and departmental level to meet customer requirements in a timely and effective manner.

    Circle one: 0   1   2   3   4

64. Employees have a role in tracking, evaluating and improving service standards.

    Circle one: 0   1   2   3   4

65. The organization makes commitments to promote customer trust and confidence through various mechanisms.

    Circle one: 0   1   2   3   4

66. Formal and informal complaints made to different organization units are compiled for evaluation and used throughout the organization as appropriate.

    Circle one: 0   1   2   3   4

67. Complaints are analyzed to determine underlying causes and findings are translated into improvements.

    Circle one: 0   1   2   3   4

68. We have an updated, objective and valid process to determine customer satisfaction.

    Circle one: 0   1   2   3   4

69. Customer satisfaction data are analyzed and compared with other indicators such as various utilization rates.

    Circle one: 0   1   2   3   4

70. We monitor trends and current levels of customer satisfaction and segment results by customer groups.

    Circle one: 0   1   2   3   4

71. We monitor major indicators of adverse customer response.

    Circle one: 0   1   2   3   4

Self-Rating Scale
0   NOT SURE how my organization compares to this statement.

1   STRONGLY DISAGREE: This statement DOES NOT DESCRIBE my organization AT ALL. There is no evidence of this activity in our facility.

2   DISAGREE: This statement generally DOES NOT DESCRIBE my organization. There is little evidence of this activity in our organization.

3   AGREE: This statement GENERALLY DESCRIBES my organization. There is a great deal of evidence of this activity in our organization.

4   STRONGLY AGREE: This statement DEFINITELY DESCRIBES my organization. This activity pervades our organization.

72. We compare our customer satisfaction results with industry averages, key competitors and industry and national leaders.

Circle one: 0   1   2   3   4

73. Our organization has received quality-related awards, recognition or ratings from independent organizations, including customers.

Circle one: 0   1   2   3   4

74. We have steadily gained customers and improved customer satisfaction.

Circle one: 0   1   2   3   4

75. Customer feedback indicates that our patients believe we deliver a high quality of care.

Circle one: 0   1   2   3   4

Comments regarding key facts, strengths and areas of improvement:

_____

_____

_____

_____

_____

_____

_____

_____

Scoring Summary

Date: _____ Name: _____

Instructions

1. Transcribe your scores for each category onto this score grid under the column "YOUR SCORE."
2. Place the scores from your fellow staff members in the grid as they become available. You may elect not to reveal the scores of your peers at this time, in which case just leave the "SCORE" columns blank.
3. Record the group average for each category and the range for each category in the columns provided.
4. Sum the total for each column and record it in the "TOTAL" line provided at the bottom of the grid.
5. The "TOTAL," "GROUP SCORE," and "RANGE" columns will be the basis of your initial assessment of your organization.
6. Refer to page 209 and page 231 for scoring interpretation instructions.

CATEGORY	YOUR SCORE	SCORE 2	SCORE 3	SCORE 4	SCORE 5	SCORE 6	SCORE 7	SCORE 8	POSSIBLE SCORE	GROUP SCORE	RANGE
I. Leadership									48		
II. Information and Analysis									20		
III. Strategic Quality Planning									24		
IV. Human Resource Development and Management									48		
V. Quality Assessment									48		
VI. Quality and Operational Results									28		
VII. Customer Focus and Satisfaction									84		
TOTAL									300		

SCORING INTERPRETATIONS

When evaluating the scores for the individual categories, the assessment team should review both the group scores (average) and the range of scores (highest score minus lowest score) for each category.

Reviewing Total Scores

- Discuss whether or not the group score for each category was what the assessment team expected it to be. Discuss your expectations.

- Discuss any variances from your expectations. Use the comments section after each category on your individual survey forms to guide your discussion of that category.

- Develop short- and long-range plans to increase the group score for each category.

Reviewing Ranges

- Determine the ranges for each category.

- In each category where there is a significant difference in the high and low scores, the assessment team should discuss the reasons behind the differing perceptions of organizational performance.

- The assessment team needs to come to a consensus regarding the actual performance of the organization in each category.

Appendix F

Capital Budget Flowchart and Product Development Flowchart

Annual Capital Budgeting Process

Goal: To distribute capital in a way
that supports the hospital's vision
of being the best-value Atlanta
health system by 1996 and
recognized as such.

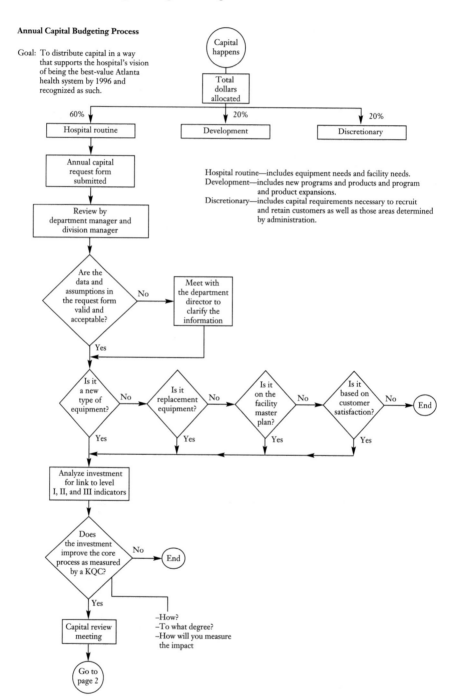

Hospital routine—includes equipment needs and facility needs.
Development—includes new programs and products and program
and product expansions.
Discretionary—includes capital requirements necessary to recruit
and retain customers as well as those areas determined
by administration.

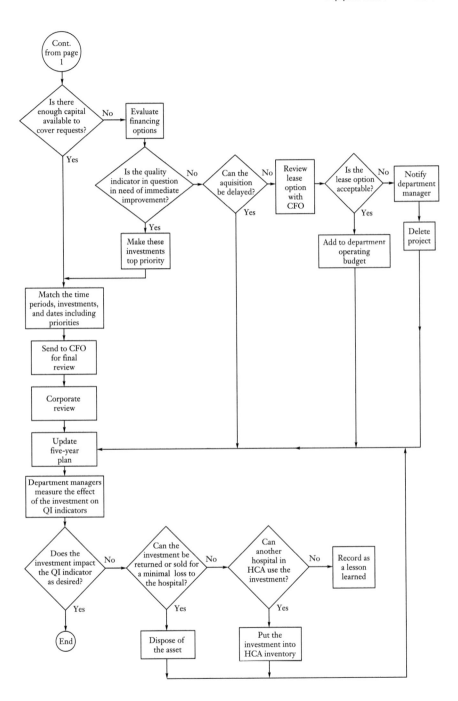

Product Development Flowchart

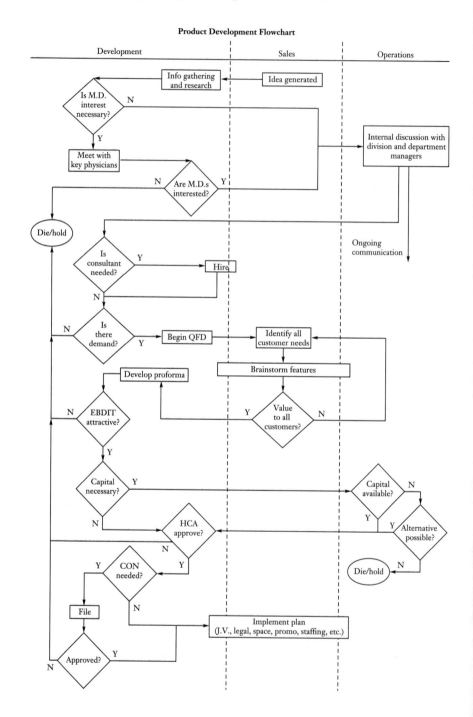

Department capital expenditure request form

Expenditure name: Date form completed:
Department: Department number:
Requested by: Total estimated cost:
Vendor name: (from proforma) $
Equipment category:

Equipment or expenditure description (include make, model, specification preferences, supplier, cost, labor, etc.) _____

_____

_____

_____

_____

_____

_____

_____

_____

What customer(s) of your department (suppliers, physicians, employees, payors, outside auditors, and/or patients) does this investment create value for?

_____

_____

What data have you collected or will collect that will support the assertion that this investment is needed to improve customer satisfaction and/or a departmental quality indicator? (For example, negative trends in rework, accuracy, downtime, increased costs, employee or customer feedback, etc.)

_____

_____

_____

_____

_____

_____

_____

Please describe how this investment will add value in the form of process improvement or increased customer satisfaction. Attach a flowchart of the process that this investment will be a part of.

_____
_____
_____
_____
_____
_____
_____
_____

How will you measure the impact of the investment on customer satisfaction or process improvement? (For example: cycle time, customer brag abouts, downtime, accuracy, etc.)

_____
_____
_____
_____
_____

Is this investment an attempt to improve a departmental quality indicator? If so, which indicator(s)?

_____
_____

Economic cash flow information. Please provide a proforma financial statement for both purchase and lease options (if applicable). To aid you in the development of proformas, a step-by-step guide is included. Please briefly summarized the results below.

_____
_____
_____
_____
_____
_____
_____

Submitted by: _____
Reviewed by: _____

Appendix G

MedFirst Integrated Health System Quality Improvement Plan

Inefficient delivery system

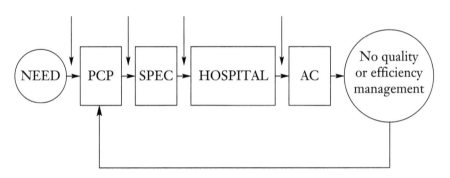

Figure G.1. Inefficient delivery system.

MedFirst health system

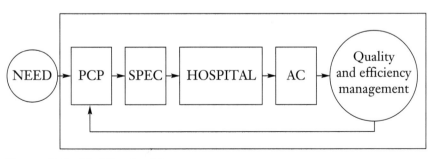

Figure G.2. MedFirst health system.

HCA MedFirst Health System Quality Improvement Plan

August 22, 1993

I. Vision: To be the best-value Atlanta health system by 1996 and recognized as such.

II. Guiding Principles:

    a. TQM-based, in the pursuit of error-free design and reduction of variation in clinical support processes.

    b. Physician and specialist selection will follow an inclusive methodology rather than an exclusive one.

    c. Tailor-made integrated health systems are our primary product, and we will strive to include all desired providers if they make quality standards and agree to TQM participation.

    d. Capitation is the preferred reimbursement method for most providers, except hospitals, in order to align the incentives of all parties towards the improvement of quality and the reduction of clinical utilization.

    e. The best-value integration system will be driven by primary care physicians, utilizing TQM-based seamless flow of information and clinical processes between primary care physicians, specialists, hospitals, and allied providers.

    f. Best-value can only be achieved and maintained through the selection of specialists who are most efficient, lowest resource users, and focus on their patients' achievement of highest health status. In addition they must be champions of a continuous improvement methodology.

    g. Overhead inspection, rework and waste is a deterrent to maintaining best-value. Error-free design is the road to success, using FOCUS-PDCA.

    h. Benchmarking, internal among physicians and external among others, is the primary engine to reduce variation.

    i. Information is the vitamin of continuous improvement and should be widely shared with all partners.

    j. We will seek continuously to manage upstream in the health system as far as possible, drawing an ever larger box around the integrated health system. However, our responsibility for generating measurable benefits to our stockholders will prevent us from expanding the health system beyond our reimbursement boundaries; that is, we will seek to maximize earnings within the reimbursement paradigm accepted by the purchaser of care.

k. We seek long-term partners who share our TQM philosophy. Provider contracts will seek to achieve the gross margin required by each provider while sharing variation in costs within the network so that internal benchmarking will increase the value of the entire MedFirst Health System, while achieving each entity's financial requirements.

l. Utilization reviews, medical director reviews, and other forms of inspection are inherently wasteful to the efficient performance of an integrated health system. Every effort will be made to create error-free clinical processes through the use of internal and external benchmarking selection of efficient specialists by employing FOCUS-PDCA to reduce variation so that inspection and rework are minimized.

III. Methods:

a. Each participating organization is required to maintain an active TQM program, using FOCUS-PDCA or equivalent. A written quality improvement plan with targets will be monitored through the use of the Management Feedback Report.

b. Physicians agree to receive TQM training and to participate in health system sponsored TQM activities.

c. Internal and external benchmarking, seeking to drive in error-free design and reduce variation, serve as the primary continuous quality improvement tool of the health system.

d. Quarterly variation reports will be submitted to all physicians and hospitals as information tools to help us achieve our vision.

e. The five-step strategy deployment process is:

1. Identify a set of objective strategic measures, with hoshin targets, that signify, when achieved, that best-value has been achieved.

2. Determine those few high leverage diagnostic-specific and support processes which should receive most attention and determine objective strategic measures, with hoshin targets, that signify, when achieved that best-value has been achieved in a specific process.

3. Identify "drivers" that will accelerate achievement of best-value and inhibitors to achievement.

4. Structure education and training to maximize drivers and minimize inhibitors.

5. Celebrate achievement of Hoshin targets and craft action plans for below target results.

IV. Structure:

   a. The President of MedFirst Health System serves as the Chief Quality Officer and the Medical Director is the clinical leader.

   b. Quality initiatives are three tiered:

1. MedFirst Health System vision is measured in aggregate form through the use of the Value Compass which balances health status, costs, efficiency, and patient satisfaction, with hoshin targets established using Kano's Level I and Level III in methodology.

2. Second-tier measures are locally based initiatives from each hospital's quality plans.

3. Tertiary activities are health system-wide, diagnostic-specific quality improvement team initiatives.

Appendix H

Sample Quality Audit Plan

Results of quality audits and assessments that relate to peer review are protected from discoverability by Georgia Code 31-7-140 and the Health Care Quality Improvement Act of 1986 PL 99-660. Most of the results of audits and assessments that relate to other areas are not publicly available. Information will be furnished on request.

Quality Audits and Assessments

Function	Type of audit or review	Frequency	Methodology	Auditor
Leadership	Customer feedback	Annually	Questionnaire	Headquarters (HQT) staff
		Ongoing	Questionnaire	Customer service
Ancillary support				
Living arrangements	Customer feedback	Semi-annually	Questionnaire	HQT staff
		Ongoing	Questionnaire	Customer service
	Preventive maintenance checks	Weekly, monthly, or quarterly, depending on type of equipment	Observation, testing equipment	Facility services
	Safety inspection	Annually	Observation	State fire marshall
			Documentation review	
	Safety inspection	Every 3 years	Observation	JCAHO
			Documentation review	
	Analysis of critical incidents	Ongoing	Documentation review	Risk management
			Review of data	
Information	Analysis of medical records for content	Each record after discharge	Documentation review	Medical records
				JCAHO surveys
	Analysis of medical records for timeliness	Each record after discharge	Documentation review	Medical records
	Inventory of delinquent records	Monthly	Review of data	QM/UR/MR committee
				JCAHO surveys
	Analysis of medical records for content	Every 2–3 days	Documentation review	Payers utilization review
	Analysis of medical records for content and timeliness	Monthly	Documentation review	Peer review organization

Function	Type of audit or review	Frequency	Methodology	Auditor
	Analysis of medical records for content	Annually	Documentation review	Blue Cross
Housekeeping	Customer feedback	Semi-annually	Questionnaire	
		Ongoing	Questionnaire	
	Safety/cleanliness	Annually	Observation	
			Documentation review	
	Safety/staff compliance	Unknown	Observation	OSHA
			Documentation review	
			Interviews	
	Analysis of potentially-compensable events	Ongoing	Documentation review	Risk management
Ancillary clinical processes	Quality alarms	Ongoing	Observation of practices	All staff
			Review of data	
			Documentation review	
	Safety/cleanliness	Every 3 years	Observation	JCAHO
			Documentation review	
	Safety/cleanliness	Annually	Observation	JCAHO
			Documentation review	
	Safety/cleanliness	Annually	Observation	College of American Pathologists
			Documentation review	
	Safety/cleanliness	Annually	Observation	State licensure
		Response to complaints	Documentation review	
Complaints	Safety/staff compliance	Unknown	Observation	OSHA
			Documentation review	
	Policy/procedure review	Every 3 years	Documentation review	JCAHO
			Interviews	

Function	Type of audit or review	Frequency	Methodology	Auditor
	Policy/procedure review	Annually Response to complaints	Documentation review	State licensure
	Appropriateness/effectiveness	Every 3 years	Documentation review Interviews Review of data	JCAHO
	Appropriatenesss/effectivenes	Annually Response to complaints	Documentation review Interviews Review of data	State licensure
	Analysis of potentially-compensable events	Ongoing	Documentation review Review of data	Risk management
Billing	Charge justification	Each record after discharge	Documentation review	Medcorp
	Timeliness in bill preparation	Monthly	Documentation review Review of data	Medical records (PPMAP)
	Accuracy of coding	Monthly	Documentation review	Medical records staff
	Accuracy of coding	Monthly	Documentation review	Peer review organization
	Compliance with Medicare regulations	Monthly	Documentation review	Peer review organization
	Compliance with Medicare regulations	Annually	Documentation review	Medicare auditors
	Policy/procedure review	Annually	Documentation review	Medicare auditors
	Policy/procedure review	Annually	Documentation review	HCA internal auditors
	Compliance with regulations/standards	Annually	Documentation review	HCA internal auditors

Function	Type of audit or review	Frequency	Methodology	Auditor
Direct patient care processes				
Admitting	Appropriateness	All admissions except HMO	Documentation review	Quality management
	Appropriateness	Monthly	Documentation review	Peer review organization
	Appropriateness	Monthly	Review of data	Quality management
	Appropriateness	Annually	Documentation review	Blue Cross
	Appropriateness	Every 2 weeks	Review of data	Contractual Adjustment Team
Daily care	Customer feedback	Semi-annually	Questionnaire	HQT staff
		Ongoing	Questionnaire	Customer service
	Analysis of potentially compensible events	Ongoing	Documentation review	Risk management
	Safety/Staff compliance	Unknown	Review of data Observation Documentation review Interviews	OSHA
	Appropriateness /effectiveness	Every 3 years	Observation Documentation review	JCAHO (Food service)
	Appropriatenesss /effectivenes	Annually	Observation Documentation review	State licensure (Food service)
Discharging	Appropriateness	Monthly	Documentation review	Peer review organization
	Appropriateness	Monthly	Review of data	Quality management (PPMAP)
	Appropriateness	Annually	Documentation review	Blue Cross

Function	Type of audit or review	Frequency	Methodology	Auditor
Direct patient care				
	Appropriateness	Every 2 weeks	Review of data	Contractual adjustment team
Doctoring	Credentialling	Initial staff appointment	Documentation review Interview Review of data	Medical staff office/medical staff dept./general staff committee board of trustees
	Reappointment	Every 2 years	Documentation review Review of data	Medical staff office/medical staff dept./general staff committee board of trustees
	Quality alarms	Ongoing	Observation Review of data Documentation review	All staff
	JCAHO pilot indicators for obstetrics and oncology	Monthly	Documentation review	Quality management oncology coordinator/medical staff
	Safety/staff compliance	Unknown	Observation Interviews	OSHA
	Analysis of potentially compensible events	Ongoing	Documentation review Review of data	Risk management
	Bylaws review	Every 3 years	Documentation review	JCAHO
	Appropriateness/effectiveness	Every 3 years	Documentation review Interviews	JCAHO

Function	Type of audit or review	Frequency	Methodology	Auditor
	Appropriateness/ effectivenes	Monthly	Review of data Documentation review	Peer review organization
	Appropriateness/ effectiveness	Annually Response to complaints	Documentation review Interviews Review of data	State licensure
Nursing	Licensure verification	Initial Biannually	Documentation review	Personnel
	Inventory of skills	Initial	Documentation review	Education
	Performance evaluation	Annually	Observation Documentation review	Nursing management
	Quality alarms	Ongoing	Observation Review of data Documentation review	All staff
	JCAHO pilot indicators for obstetrics and oncology	Monthly	Documentation review	Quality management Oncology coordinator
	Safety/staff compliance	Unknown	Observation Interviews Documentation review	OSHA
	Analysis of potentially compensible events	Ongoing	Documentation review Review of data	Risk management
	Appropriateness/ effectiveness	Every 3 years	Documentation review Interviews	JCAHO
	Appropriateness/ effectiveness	Monthly	Documentation review	Peer review organization
	Appropriateness/ effectiveness	Annually Response to complaints	Documentation review	State licensure

Appendix I

Some Data Collection Plans

Data Collection Plan

Department: Food Service

Process: Nutritional screening

Date: April 18, 1994

Why?

To increase the awareness of moderate- or high-
risk patients to physicians

To decrease the patients stay therefore decreasing
hospital cost

What data will be collected?

The number of orders by physician on patients with
moderate/high-risk nutritional status

When will the data be collected?

Daily

Data Collection Plan-Page 2

Process: Nutritional Screenings

How long will the data be collected before the initial analysis?

One month—May 1

Who will collect the data?

Dietitians

How will the data be collected?

The dietitian will check the number of referrals of moderate- and high-risk patients. The number of check will be counted at the end of the month. Keep the number of patients at moderate/high risk

How will the data be analyzed?

Referrals

What point will be plotted monthly on the storyboard?

The percentage of orders by the physician of moderate and high-risk patients

Data Collection Plan-Page 2

Process: <u>Nutritional Screenings</u>

What training is needed and how will it be accomplished?

<u>Hold a meeting with dietitians to explain data</u>

<u>collection</u>

_____

_____

_____

_____

MAR Accuracy

Month _____

Number of Rx Errors	Number of Transactions	Percent Error
1.		
2.		
3.		
4.		
5.		
6.		
7.		
8.		
9.		
10.		
11.		
12.		
13.		
14.		
15.		
16.		
17.		
18.		
19.		
20.		
21.		
22.		
23.		
24.		
25.		
26.		
27.		
28.		
29.		
30.		
31.		

Index